Dolomites

Book 1: North and West

Florian Fritz and Dietrich Höllhuber

SUNFLOWER BOOKS

First edition © 2023
Sunflower Books™
PO Box 36160
London SW7 3WS, UK
www.sunflowerbooks.co.uk

All rights reserved. No part of this publication may be reproduced, stored in a retrieval system, or transmitted by any form or by any means, electronic, mechanical, photocopying, recording or otherwise, without the prior written permission of the publishers.

ISBN 978-1-85691-541-0

Important note to readers

This book is a translation from guides originally published in Germany (see Publisher's note on page 6). We have tried to ensure that the descriptions and maps are error-free at press date. The book will be updated, where necessary, whenever future editions permit. It will be very helpful for us to receive your comments (sent to info@sunflowerbooks.co.uk, please) for the updating of future editions and for our online update service.

We also rely on those who use this book — especially walkers — to take along a good supply of common sense when they explore. Conditions can change fairly rapidly due to storm damage. Explore *safely*, while respecting the beauty of the countryside.

Cover photo: the Villnösstal/Val di Funes and Geisler/Odle peaks, with upper St Magdalena (Santa Maddalena Alta) in the foreground (Walks 7-13)

Translated from *Dolomiten/Südtirol Ost* by Dietrich Höllhuber (and revised edition by Florian Fritz) and *Dolomiten Wanderführer* by Florian Fritz, text and maps ©2006, 2009, 2015, 2018, 2020 Michael Müller Verlag, Erlangen, Germany

Photographs: 24, 30 (both), 31 (bottom), 32, 33, 34, 35, 59, 88, 91, 92, 95, 97, 100, 102-3, 105, 107, 111, 113, 117, 127, 128-9, 130, 136-7, 138, 140-1, 142-3, 144-5, 148, 150-1, 155, 156, 167, 168-9, 171, 172, 173, 175, 176, 180, 182, 184, 187, 189, 190, 192-3, 194 (Florian Fritz); 31 (top) (Sybille Fritz); 25, 40, 42, 46, 48, 51, 62, 64, 67, 69, 72, 75, 77, 78, 81, 82, 109, 110, 118, 147, 151 (top), 162 (both) (Dietrich Höllhuber); 55, 58, 84, 164 (i-stock photo); 27 (Südtirol Marketing Board); 38 (Eisacktal Tourist Board); 160 (Eggental Tourist Board); 5, 18, 28-9, 44, 71, 86, 124, 134, 193 (right), cover (Shutterstock)

Sunflower Books is a Registered Trademark.
A CIP catalogue record for this book is available from the British Library.
Printed and bound in England by Short Run Press, Exeter

Contents

Preface	5
Publisher's note	6
Introduction	8
When to go	8
Travelling to the Dolomites	9
By air • By train • By car	
Getting around the area	10
By car • By bus • By train • By cycle	
Where to stay	13
Hotels • Farmhouse holidays • Mountain huts, youth hostels, campsites	
Cuisine	14
Practicalities A-Z	16
Climate and weather • Communications • Festivals, customs and events • Information • Maps • Medical care • Money/banks • Opening times • Shopping and souvenirs • Sports	
Short historical summary	24
Walking in the Dolomites	27
Walking areas • Weather and best times to walk • Flora • Fauna • Equipment and food • Emergencies and emergency phone numbers • Planning your walks and getting to them • Waymarks and signposts, grades, maps, GPS	
1 Pustertal/Val Pusteria: the lower valley	36
Walking tips: ● Lindenweg from Mühlbach; ● Mills Nature Trail; *Cycling tip:* From St Lorenzen/San Lorenzo to Mühlbach/Rio di Pusteria	
2 Hochpustertal/Alta Pusteria	45
●• Walk 1: From Lake Prags/Lago di Braies to the Seekofel Hut/Rifugio Biella	55
● Walk 2: To the Drei Zinnen/Tre Cime di Lavaredo	57
● Walk 3: Circuit under the Rotwand/Croda Rossa di Sesto	59
● Walk 4: To Helm/Monte Elmo and the Sillianer Hut	61
Cycling tips: from Toblach through the Höhlensteintal; Pustertal cycle path between Mühlbach and Lienz	
3 Tauferer Tal and Ahrntal/Val di Tures and Valle Aurina	63
● Walk 6: From Kasern/Casere to the Birnlücken Hut/Rifugio Tridentina	70
Walking tips: ● Visit to Kofler zwischen den Wänden; ● Franziskusweg; ● Lake Klaus/Chiusetta; ● Kehreralm; ● Krimmler Tauern; *Cycling tip:* from Bruneck to Sand in Taufers	

●●● Symbols indicating grading of the walks: see page 35

4 Dolomites, Book 1: North and West

4 Antholzer Tal and Gsieser Tal/Val di Anterselva and Valle di Casies 72
Walking tips: ● Grentealm and Kumpfleralm; ● Lake Antholz/Lago di Anterselva

5 Eisacktal/Valle Isarco 76
- ● Walk 6: Circuit from Kreuztal/Val Croce on the Plose summit via the Telegraph 85
- ● Walk 7: Circuit from St Peter/San Pietro on the Bergbauernweg 87
- ● Walk 8: Circuit from Zans via the Gampenalm 90
- ● Walk 9: From Zans to the Schlüterhütte/Rifugio Genova 93
- ● Walk 10: On the Adolf Munkel Trail (the Sentiero delle Odle) 96
- ● Walk 11: In Reinhold Messner's footsteps — circuit from Zans via the Gschnagenhardt Alm 101
- ● Walk 12: From Zans to the Wörndleloch Alm 105
- ● Walk 13: Around the Aferer Geisler/Odles Deores 108
- ● Walk 14: The Postal Trail from Lajen/Laion to St Ulrich/Ortisei 111

6 Seiser Alm area/Alpe di Siusi 115
- ● Walk 15: From Kastelruth/Castelrotto to Seis/Siusi via St Valentin 123
- ● Walk 16: From Völs/Fiè to the Tuffalm and Hofer Alpl 125
- ● Walk 17: On the Oswald von Wolkenstein Trail 128
- ● Walk 18: Circuit from Compatsch to the Puflatsch/Bullaccia summit 131
- ● Walk 19: From Compatsch across the Seiser Alm/Alpe di Siusi plateau 135
- ●❗ Walk 20: From Compatsch to Schlern/Sciliar 139
- ●❗ Walk 21: From the Schlernhaus/Rifugio Bolzano to the Saltria chair lift 144
- ●❗ Walk 22: From the Seiser Alm/Alpe di Siusi to Schlern/Sciliar and the Tierser Alpl Hut 149
- ●❗ Walk 23: Circuit from Compatsch via the Tierser Alpl Hut/Rifugio di Tires 153

Walking tips: ● Hauenstein Castle ruins and Sagenweg; ● Laranz Woods; ● Tisens and Tagusens

3 The Rosengarten/Catinaccio area 158
- ● Walk 24: The Farm Trail from Prösels/Presule Castle to St Katharina/Santa Caterina 167
- ● Walk 25: Tschamintal/Val di Ciamin 173
- ● Walk 26: From the Niger/Nigra Pass to St Zyprian/San Cipriano 177
- ●❗ Walk 27: From the Kölner Hut/Rifugio Fronza through the Tschamintal/Val di Ciamin 181
- ● Walk 28: From the Paolina Hut round Rotwand/Roda di Vael 187
- ● Walk 29: From the Kölner Hut/Rifugio Fronza to the Karer/Carezza Pass 190
- ●❗ Walk 30: Below the Vajolet Towers 194

Walking tips: ● Weisslahnbad; ● 'Elizabeth Promenade'; ● Lake Karer circuit

Index 196

Fold-out area map *inside back cover*

Preface

In 1788 the head of the Department of Mineralogy at the Ecole des Mines in Paris, Deodat de Dolomieu, visited the southern Tyrol to explore the mountains. At that time there was no special name for these steep-sided, isolated mountains with their brightly coloured rock. In those days hardly anyone was interested in the new sciences of mineralogy and geology; most people believed that God had created the world 6000 years earlier — why worry about exactly *how* it came about?

Dolomieu found petrified tropical corals and other fossils at a height of 3000 metres, which told him that these mountains were once under the sea. Above all, he found a stone that, after his scientific studies were published, was named for him: dolomite. In dolomitic rock the calcium in the original limestone sediment from the sea bed or coral reefs is transformed to incorporate magnesium. Gradually the term 'Dolomites' began to appear in the scientific literature when this part of Tyrol was discussed, and it finally filtered down to common use.

The dramatically sited Christomannos eagle (see Walks 28 and 29)

Up to 240 million years old, these coral reefs rose from the sea bed in an almighty upheaval some 65 million years ago. These tectonic events, coupled with ongoing erosion from glaciers, snow, rain and wind have created deep valleys which today make a first-class holiday base. The Dolomites are a mecca for walkers, mountain bikers, climbers, skiers and paragliders. But you don't have to be an *aficionado* of any of these sports to enjoy the fresh air in the upper valleys, the healthy mountain setting and home-made cooking, visits to working alms or taking a lift up to the high peaks.

Publisher's note

Sunflower's original guide to the Dolomites, published in 2010, was translated from a German *general* guide, with 35 long and short walks. The Preface above is taken from that book, authored by the late Dietrich Höllhuber. His guide was updated by Florian Fritz, who has since written a purely *walking* guide. We're very fortunate to have these authors, who both started walking and climbing in the Dolomites in their teens; their enthusiasm shines through on every page.

Sunflower always wanted to offer readers more walks in the fabulous Dolomites, so we've put both books together — giving a total of 70 long and short walks. But because we wanted to keep all the other information in the general guide (everything from history to cuisine, from town plans to lift opening times and prices), this called for *two* books. To keep both guides to the same size and with an equal number of walks in each, we've split the guides in a rather unorthodox way — not in the usual east/west division.

The 'chapters' in **Book 1** cover **the north** (areas along the SS49 and Rienz/Rienzo River) **and west** (regions east of the A22 motorway/SS12 and Eisack/Isarco River). Those in **Book 2** cover areas more 'inland' of these roads: **Gröden/Val Gardena**, **Gadertal/Val Badia**, and regions further **east and south**. *Neither guide takes in the Brenta Dolomites west of the A22 motorway.*

The way we have split the guides has resulted in certain anomalies: for instance, walks to the Drei Zinnen/Tre Cime di Lavaredo feature in *both* books: they are approached from the north (from Sexten/Sesto) in Book 1 and from the south (from Lake Misurina near Cortina) in Book 2. There are several similar overlaps: *the walks are based on where you leave your transport — either to start the walk itself or to take a lift to a mountain station to start the walk.*

The format in these introductory guides is a bit different from the usual Sunflower style: instead of car tours, each 'chapter' covers a specific holiday area (see fold-out maps), with information about the towns and villages — from the 'sights' to lift opening times and prices. The **35 long and short walks** are described, with maps, following each chapter. But there are also dozens of other **detailed walking and cycling 'tips'** and suggestions for more of the authors' favourite hikes in each chapter — which you can follow using the relevant Tabacco 1:25,000 map (see page 35).

While it is usual for English-language guide books about the Dolomites to use **Italian place names**, you won't find these names taking precedence 'on the ground'. Italian is the main language in the Val di Fiemme/Fleimstal, Primiero, Agordino and Cadore; Ladin in the Fassatal/Val di Fassa, Buchenstein and Ampezzo. German is so widely spoken in South Tyrol (where a good many of these walks are based) that even Italians may use German place names (many of the Italian names were created under Mussolini: the original, German, names were simply translated into Italian). Sign-posting usually gives both names (or three, in **Ladin** areas). Since the maps in this book were produced in Germany, with **German place names**, we generally use these names in the text, but always show the Italian name when the place is first mentioned — or we list *all three* names, if the village is Ladin (see Book 2). The Index of course lists all names.

Those of you unfamiliar with the area may be puzzled by the German word '**alm**', which can be used in several contexts. An alm is a mountain pasture above tree line, usually with a 'hut' (German 'Hütte', Italian 'Malga'), often used for dairy farming. Many of the 'huts' welcome visitors, selling fresh milk and cheese ... and enticing meals.

Finally, please take into account that Dietrich and Fritz were/are very strong hillwalkers, completely at home in this mountainous environment. It would certainly be wise to build in *plenty of additional time* for these walks, until you feel at home following in their footsteps! And of course, we advise you *never to walk alone*.

Introduction

The Dolomites — a UNESCO World Heritage Site since 2009 — are located just south of the Austrian border, between the Eisack/Isarco Valley to the west and the Sexten/Sesto and Piave valleys to the east. The southern boundary lies on a line that curves roughly northeast from Trento to Belluno.

When to go

The whole Dolomites, whether it be the northern Pustertal/Val Pusteria or the southern Cadore, have a continental alpine climate. **Summers** are hot and dry, especially in the valleys. Only in areas affected by the famous 'Adriatic lows' is there significant rainfall. On the highest terrain it can freeze up and snow even in high summer! **Autumn** comes late and is mostly dry, perfect for outings. Unfortunately, most hotels in the Dolomites close by the middle or end of September; if you plan to come after this, be sure to book ahead and remember that *many lifts may be closed*. By mid-December all the lifts are open again, and Dolomiti Superski — the largest collection of lifts and runs in the world — is in full swing. **Winter** precipitation is not very high in the Dolomites, so the pistes must be carefully (and often

UNESCO World Heritage Dolomites

The nine most important areas of the Dolomites have been part of the UNESCO World Heritage since 2009. More than 231,000 hectares of mountainous land in the provinces of Belluno, South Tyrol, Pordenone, Trento and Udine were placed under its protection. The universal value of the Dolomites was justified by the extraordinarily varied mountain formations, the enormous importance for geological science (the wealth of fossils from the Triassic Era), and its 'sublime, monumental, lush and colourful landscape'. This means that cultural elements are also included in the justification, because landscape is not just nature: man has shaped it very significantly.

The protected areas of the Dolomites are:
- *Pelmo, Croda da Lago (Belluno)*
- *Marmolada (Belluno, Trento)*
- *Pale di San Martino, Pale di San Lucano, Dolomiti Bellunesi, Vette Feltrine (Belluno, Trento)*
- *Dolomiti Friulane e d'Oltre Piave (Belluno, Pordenone, Udine)*
- *Northern Dolomites (Belluno, South Tyrol)*
- *Puez-Geisler (South Tyrol)*
- *Schlern-Rosengarten, Latemar (South Tyrol, Trento)*
- *Bletterbach (South Tyrol)*
- *Dolomiti di Brenta (Trento)*

The province of Belluno has 41.2% of the core zone, South Tyrol 31% of the core and 51.8% of the buffer zone. Trento, Pordenone and Udine have only smaller areas (14.6/10.7/2.5% of the core and 8.9/16.9/6.5% of the buffer zone respectively).

Introduction: getting to the Dolomites

very artistically) prepared. Sunny days are far more frequent than they are north of the Alps, and the view from the top of many ski slopes takes in about half the range. **Spring** begins late, no earlier than April/May in the valleys and June higher up — that's the time to explore the Dolomites on foot! Read more about the weather on pages 28-30.

Getting to the Dolomites
By air
There is an airport in the Dolomites, at Bozen/Bolzano, but as of press date there are no flights from the UK. The three airports handiest for the Dolomites are Innsbruck to the north and Verona and Venice to the south — with onward travel by rail, bus or car taking about two hours. Other gateways are Milan or Bergamo (onward travel about four hours), Treviso (onward travel under three hours) or Munich (four hours away). To see some flight suggestions, log on to South Tyrol's website: www.suedtirol.info.

By train
The Dolomites *can* be reached by rail from London St Pancras International in under 24 hours, but at least two changes of train will be involved (with a change of *station* as well). If your heart is set on going by train, details can be found at www.bahn.de (German railways), www.trenitalia.it (Italian railways) or trainline.com.

The main railway stations in the Dolomites, served by the fast Eurocity trains, are at Trento, Bozen/Bolzano, and Brixen/Bressanone. From these stations there are direct bus services to the northern and western holiday areas in the range. Only the far south-

Travelling by train is comfortable, but, unfortunately, quite a long-drawn-out affair from the UK

eastern side of the Dolomites, near Belluno, is more quickly reached by train from Padua or Venice. The Franzensfeste/Fortezza station is where you should change for trains to the northern areas near the Pustertal/Val Pusteria; these stop at Bruneck/Brunico, Toblach/Dobbiaco and Innichen/San Candido.

For copious details about rail connections — including any of the few remaining **motorail** possibilities (unfortunately most have closed), log on to www.seat 61.com, a cornucopia of train information.

By car
Driving to the Dolomites is an option recommended for those who enjoy the flexibility and freedom of having their own

transport. After crossing the English Channel by tunnel or ferry (there are also ferries from Hull and Rosyth in Scotland to Zeebrugge) it is an easy drive of about 12 hours on the Continent's excellent motorways. (For an overview of the route, motorway tolls and approximate fuel costs, log on to www.viamichelin.com.)

The best approach to the Dolomites is via the A22 motorway over the Brenner Pass. This gives quick access to the western and northern parts of the range, and there are exits at Brixen/Bressanone, Klausen/Chiusa, Bozen/Bolzano and Trento, from where you can head east and south on good roads. (Other motorways which you might use if you are only visiting the southern and eastern Dolomites covered in Book 2, include the very busy A4 linking Milan and Venice. From Mestre near Venice the less-travelled A27 gives access to Belluno, with a good national road, the SS51, continuing to Cortina.)

In addition to your passports, be sure to have a valid **UK photocard driver's licence** (if you do not have a *photocard* licence, you will need an international driving permit). You must also have a **vehicle registration document** and **green card insurance** (guaranteeing that you have third party cover). If you are involved in an accident, all three documents will be required.

You will also need a **GB sticker**, **spare bulbs**, **warning triangle**, and a fluorescent yellow jacket for each person in the car. If you have a new or valuable car, it is worth getting special vehicle recovery insurance for the trip, offered by all automobile clubs and insurers. This covers the costs of transporting the vehicle to the nearest garage, getting you and your car back home, the cost of sending spare parts, any accommodation costs incurred, etc. Not all insurance contracts are the same, so read the small print!

Do contact your motoring insurer or log on to www.gov.uk before travelling, to check for any late Brexit-related changes!

Getting around the area
By car

Naturally the same rules apply in the Dolomites as north of the Brenner Pass, although Italians drive more on instinct than by 'rules'. But on the whole respect for motoring laws is better in the north of the country than in the south … so you can pretty much rely on traffic halting at red lights!

Roads in the Dolomites demand the utmost concentration. When holiday traffic is heavy, you'll be crossing the more difficult passes at a snail's pace.

The **speed limit** on **motorways** for cars and motorbikes is 130km/h (80mph), for cars with trailers 80km/h (50mph), for caravans above 3.5t 100km/h (60mph). Motorbikes under 150ccm are not allowed. On **main roads** the speed limit for cars and motorbikes is 110km/h (70mph), for cars with trailers 70km/h (45mph), for caravans above 3.5t 80km/h (50mph). On **secondary and minor roads** the speed limit for cars and motorbikes is 90km/h, for cars with trailers 70km/h, for caravans above 3.5t 80km/h.

Dipped headlights are mandatory when driving, *even in daylight*.

At **red lights**, you are allowed to turn right if no traffic is approaching from the left.

Introduction: Getting around the area 11

Frequently seen traffic signs
Baccendere i fari: put on your lights;
attenzione: caution;
deviazione: detour;
divieto di accesso: entry forbidden;
lavori in corso: works in progress;
parcheggio: car parking;
rallentare: slow down;
senso unico: one way;
strada senza uscita: one-way street;
tutte direcioni: all directions;
uscita veicoli: caution: vehicle exit;
zona a traffico limitado: limited vehicle access;
zona disco: parking only with disc;
zona pedonale: pedestrian zone.

Seat belts must be worn in both front and rear seats, and an appropriate harness is obligatory for children aged 3-12.

The permitted **alcohol level** is 0.5mg/l; this means that you cannot drink more than one glass of wine without risking going over the limit. Motorists driving over the limit will have their licences revoked for two weeks to three months and pay high fines. If you have an **accident** the car will be impounded (these rules apply to foreigners as well as Italians).

There are **emergency** phone boxes at 2km intervals along the motorways. Private emergency services are not allowed. The service vans of the ACI (Italian Automobile Club) can be reached 24 hours a day on ℂ 116 but, since they will not always speak English fluently, speak slowly and carefully.

For **full information about**
driving to and in Italy, see www.italia.it.

Petrol prices are about the same as in surrounding Continental countries. For lead-free ask for *senza piombo;* super = *super* and diesel = *gasolio;* octane and quality are the same as in other Continental countries.

Petrol stations are only open 24 hours on the motorways; on main roads and in towns and villages they are usually *closed* from 20.00-7.00 and from 12.00-15.00 as well as *all day Sundays.* More and more petrol pumps are fitted with credit card automats which also take euro notes.

Charging stations for electric cars are steadily increasing on the motorways and in towns. At the Brenner Pass there are many dispensers for varying marques of car; in towns there are often special parking places with charging stations. Many hotels — and not just the high-priced ones — have charging points in their garages, some even offer rental of high-powered electric cars.

By bus
Buses in the three Dolomites provinces of South Tyrol, Trentino and Belluno are a fast, economical and reliable way of getting about — as long as you aren't trying to travel on a Sunday, when many of the smaller places are not served by bus.

On all three traffic networks (see below) you can buy tickets when boarding the bus, in the office of the bus operator, or at local shops and kiosks (usually tobacconists). Buying a ticket on boarding is significantly more expensive.

Both individual tickets and passes are on offer; the latter are good for all buses and also the trains. The ticket or pass must be validated on boarding, or you will face a hefty fine.

Some of the operators offer **free (or very cheap) bus travel for skiers and hikers** in winter, even serving isolated hotels and the valley stations of the lifts. In a very few cases (like the Lake Karer/Carezza area), this is also true in summer. Ask at the operators' offices for information.

SAD (www.sad.it) is the bus operator in **South Tyrol**, with its offices in Bozen/Bolzano, from where a good number of their orange-red and green buses also depart. Other centres are in Brixen/Bressanone and Bruneck/Brunico. SAD also travels to some places outside South Tyrol, for instance to the Fassa Valley in Trentino (from Bolzano) and Cortina d'Ampezzo in Belluno (from Toblach).

The two other operators are **Trentino Trasporti** (www.ttspa.it) in **Trentino** and **Dolomitibus** (www.dolomitibus.it) in **Belluno**.

By train

The Brenner railway line and the railway in the Pustertal/Val Pusteria offer good services for those based at Bozen/Bolzano, Brixen/Bressanone, Bruneck/Brunico and Toblach/Dobbiaco or

> **Mobilcard and other guest cards**
>
> If you plan to use buses and trains to any extent, you will come to appreciate a **Mobilcard**. You can get them for the whole South Tyrol region — for all buses and trains and even some ski lifts (1 day for 15 €, 3 days for 23 €, 7 days for 28 €; see www.mobilcard.info). Cards must be validated whenever you travel. They are available from tourist offices or automats in local train stations.
>
> Or you can buy a **Museum Mobilcard** offering the same transport options but including free entrance to almost all South Tyrol's 128 museums: 3 days 30 €, 7 days 34 €.
>
> Accommodation providers sometimes give their guests free **local mobile cards** — of which there is such a confusing variety that it's best to search the web beforehand.
>
> For **cyclists** there's the **Bikemobil Card** (1 day for 25 €, 3 days for 30 €, 7 days for 35 €).
>
> For those exploring the whole range, there's the **Dolomiti Super Summer Card** (see page 22).

Bus station at Bozen/Bolzano

Innichen/San Candido. Trains travel almost hourly every day from Innichen to Franzensfeste/Fortezza via Toblach and Bruneck. From there you change to trains for Brixen, Klausen and Bolzano as well as Auer and Neumarkt. For information see www.trenitalia.com.

Since many stations are unmanned, buy tickets at automats or from *bus* drivers. Only when there is no automat can you pay on the train. In Italy train tickets **must always be validated** before you board the train, otherwise you may be subject to a high fine. Single tickets — unless they are passes — are only good for a bus *or* a rail journey; they are *not* interchangeable.

By cycle
Because of the strenuous gradients, the Dolomites are not suited for long-distance cycling. But they *are* ideal for mountain bikes. Almost all **trains** will accept mountain bikes (see www.trenitalia.it for more information). Carriages for bikes are at the start or end of the train. One-day tickets cost about 6 €. All **bus** companies will take bikes *if there is room* (not usually the case on weekends).

Where to stay
Hotels
The number of rooms in hotels, *pensions,* apartments and farmhouses in the Dolomites is huge.

South Tyrol has an especially large choice. Prices are pretty much the same throughout the Dolomites — and on the high side overall. The most economical places to stay are in South Tyrol.

Accommodation standards are quite high whatever the category: all hotel rooms have bath or shower, WC, telephone, TV (usually satellite), hairdryers, internet (usually free, but it may not work very well in individual rooms). Most have mini-bars as well. A balcony, usually flower-filled, is standard, except in historical houses and the small houses where individuals rent out private rooms. A common feature of many 3-4 star hotels is a very luxurious 'wellness centre', with saunas, whirlpools, in- and outdoor swimming pools, gym equipment and solaria.

In many places, especially *pensions,* three nights is the **minimum stay**. In high season you will also be expected to take half-board terms. Room and breakfast is generally only available in low season.

Unless you are using a travel agent or booking a package holiday, surf the web to find a place that appeals to you. Most of the sites have an English version with e-mail facility, should you have any questions. You can then **book the accommodation** on the web, or by phone or letter.

While **seasonal opening** varies, **high season** in all the provinces is from the 4th week in July until the 3rd week in August, and from Christmas to 6 January; in skiing areas only, also from February to mid-March.

Hotels in the **family-friendly group** (usually 3-5 stars) take special care of the children, with playgrounds or playrooms and sometimes special programmes for kids. Log on to www.familien hotels.com (English pages).

There are also 3-4 star **hotels for walkers** and their families, with equipment hire, mini-bus for walk access, guided walks, walk

'libraries' with maps and guides. See www.wanderhotels.com (English pages).

Farmhouse holidays

Farmhouse holidays *(agriturismo)*, while less common in Trentino and Belluno, are possible in many areas of South Tyrol, where they are known as *Buschenschank*. For details log on to the relevant website: www.roterhahn.it.

Mountain huts, youth hostels, campsites

Mountain huts are reserved for mountain climbers and are not included in any list of accommodation *unless* they are run as guest houses for tourists. In summer, from 20 June to 20 September, virtually all mountain huts are open, and many stay open until mid-October or later. The tourist boards know all the opening dates and will supply lists on request.

Youth hostels are in short supply. The provinces in the Dolomites don't appreciate tourists who don't spend! Exceptions are the lovely youth hostel in the old Grand Hotel in Toblach/Dobbiaco, the hostel in Bolzano and some church centres like the Kassianeum in Brixen.

Campsites are also very thin on the ground, with just one place in South Tyrol — in Völs. For what there is, log on to www.camping.it.

Cuisine

Food in the Dolomites is a unique combination of Tyrolean, Imperial Viennese and Italian cooking. On top of that you have the pleasure of Tyrolean wines, from the dry white Sylvaners from the Eisack/Isarco Valley to the elegant Pinot Noir from the lower Etsch/Adige.

Broadly speaking, the Dolomites can be divided into three culinary regions where either dumplings, potato-based gnocchi or pasta predominate. In South Tyrol (the focus of this book), even in the Ladin areas, dumplings dominate: bacon dumplings with sauerkraut and little dumplings in the soup. In Trentino's Fassa Valley the preference is for gnocchi, like the spinach-green *strangolapreti* ('priest chokers' — though no one knows how it came by this name). This is also true in the formerly Austrian Buchenstein and the Ampezzo Valley with Cortina. South of the old Austrian border, in Belluno province, pasta comes second only to polenta, the thick maize porridge.

This Italo/Tyrolean/old Austrian 'fusion' is at its most interesting in South Tyrol, where there are the most high-class restaurants, but in other provinces it also attains high standards. So traditional eating in the Dolomites is very simple: there are dumplings or the ravioli-like 'Schlutzer' or polenta, and with it maybe bacon or a soup with dumplings or little dumplings. Bacon and smoked sausages are available everywhere, although 'bacon' here means something different from what you would find in Germany, Austria or Switzerland (see below).

Dolomites specialities

Bacon *(Speck)* is made by stripping the hind legs of fat then soaking the meat in a bath of salt with cabbage. After this it is cold-smoked over juniper wood and stored for a long time. This makes the bacon extremely tender, with a mild flavour. In Tyrolean style this is cut into thick chunks and, once on the table, cut again into rashers and served on bread with a glass of

Introduction: Where to stay/Cuisine

> **Buschenschank and Törggelen**
>
> 'Törggelen' has almost become synonymous with the culinary way of life in South Tyrol. The meaning itself comes from the word 'Torggel', or wine press, and 'törggelen' means going to taste the new wines at the vintner's. Naturally this is best done with a little food on the side!
>
> In the autumn people walk up to the high ground, where the sun seems to linger longer, and the vintners open their premises for a short time — offering wine-tastings and home-cooked titbits. Traditionally this took place between saints' days — St Martin (11 November) and St Catherine (25 November) but, like all other customs today, the period has been stretched and now lasts from late October to the end of the year!
>
> A bouquet above the entrance draws attention to the fact that the 'Buschenschank' is now open. The new wine ('Nuie') to be tasted is displayed in the farmer's room or on a table in front of the house ... together with 'Schlachtschüssel' (cooked bacon, liver sausage and fresh blood sausage), roasted chestnuts, 'Speck', 'Krapfen' and perhaps a strong barley soup with dumplings and cabbage. Even if the vineyard is accessible by car, it's the walk (or cycle ride) that 'makes' the day's outing.

'Speck' appetizer in Cortina

red wine for the *merende* (the equivalent of a very hearty English afternoon tea). Done in the Italian way it is (like all other hams) cut paper-thin and served as an appetiser. Unfortunately it is still legal to call packaged bacon 'Südtiroler Speck' — so if you are buying it in a shop, *beware;* better still, buy it direct from the farmer. (For an interesting treatise on South Tyrolean bacon, see www.recla.it/en/.)

There are various **local cheeses** from the Alpine pastures. The local cheese is often grated over pasta; from Trentino, for example, there's the very good, parmesan-like *grana* cheese. In the Val di Fassa and Val di Fiemme they make the strong-smelling *puzzone*, covered with a light ochre skin. *Ziger* is a cone-shaped fresh cheese with chives; widely available in South Tyrol, it is eaten on black bread with vinegar, oil and onions.

All **desserts** in the Dolomites hark back to Austrian days: strudel, especially apple strudel, *Kaiserschmarrn* — Austrian pancakes with raisins, the famous *Sachertorte*, and buckwheat gateau with red berry filling. You can also expect to find *Zelten*, a fruit bread, and from Trentino a gingerbread biscuit with lots of lemon and orange zest. *Krapfen* are a Ladin speciality — an elongated deep-fried doughnut with poppy seeds.

Practicalities A-Z

Climate and weather

The Dolomites encompass several climate zones, from the mild climate of western Lombardy in northern Italy (with an average annual temperature above 10°C) to the hard mountain climate (average annual temperature about 0°C). Few settlements lie above the upper sub-alpine border (1600m) and none at all in the alpine zone. For full details of climate and weather, see under 'Walking' on page 28-30.

> **Weather forecasts on the web**
> *South Tyrol:* www.provinz.bz.it/wetter (in English); other weather forecasts at www.data meteo.com (also in English).

Communications

In almost all tourist centres there are **post offices** and (card) **telephone kiosks** (buy cards from tobacconists). The **post** is slow and expensive: *posta prioritaria* is recommended, as it is a bit faster, although more expensive. Many towns and villages have **internet points**; more are added every year, and several villages have free hot spots. Take your **mobile/smartphone**: there is an excellent network of masts — and ever fewer public phone boxes. **Television** is pretty well confined to programmes in Italian or German, but most 3- and 4-star hotels and apartments have satellite television receiving news from Sky, the BBC or CNN.

For **telephone information** in Italy call ℂ 12, for outside the country ℂ 186. When making **international calls** from Italy to the UK preface the number with 0044; to North America with 001.

Calling from outside the country to Italy, preface the number with 0039 and *include the zero* from the area code (eg for a number in the Bolzano area call 0039/0471 + the number).

The general **emergency service** (including helicopter ambulance) is ℂ 118; **police** ℂ 112; **fire department** ℂ 115; **breakdown/vehicle recovery service (ACI)** ℂ 116. Other emergency numbers, specifically for walkers, are on page 33.

Festivals, customs and events

Even without the events organised by the tourist boards, there is always enough to see and do in the Dolomites. One sees people in local costume in the farmers' markets or on Sundays going to church. The brass bands and 'Schützen' (see opposite), with their attendants, gather together at church festivals, processions, annual fairs, the many pilgrimages and the autumnal transhumance with decorated cattle.

The following festivals and events take place annually throughout the Dolomites:

Prozesso alle Streghe, a folk festival in remembrance of the witches' trials (Cavalese, 1st week in January);

Hay-sleigh and **horse-drawn sleigh races** (Stern/La Villa, February);

Good Friday processions in most places that have a church;

Corpus Christi processions take place on the Sunday after Corpus Christi, since Corpus Christi is not a holiday in Italy;

Oswald von Wolkenstein Ride, mock historical battles on the Seis plateau, end May/early June (see panel on page 116 and Walk 17 on page 128);

Sacred Heart Festival in June, with processions in many places. In the evening eye-catching fires are lit on the surrounding mountains, showing, for instance, the flaming heart symbol surmounted by a cross;

International Choirs Festival (in the Hochpustertal/Alta Pusteria;

Jazz Festival (in Bruneck/Brunico, July);

Estate Musicale di Fiemme, a festival of classical music, choirs, jazz and operettas (in the Fleimstal/Val di Fiemme, July/August);

I suoni delle Dolomiti spread among the mountains in Trentino during July and August — music from classical and chamber to jazz and pop. A highlight is the 'Sunrise in the Dolomites' concert held on Col Margherita, starting with a cable car ride to the col at 3am;

Schützen

'Schützen' were Tyrolean citizens charged since the early 16th century with the protection of the homeland. They played an important role in 1797, when Napoleon's troops invaded. Associations of Schützen still exist, and members see themselves in the true sense of the word as 'defenders of the homeland' and as followers of the first defenders of Tyrol.

But there are not only Schützen in South Tyrol: everywhere in the old Austrian parts of the Dolomites you will see a growing number of Schützen at all possible festivals.

Schützen association websites are mostly in German, but if you key the word into an advanced search in English, there are some interesting references.

Gustav Mahler Weeks (in Toblach/Dobbiaco, mid-July to mid-August) — classical music by Mahler, who lived and composed here during three summers, but also by others;

Festa delle Bande: brass-band

Kastelruth/Castelrotto

festival (in Cortina d'Ampezzo, August);

Ascension Day (15th August), holiday processions throughout the Dolomites, with various guilds and associations (including Schützen) in traditional costume; especially noteworthy at pilgrimage churches dedicated to the Virgin Mary, like Maria Weissenstein near Deutschnofen;

Palio della Sloiza: folk festival when the hay is cut, with traditional sledges (in Primiero, end August);

Folk music and folk-dancing day: in the folk museum at Dietenheim (September);

Spectaculum, a three-day Middle Ages festival (in the streets of Bolzano and at Runkelstein Castle, September);

Almabtrieb/Desmontegada are the German/Italian words for the annual transhumance in the autumn, when the cattle come back down from their alpine pastures. This festival is celebrated in many places, but is especially interesting when the goats are brought down in Cavalese on the 3rd of September;

Harvest: a procession giving thanks for the harvest (many places, on the first Sunday in October)

Speckfest in Villnöss/Funes, early October, samplings of difference bacons, music

Kuchlkirchtag in Brixen/Bressanone with guided culinary walks; also **Kuchlkastl** in Völs/Fiè, a culinary folk festival on Schlern/Sciliar (both in October);

Leonhard-Ritt, a religious procession featuring riders on horseback, horse-drawn carriages, etc (in St Leonhard/San Leonardo in the Abteital/Val Badia on the second Sunday in November);

Krampus Day (5 December) and the **Krampus Lauf** in Toblach/Dobbiaco (see page 47);

Christmas markets in Bolzano, Brixen/Bressanone (the oldest) and other places, in the style of German and Austrian Christmas markets (in December).

Information

Tourist boards outside South Tyrol all have the abbreviation APT (Azienda Promozione Turistica) or IAT (Ufficio Informazioni Assistenza/Accoglienza Turistica). Websites for the various tourist boards are shown at the top of each chapter. Naturally you can also consult the **Italian Tourist Board** (www.italia.it or www.italiantourism.com), but they usually have less local information to offer than the bodies mentioned above.

There are excellent **internet sites and apps** for the Dolomites and South Tyrol — right down to room rentals, sports opportunities, government departments and public places. *Most of the sites have English pages.*

www.suedtirol.info is the official site of the South Tyrol Tourist Board — very informative and user-friendly.

www.suedtirolerland.it has wide-ranging information about accommodation and leisure activities.

www.suedtirol3d.it offers delightful panoramas to inspire you or to remind you of your visit when you're back home.

www.naturparks.provinz.bz.it, info about the nature parks in South Tyrol.

www.trenitalia is the official site of the Italian railways.

For **smartphone** users there is an ever-increasing number of apps, some more useful than others.

Sentres is a very comprehensive outdoor databank with walks and cycle tours of all grades; great for planning.

Südtirol to go is an app where you can check all public transport. Available in English, but some pages only in Italian, German or Ladin.

ArchApp (South Tyrol) gives an overview of the most interesting architecture in South Tyrol. It's especially useful if you're touring the area by car.

Other apps are mentioned in the book where appropriate and, unless otherwise specified, all are free.

Maps

Free maps from tourist offices are only useful for general orientation. Many commercial touring maps leave off the less-visited south of the range. An exception is **Michelin**'s 1:400,000 Regional Map 562 ('Italy Northeast'). The map of South Tyrol published by Tabacco (1:160,000) shows almost all the Dolomites and is good for touring by car and motorcycle, or for planning long-distance treks. Excellent large-scale maps (scale 1:25,000) are produced by the same publisher; see page 35.

Medical care

Before travelling, you may wish to get a Global Health Insurance Card (**GHIC**) which gives you the right to free emergency healthcare. For more information, log on to gov.uk.

You are also strongly advised to take out **travel insurance** which includes health cover since, for instance, mountain rescue will not be covered by a GHIC.

In case of illness, do *not* go to the doctor first, but to the USL (Unità Sanitaria Locale; the local medical centre), which is specially set up to deal with tourists. They will send you to a doctor or hospital. Since the opening dates and times of the USLs vary enormously, we have not given them in this book; check at the tourist office when you arrive — or look in the town halls, where opening hours are posted. If you are treated by a registered doctor with a private practice (thus not at the medical centre or a hospital), you will usually be expected to pay, then claim it back on your travel insurance when you return home.

Pharmacies and doctors open or on call at night and on

weekends are posted at the town hall and on the doors of pharmacies. They are also listed in the daily newspapers like *Dolomiten* in South Tyrol.

The only **hospitals** in the area covered by this book are at Bolzano, Brixen/Bressanone and Bruneck/Brunico. People suffering serious accidents or illnesses are often flown by air rescue to Trient/Trento or Innsbruck for treatment.

Money/banks

The euro (€) is the local currency. Almost every town and village has an automatic bill dispenser (if you hold the appropriate debit card); the relevant charge on your card will be upwards of 5 €. If you make withdrawals with a credit card, reckon on a surcharge of about 3%. All Cirrus, Maestro and Visa credit cards — with or without chip — should be accepted.

Opening times

In South Tyrol many shops used to be closed on Saturday afternoons, but that has been changing in the last few years. **Banks** are usually open Mon-Fri from 08.00-13.00/14.30-15.30; post offices Mon-Fri from 08.15-13.00.

Shopping and souvenirs

Shopping, usually confined to rainy days, can be quite fun on good days, if it's combined with an excursion or a walk. Products from the farms are the best souvenirs to take home (see 'Dolomite specialities' on page 14).

Traditional handicrafts, including wood carvings, fabrics (like loden wear), embroideries, *Speck*, wine and schnapps are the best-loved gifts. More fanciful would be a bouquet of dried flowers, a reverse painting on glass, a book about local cuisine…

Loden wear: This attractive dress never goes out of style, so it's always a good investment. It's worth shopping around: prices are cheaper in Toblach/Dobbiaco, for example, than in Bolzano.

Fabrics and lace: Good places to buy hand-made linen or cotton/linen tablecloths are in the Pustertal/Val Pusteria (for instance, shops in Bruneck/Brunico). In the upper Tauferer Ahrntal/Valle Aurina you can also get pillow lace (for instance in Prettau/Predoi).

South Tyrolean *Speck* (see page 14) is world-famous and available in all good-quality food shops. Avoid all packaged *Speck;* buy it from the farmer who has smoked it himself, to get the best, old-style quality — mild and tender.

Mushrooms: Italians go mad for the dried porcini mushrooms *(Boletus edulis)*, also called ceps. Specialist purveyors (like 'Tutto Funghi' in Bruneck/Brunico) guarantee fine-quality produce.

Cheeses: Cheese from the alpine pastures is a good choice, especially the semi-hard and mature cheeses. The products of the Sexten/Sesto and Toblach/Dobbiaco dairies are especially recommended.

Sports

In both summer and winter the Dolomites are an ideal destination for sports enthusiasts. In summer the landscape is perfect for walking, long-distance hiking, climbing and mountain biking. With the first snows, the landscape changes to a paradise for skiing, snowshoe walking and snowboarding. It's a wonder people aren't tripping over each other, but

Practicalities A-Z 21

there's such a choice of sports that this only seems to happen in a few places.

The classic Dolomite sport of mountain climbing has now threaded out into many different strands, since **walkers, mountain climbers, rock- and free-climbers** not only all have different goals but different equipment. Whatever your choice, there's an excellent network of walking routes and many climbing 'gardens' and climbing walls.

A special feature of the Dolomites is the ***via ferrata*** (literally 'iron road'). There are many of these protected climbing trails: iron grips, pegs and cables enable those who are not technical experts to scale walls that would usually only be the province of Grade IV climbers or beyond. But you still have to have a helmet and

Autumnal landscape on the Aica Farm Trail (Walk 24)

Dolomiti Superski

'One ski pass, 12 ski areas, 1200km of pistes' — that's Dolomiti Superski's advertising slogan. It offers the largest selection of lifts and pistes anywhere.

One of their pistes (Gran Risa in Stern/La Villa) counts among the most interesting, fastest and most popular in the world. Names like Wolkenstein/Selva, St Ulrich/Ortisei, Stern/La Villa, Plose, Kronplatz/Plan de Corones, Cortina d'Ampezzo (1956 Olympics), Canazei, Fleimstal/Val di Fiemme (FIS World Cup/Nordic Championships 2003) make winter sports enthusiasts' hearts beat faster. The Sella Ronda, which circles the Sella group, and the Marcialonga, the Nordic marathon in the Val di Fiemme, have attained mythical status. Most places have taken snowboarding and cross-country snowshoe walking to heart.

The **Dolomiti Superski pass** encompasses almost the whole of the range (with the exception of the western Brenta Dolomites and the Adamello group). The pass isn't exactly cheap and is only worth buying if you want to travel to more than one of the ski centres mentioned here or if you are staying in a place from where various ski resorts are easily reached — for instance in Brixen/Bressanone, with the nearby Eisack/Isarco Valley, Gröden/Val Gardena, and the Seiser Alm/Alpe di Siusi or Bolzano, with its good connections to almost all areas.

The pass encompasses **12 skiing regions**: 1 Cortina d'Ampezzo; 2 Kronplatz/Plan de Corones; 3 Hochabteital/Alta Badia; 4 Grödnertal and Seiser Alm/Val Gardena and Alpe di Siusi; 5 Fassa Valley and Lake Karer/Lago di Carezza; 6 Arabba; 7 Hochpustertal/Alta Pusteria; 8 Fleimstal/Val di Fiemme and Obereggen; 9 San Martino di Castrozza and the Rolle Pass; 10 Eisack/Isarco Valley; 11 Tre Valli (Moèna, Lusia, Falcade); 12 Civetta.

Anyone who is visiting the whole range should consider the **Dolomiti SuperSummer Card** (www.dolomitisupersummer.com), which offers discounted rates on more than 100 lifts (ascents reduced 20%, descents 35%). And if you are planning a longer stay or visiting several times during the season, it may even be worthwhile considering a season ticket costing about 350 €, since the price of single tickets mounts up faster than you think!

Ski pass offices are in all towns and villages where they may be used, often at the lower lift stations.

For **information** and up-to-date prices and concessions see www.dolomitisuperski.com.

---

other equipment — and, naturally, experience in Alpine terrain. For information contact the AVS (the South Tyrol Alpine Association; www.alpenverein.it). Only a couple of walks in our two-book guide involve a *via ferrata* — and they would be categorised as 'easy' by *via ferrata* standards.

Walking is covered on pages 27-35.

Fishing is allowed in the many clear watercourses in the range. Licences for foreigners are easily obtained from tourist offices or even tobacconists. Private fishing areas are marked in Italian with *Divieto di pesca* or *Pesca privata*.

Practicalities A-Z

The only people who come to the Dolomites to **swim** are those who like indoor hotel swimming pools. Actually, that's even becoming a pleasure now in the 4-star hotels, with their 'wellness' areas, saunas, whirlpools, etc. Whoever wants to swim 'naturally' can do so in Lake Vahrn near Brixen/Bressanone or in Völs/Fiè. Or in one of the many ice-cold mountain lakes — very refreshing, if you can stand it!

The lack of level terrain is a hindrance to building **golf courses**, but there are a couple in the area covered by this guide — at Deutschnofen/Nova Ponente and Reischach (Bruneck/Brunico).

The strong up-currents which characterise weather in the Dolomites (especially on fine mornings before noon) make the range a superb meeting place for **paragliding**. The best starting points are the mountain stations of the lifts or nearby places, like on Plose above Brixen/Bressanone or the Spitzbühel Hut on the Seiser Alm/Alpe di Siusi. For South Tyrol you can get up-to-date information at www.paragliding.it.

Cycling and mountain biking are two of the top sports in the Dolomites. **Cyclists** on racing bikes swarm along the major roads, especially around the Sella group. Mountain bikers are competing more and more with walkers, and there are some fine cycle routes for families, for instance on the level terrain between Toblach/Dobbiaco and Lienz (see cycling tip on page 52). Since you can take your bike with you on the bus anywhere in the Dolomites (provided there is room), you can cover long distances without having a car at your disposal. **Cycle hire** is available almost everywhere. Many tourist boards hand out free MTB guides and maps and/or offer biking guides.

The network of old mountain roads dating from the First World War, originally built as mule tracks, is an Eldorado for mountain bikers. These roads are generally only moderately steep, most are very well maintained, and they are closed to all motor traffic.

The Dolomites are not very suitable for **horse-riding**, which is mostly concentrated in the outlying wooded mountains and on the large plateaus like Seis/Siusi. In the valleys north of the Pustertal/Val Pusteria there are some riding stables which specialise in trekking; more information on this from the Tauferer Tal Tourist Board: www.tauferer.ahrntal.com. For South Tyrol you can get information about riding stables and farms with horses from the Tourist Board (www.suedtirol.info). If you like Haflinger horses, contact the South Tyrol Haflinger Breeders' Association, www.haflinger-suedtirol.com.

Every tourist centre has **tennis courts**, and you can rely on all 4-star hotels having them.

Winter sports — like **snow-shoe walking** and **hiking** — are becoming ever more popular: February is now considered high season; accommodation must be booked well in advance. The mountain lifts and pistes, as well as the region's ski runs are managed in cooperation with Dolomiti Superski (www.dolomitisuperski.com). There is now an impressive network of **winter walking trails** — perhaps with a cosy inn as the focal point.

Short historical summary

From about 12,000 BC: After the Ice Age the first hunting expeditions in the area of the Dolomites.

From about 5000 BC: First Stone Age farming settlements in the wide valleys, soon followed by cattle husbandry on the mountain slopes (for example at the Seiser Alm/Alpe di Siusi or the alm south of Croda da Lago).

About 3500 BC: Ötzi, the man from the Schnalstal north of Merano, dies on a high mountain pass. When he was found in 1999, he had metal objects and goods that came from far away (flint from Monte Lessini near Verona).

From about 500 BC: Celtic invaders populate areas around the Eisack/Isarco and Etsch/Adige valleys.

16/15 BC: Roman Legions under Drusus conquer the area now known as Trentino-South Tyrol; incorporation in the province of Raetia; Romanisation of the Celtic population.

493-526: Rule from Verona under the Goth Theoderich I, otherwise known as 'Dietrich of Bern', the Ladin hero associated with the Laurin/Rosengarten legend (see page 163).

568-773: Lombards invade from the south, the alpine Romans are cut off from direct contact with other Roman groups south of the river Po. This results in a series of Raeto-Roman languages (for example Ladin in the Dolomites).

8th C: Expansion of the Bavarian influence south of the Brenner Pass; in 769 Duke Tassilo founds Innichen Monastery to promote the Germanisation of the Pustertal/Val Pusteria, which has been inhabited by Slavs since the 6th century. The Ladinised inhabitants retreat into the deeper valleys, preserving their language and culture.

773: Charlemagne conquers the area; the whole Dolomites are under Frankish control.

814: Charlemagne dies, precipitating the end of the Carolingian Empire.

843: Under the Treaty of Verdun the area of the Dolomites is split between the Italian and German kingdoms.

1004/1027: Trient/Trento and Brixen/Bressanone (bishoprics since 381/571) become Episcopal principalities, thus independent territories.

1282: The County of Tyrol also becomes sovereign territory, following which the Counts of Tyrol extend their holdings in the south and bring the principalities of Brixen and Trient under their influence. Gradually the three-language culture spreads throughout Tyrol.

1363: On the death of the last remaining member of the Tyrol family, the county falls to the House of Habsburg (up until 1918!).

1511: Kaiser Maximilian I, the Habsburg Emperor, releases the Tyroleans from war duty outside Tyrol, but obliges them to defend the land. This obligation builds the foundations for conscription in 1915, to defend the borders of the Dolomites until 1918.

1525/1526: The German Peasants' Revolt, Neustift Monastery plundered, Brixen's High Commander murdered (1532).

From about 1600: Agreements between landowners and farmers

Short historical summary

Fresco at Rodeneck Castle dating from the Middle Ages: horseman from King Arthur's Round Table

put use of alpine pastures on a sound footing.

16th/17th C: Due to cheap exports from America, metal prices fall back sharply; mining in the Dolomites (Primiero) and the northern side-valleys of the Pustertal comes to a standstill.

1784: Kaiser Joseph II decrees German to be the official language of the Habsburg Empire.

1788/1789: French geologist Deodat de Dolomieu discovers an unusual calcium magnesium carbonate rock in the Eisacktal/Valle Isarco; the new mineral is named after him and later is applied to the entire mountain range.

1796/1797: First war of the French/Bavarian coalition.

1803: The principalities of the German Holy Roman Empire are shattered and pull back to Brixen and Trient.

1805-1806: After the defeat by Napoleon at Austerlitz, Austria cedes Tyrol to Bavaria; other temporary boundary changes ensue.

1809/1810: Tyrolean Revolt against Bavaria and France, led by Andreas Hofer, fails.

1815: Following Napoleon's defeat, the Congress of Vienna gives all of the Dolomites to Austria, which already holds Venice and Lombardy.

1864-1867: A railroad is built over the Brenner Pass.

1866: Austria loses Venice to the Italians. The Dolomites south and southeast of Cortina (the Cadore) join the new Kingdom of Italy. Cortina and the northern and western valleys remain with Austria.

1912: The Great Dolomite Road crosses the Austrian Dolomites from Bolzano to Cortina.

1914-1918: First World War. In 1915 Italy joins the Allies; bloody fighting in the mountains between Italy and Austria, with emplacements as high as 3000m (almost 10,000ft) across the range, from the Lagorai group to the Sexten Dolomites. Areas at the Front (like Arabba) are evacuated and eventually destroyed by shelling (for example Toblach/Dobbiaco). In the Italian enclaves there is resistance, with many from the province of Trentino fighting on the Italian side. Heroes of the Italian resistance (the 'Irridentisti'), such as Cesare Battisti from Trient/Trento, are executed by the Austrians and become martyrs; many Italian streets and squares are still named in their memory.

1918: Tyrol south of the Brenner Pass falls to the Italians.

1919: The Treaty of St Germain establishes the present border between Austria and Italy. All the Dolomites become part of Italy. New borders divide the area into three new provinces: Bolzano/Bozen, Trentino and Belluno.

1922: The Fascists take over government offices in South Tyrol by force.

1923: Edict forbidding the use of the German language in schools in South Tyrol. Illegal schools spring up throughout the area. All public offices, notices, etc must be exclusively in Italian. In the same year the Fascists forbid the name 'Tyrol' and substitute a made-up word: Alto Adige (translation from the German 'Upper Etsch Valley'). They try to break the cultural identity of the German- and Ladin-speaking people and Italianise the population.

1935: With the building of an industrial zone in south Bolzano and the massive influx of workers from southern Italy the Italianisation is accelerated.

1938: After Austria is annexed by the German Reich, South Tyrol expects to be annexed as well. But Hitler promises his ally Mussolini that the Brenner Pass border will be inviolate.

1939-1945: Second World War; even before the opening of hostilities, Italians and Germans unite in a settlement in the German-speaking part of South Tyrol. Up until the end of 1939 the option remains open for Italians to stay in their homeland or for people of German origin to emigrate to the German Reich: 86% of South Tyroleans opt for emigration but, because of the war, only 30% actually do so.

1946: The Paris Peace Conference reconfirms for Italy the borders that existed before the war.

1948: The provinces of Bozen/Bolzano and Trient/Trento are given administrative autonomy. This means that German can again be taught in schools. But the administration remains in Trient/Trento, where German-speaking people are in the minority. In the following years the provinces' autonomy is constantly undermined: for instance, in 1955 a law is passed forbidding children to be christened with non-Italian names — a reminder of the Fascist era.

1956: Winter Olympics in Cortina d'Ampezzo, greatly promoting the appeal of the Dolomites as a tourist destination.

1959-1967: Austria brings the question of South Tyrolean autonomy before the full congress of the UN, which offers to help negotiations. Terrorist attacks against Italian establishments. By 1967 all parties in negotiations.

1972: Autonomy for South Tyrol grows in strength; the administration in Bozen/Bolzano receives much more authority. Equality between the Italian and German languages.

2002: Italy passes a bill allowing provincial borders to change, even when it's a matter of an autonomous province (something not previously allowed). The way is open for Ladin areas (Ampezzo, Buchenstein and the Fassatal) to become part of South Tyrol, with its political and cultural guarantees for German and Ladin people.

2008: The SVP (South Tyrolean People's Party), the main representative of the German and Ladin electorate, loses its majority for the first time. People appear to be voting less on ethnic criteria.

2018-to date: Elections in 2018 lead to a massive loss in support for German-speaking secessionist parties in South Tyrol. The SVP is also at a low ebb, forced to form a coalition with the populist/conservative LN party. There are more Italian-speaking MPs. In Trentino there is a centre-right government.

Walking in the Dolomites

You may think of bare crags, steep ridges, the alpine glow and King Laurin's kingdom in the rose garden. The fact that the famous legends, which have been handed down for centuries in the Ladin-speaking area, have survived to this day are proof that the Dolomites are a deeply mysterious, mystical region. This is not limited to the rocky summits, but extends to the dark pine forests, the flaming larch groves, flower-strewn alpine meadows down to steep valley gorges, on the slopes of which ancient farmhouses cling like eagle's nests. And you can hike in all these altitude zones!

The walks in this book range from simple strolls across alm meadows with 'inn crawls' for culinary delights to high alpine hut-hopping — and everything in between. And the best part of it is that as long as you keep off the main trails, start out early in the morning, and don't pick August for your walking break, you are often on your own. And then there is sure to be a hut somewhere to take a break… with a hearty meal of dumplings or a spicy ham platter, maybe with a glass of red wine to go with it.

Walking areas

The walks in this guide cover the areas closest to the main valley roads: the Pustertal/Val Pusteria embracing the S49 (the main west-east road in the northern part of the range) and the A22 motorway/S12 in the Eisacktal/Valle Isarco. The companion volume (Book 2) covers the Grödnertal/Val Gardena, Gadertal/Val Badia and the eastern Dolomites — 'inland' of these two main arteries. Between them, the walks cover many of the UNESCO World Heritage regions (see panel on page 8).

This volume explores not only the **lower and upper Pustertal/Val Pusteria**, but three interesting valleys north of the S49: the Tauferertal/Val di Tures and Ahrntal/Valle Aurina and the more easterly Antholzertal/Valle de Anterselva. East of the Eisacktal the main focus for the walks are the Villnösstal/Val di Funes, the Seiser Alm/Alpe di Siusi and the Rosengarten/Catinaccio area.

The lower **Pustertal** is narrow and shady; the walks in this guide are concentrated in the upper valley — where you'll find some of the most famous motifs of the Dolomites, like the Drei Zinnen/Tre Cime di Lavaredo … and plenty of other walkers.

The **Villnösstal/Val di Funes** is by far the quietest and most unspoilt walking area. That might be because there are no lifts at the foot of the mighty Geisler/Odle peaks. Not all the inhabitants of the valley are happy about this! For

View across the Seiser Alm/Alpe di Siusi meadows to Schlern/Sciliar and the Santner peaks

years they've been talking about linking the valley with Seceda — luckily, so far these talks have come to nothing.

The villages of Kastelruth/Castelrotto, Seis/Siusi and Völs/Fiè, below the **Seiser Alm/Alpe di Siusi** have kept their rural character, even though they are very touristic. Vines are cultivated in the area, and there are many well-preserved medieval farms. The alm itself, the largest alpine pasture in Europe, is for the most part car-free. Although it's full of people for most of the year, you will usually be able to find a quiet place for yourself on this huge plateau. Between Schlern/Sciliar and the Rosszähne/Denti di Terrarossa you can also be sure of plenty of high-alpine walking options.

The **Rosengarten/Catinaccio area** is an alpine surprise bag, filled with boulders, scree-filled gullies and cauldrons, rock teeth, ridges and mighty walls. But it also offers gentler walking — like the isolated Tschamintal/Valle di Ciamin and the track to the idyllicly sited Haniger Schwaige (dairy) in the Tiersertal/Val di Tires (Walk 26).

Weather and best times to walk

In the Dolomites it is basically warmer and milder than north of the Alps — and usually drier, since the main Alpine ridge protects the range from cold winds and storms. It's not for nothing that the South Tyrol tourist board has been promoting the slogan guaranteeing '300 days of sunshine a year'.

When bad weather builds up in the south, it sometimes leads to the notorious 'Föhn' north of the Alps. The so-called 'Northföhn' is less well known. It can be caused by bad weather on the northern side of the Alps or a cold front coming in from the west. In the first case, it ensures sunny, mild weather in the valleys, in the second case the weather is nice, but there is a stormy, icy wind.

You can go through all five climatic zones in the Dolomites if you travel from the Etschtal/Adige Valley west of Bolzano into the mountains. You would start out in an **insubric climate**, in a region where the average annual temperature is above 10°C/50°F. The winter is mild, there's seldom any frost, precipitation is about 700-900mm/27-30in, there are

Winter walking is increasingly popular

not many long dry periods. The southern slopes are usually snow-free in winter. But a little bit higher, the **submontane central European climate** begins, with changeable precipitation patterns. It's dry in the Eisacktal/Valle Isarco, but in other places precipitation can reach 1400mm/55in. Downy oak, hop beech and cultivated sweet chestnut characterise this climate zone. The average yearly temperature is between 9° and 10°C, and winter frosts are quite common. When you get to the **montane central European climate** zone, the annual mean temperature sinks to under 7°C/45°F, with precipitation between 900-1400mm/30-55in. Once in the mountains, up to 2200m/7200ft, there's a **subalpine climate**. The annual mean temperatures are around 4°C/39°F, with most precipitation in winter and staying on the ground as snow for quite some time. The **alpine climate** is limited to the high alpine peaks. With a yearly average temperature of about 0°C/32°F the subsoil is frozen year-round and snow lies at least half of the year — usually for eight months.

So basically it depends on the height of where you want to walk in the Dolomites. You can hike here all year round. One of the trends in recent years is **winter walking**. Many trails are cleared in winter, and huts are generally open from December to March. And there's also snowshoeing — very popular now — as it's possible at all heights and doesn't depend on how thick the snow is. But of course, like skiing, there's always a certain danger from avalanches and abruptly changing weather. Winter walking is certainly possible on the Seiser Alm/Alpe di Siusi, in the Villnösstal/Val di Funes or in the Tschamintal/Valle di Ciamin.

But the classic walking seasons in the Dolomites are **early summer** (on lower ground from May, in higher reaches and northern slopes from mid-June to the end of the month) with its endless floral carpets, **high summer** (July and August), when it's guaranteed that the lifts and huts will all be open (disadvantage: heat and afternoon thunderstorms) and **autumn** (September/October)

— when the weather is usually stable, the yellowing larch foliage is magnificent, and the air is clear. In many years autumnal walks are possible well into November… but lifts and huts are closed, to get ready for the influx of winter visitors.

Flora

Even attempting to sketch out the abundance of flora in a guidebook like this is impossible: if you hike in the Dolomites, you will encounter subalpine and alpine vegetation.

The reason for the diversity is the different altitude zones. In addition, there are the various rocks and their effects on the plant world. All of this is influenced again by the climate, the dryness of some valleys and the high precipitation on some north-western flanks, the moisture of the soil in the valleys and in high alpine cirques, in swamps and moors and at the edge of lakes — as well as the surface heating on steep sunny slopes.

The dry **pine forests** on the southern slopes of the large valleys are still extensive. There are natural **spruce forests** in all areas of the region between 900m/3000ft and 2000m/6500ft; on the higher elevations these are widely interspersed with **larch**. There are, literally, light forests of larch — all other trees having been cut down for grazing land. Humans have been very hard on the **stone pine** forests. They were cleared to make way for alpine pastures, and the wood was much in demand (a stone pine is still the pride of every farmer today, and few new hotels being built today can do without this wood). But stone pines can still be found on the higher elevations and in inaccessible areas.

The **dwarf shrub** belt with dwarf pines, rhodendrons and junipers has also been heavily shaped by man and cleared for grazing. The high-alpine communities and plants growing in the highest mountain areas in

Alpine anemones growing high up on a slope; above: star-like edelweiss

which they can survive (over 2500m/8200ft and up to the summits) are mostly in their original state.

Among the 1500 species of flowering plants to be found in the Dolomites, there are many endemic flora — plants that only occur in this zone and have adapted to the lime. This is how new species and subspecies emerged. This can be clearly observed in the **stemless gentian**: *Gentiana kochiana* grows on crystalline rocks, *Gentiana clusii* grows on limestone. To the layperson, these two species of the classical gentian look identical; it would take a botanist to know the difference. But the Dolomites also have real endemics that can only be found here: a saxifrage species and the **Dolomite columbine**, the **Dolomite yarrow**, **Séguier's buttercup** and the beautiful, but rarely seen **crested devil's claw** that grows on steep rock faces.

Fauna

In the Dolomites humans have changed the environment according to their needs and so restricted, destroyed, but also expanded the habitat of many animals. While roe deer and red deer get enough space, the black grouse has become rare because Tyrolean hats sport its feathers…

You are most likely to encounter wild animals on high pastures and mountain meadows. On alpine grass, especially in the cirque hollows, you can often see marmot burrows and the males who give piercing whistles to warn others when you approach. **Chamois** are not uncommon, and if you are lucky you can watch the **Alpine hare**, but also **hazel grouse** and **snow grouse**. The

Above: a curious marmot

Below: the protected martagon lily

golden eagle circles over the Fanes and Puez groups. As soon as you reach a summit or hut, you are flown around by curious **alpine choughs**, and for a bite the birds come daringly close to hikers.

Capercaillie and **black grouse** are among the European grouse which used to be found in many areas and are now limited to a few areas of the Alps and northern Europe. They have been greatly decimated by the love of black grouse, mainly because of the cock's decorative tail feathers, which are popular on Tyrolean hats. Today their habitat is so reduced that only small remnants remain. The total number doesn't sound too bad: in the Alps and Carpathians there are supposedly around 43,000 black grouse, but in the north of the British Isles alone there are some 25,000! But the stocks are isolated and their numbers are getting smaller and smaller due to the destruction of nature and the environment. The annual courting ritual of the grouse is famous; the adult males fight with each other in clearings for the females, who look on nonchalantly.

Marmots belong to the squirrel family, but they are larger; they can grow up to 66cm long (over 2ft) and weigh 7kg/15lb. They are typical rodents with strong yellow teeth that they use to eat leaves, shoots, flowers and seeds. They are real winter sleepers, they spend five to seven months a year sleeping in their burrows, during which the normal 70 pulse beats per minute are reduced to five. A side cave is used as a toilet: if you wake up twice a month, you go to this part of the 'building' to urinate. In the past, the marmot had more enemies than today (the population is estimated at 50,000 animals); the extermination of lynx and wolf in the alpine habitat has only left eagles and foxes as enemies. Marmots live in large family groups. If the animals are outside the burrow, a few older males always watch to whistle in case of danger, whereupon everything disappears into the nearest hole.

Equipment and food

Many trails run over stony and loose, sometimes skiddy ground, so that for most hikes **ankle-high hiking boots with good grip** are necessary. A few simple hikes can be done with trainers, for all other walks we strongly advise you to wear suitable footwear! You should also take **sun protection**,

A pair of eagles circle above the Langental/Vallunga

sunglasses, a **first aid kit,** and appropriate **hat**, a **rain jacket** and (in spring/autumn or for high-altitude walks) a **thick jersey** or **multi-layer clothing**. In the winter months, **hats** and **gloves** will be required. **Hiking poles** are particularly advantageous on long, steep ascents and descents, but on some walks they are *indispensable* due to the great height difference, which could cause you to damage your knee and hip joints.

Don't stint on your supply of drinks: you should carry 1.5 to 2 litres of water per person — more on long hikes. Springs and fountains are only found on certain stretches and, while there may be plenty of huts, the distances between them are often considerable. The situation is similar with the provisions: better to have a couple of muesli bars or sandwiches too many with you than to struggle on the last kilometre up the mountain with a growling stomach or even to sink at the side of the path with low blood sugar.

One of the reasons we recommend hiking boots on many walks is that you may be walking over tree roots like these!

Emergencies and emergency phone numbers

You should always have a fully charged mobile with you so that you can dial the following number in an emergency: **112, the pan-European emergency number**. An emergency doctor and ambulance, as well as the **Italian mountain rescue** service can be reached at **118**.

If you don't have a mobile with you or you're in a dead zone with no signal, use these internationally recognised rescue signals: optical (eg, wave a handkerchief) or acoustic (eg, shout) **six times** in a row, leaving a space of **10 seconds** between each, then wait **one minute** and **repeat the emergency call** (six signals every 10 seconds). Smartphone owners have the advantage that they can make an emergency call directly via the emergency service app ('Emergency Service South Tyrol'). This app also lists the nearest hospitals, pharmacies and emergency doctors on a daily basis.

Planning your walks and getting to them

The walks in this book all end at the point where they started out: perhaps it's a circuit, an out-and-back walk, or a linear walk with a

34 Dolomites, Book 1: North and West

Waymarking and signposting are exemplary. The sign above, on Walk 18, shows both trail numbers and names.

bus back to the start. A lift often helps to optionally shorten the ascent or descent. You can choose from a wide range of short, easy walks through to strenuous day-long hikes. *The times quoted are pure walking times without breaks.* It can take longer if you have children or if there are some sights along the way. If you have a dog with you, please keep it on a lead. Early departures are generally recommended — to avoid the heat in summer and minimize the risk of getting caught in a thunderstorm. And outside high season, the shorter days usually force you to leave early anyway.

If you plan to be **car-free** (see 'Getting around by bus' on page 11), which is not difficult due to the good bus network and inexpensive guest cards, inquire about bus times (at www.sii.bz.it all route plans can be downloaded as PDFs), and remember that on weekends buses often only run every few hours or with a 'lunch break'. If you want to use a mountain lift, the relevant operating times are shown in the same chapter as the walk, *but double-check on the ground or in advance on the net.* (Lifts usually operate from 9am to 5pm in summer, often longer, and seasonally from mid-June to mid-September, sometimes longer.) Buses often go directly to the valley stations of the lifts.

Waymarks and signposts, grades, maps, GPS

Trails in the Dolomites are usually well cared for and maintained. **Waymarks** are clearly recognizable and mostly applied throughout. Red and white or red-white-red is the general waymarking colour found on rocks, trees, posts and signs. A few walks are **signposted** using the name of the particular trail, as in the signpost shown above left for Walk 18 ('PU' indicated the circuit trail around 'Puflatsch'). But almost all hiking trails are numbered. The identifying name or number of all trails followed during a walk is indicated in the logistics section at the top of the page. Since some trails have multiple numbers on certain stages — or there are occasional differences between the signs and hiking maps — please don't just rely on numbers! There is no danger of getting lost on any of the walks in this book. And you will rarely be on your own…

Walking in the Dolomites 35

There is a quick overview of each walk's **grade** in the Contents, with more information at the top of each walk. In outline:
- 🔵 easy-moderate; good surfaces underfoot; ascent up to 600m
- 🔴 moderate-strenuous; less good terrain, ascents often above 600m
- ⚫ difficult — only suitable for very experienced hillwalkers
- ❗ indicates exposed sections where you must be sure-footed, with a head for heights.

The **maps in this book**, drawn by the original German publisher, **are all at different scales**. We have adapted them partially, to be more in tune with our usual style, but we were not able to change the scales without redrawing them entirely. ***This can be deceptive; please check the map scale before setting off!*** Below is a key to the map symbols:

- ═══ Motorway
- ━━━ Main road
- ━━━ Secondary road, motor track
- ──── Track (motorable, jeep, farm)
- ┄┄┄┄ Footpath.Park boundary
- ──2→── Main walk and direction
- ──2→── Alternative and direction
- ●━━● Lift (chair or cable car)
- ⛨ † Church.Cross or crucifix
- ♜ ♜• Castle or palace.In ruins
- ♜ ▽ Rock.Interesting feature
- 🏛 ℹ️ Museum.Information
- 🚌 🅿️ Bus stop.Parking.
- ▬ ▬ Railway station.Building
- ⊟ ⊖ Gate/gateway.Closed
- ✿)(Viewpoint.Bridge
- 🗿 ★ Cairn.Natural attraction
- ○ ⊖ Spring.Source
- ⓦ ✴ Waterfall.Sportsground
- 🏕 🏠 Picnic area.Hut/refuge/dairy
- 🔟 ★ Waypoint.Attraction

Walkers, climbers and general enthusiasts should use the **excellent large-scale maps** (1:25,000) published by **Tabacco**, available at all bookshops and newspaper kiosks in the Dolomites. The **Kompass** and **Freytag & Berndt** maps are generally less detailed but sometimes more up-to-date, as they are reprinted more frequently. While our maps should suffice for the main walks in this book, it is

Brillenschafe ('spectacle-wearing sheep', named for the black rings round their eyes; see Walk 12) are great mountain climbers!

assumed that you will have at least the relevant Tabacco map covering your base area. There is a wealth of detail to be gleaned from these Tabacco maps, and they may be needed if you take up any of the dozens of unmapped walking or cycling tips described or mentioned in passing.

Free **GPS tracks** are available for all these walks: see the Dolomites page for Book 1 on the Sunflower website. Please bear in mind, however, that GPS readings should *never* be relied upon as your sole reference point. And those of you who cannot be bothered to use GPS on the ground *may* nevertheless enjoy opening the GPX files in Google Earth to preview the walks in advance!

1 PUSTERTAL/VAL PUSTERIA: THE LOWER VALLEY

Mühlbach and the Valser Tal • Meransen • Vintl and the Pfunderer Tal • Terenten and Pfalzen • Bruneck • Sonnenburg Nunnery

Walks: none; *walking tips:* Lindenweg (page 37); Mills Nature Trail (page 39); *cycling tip:* St Lorenzen to Mühlbach (page 43)
Websites
www.eisacktal.com
www.pustertal.org
www.gitschberg-jochtal.com
www.vintl.net
www.kronplatz.com
www.bruneck.com
www.meransen.com
www.terenten.com
www.kiens.info
www.olang.info
www.dolomitisuperski.com
Opening hours: see individual attractions

From Franzensfeste/Fortezza almost all the way to Bruneck/Brunico the valley of the Rienz River is narrow and shady. So most people stick to the sunny side-valleys or make straight for Bruneck.

The lower Pustertal is not really suitable for settlement and is sparsely populated apart from market and administrative centres like Mühlbach/Rio di Pusteria and Vintl/Vandóies. Two sunny neighbouring valleys, the Valser Tal and Pfunderer Tal, run in from the north; both of them have pretty farming villages and many solid Tyrolean twin farm buildings. From here one can climb the ice-capped peaks of the Zillertal Alps, like Hochfeiler on the Austrian border, but also explore the lovely high alpine landscape around Lake Eisbrugg.

The sunny terrace between Terenten/Terento and Pfalzen/Falzes is quite heavily populated — more grows here, the days with sunshine are more frequent than in the deep valley below or in the side-valleys. The landscape is also very suitable for strolls and short walks. Bruneck, the most important town in the whole Pustertal, lies in a wide basin; it has a well-preserved old centre, worth seeing.

Mühlbach/Rio di Pusteria and the Valser Tal/Val di Valles

The Eisacktal narrows some 2km above Mühlbach by the Mühlbacher Klause, the remains of a Middle Ages defensive wall and toll-house. A prehistoric stone-slab track, the Lindenweg, runs up to Meransen/Meranza on a sunny terrace, which can also be reached by cable car or road. Up here the old farms have been converted into apartments and hotels. In contrast, the **Valser Tal**, despite having a small ski area, has remained essentially unchanged — especially when you walk up into the end of the valley, where you can take a break on the Fane Alm, one of the few alm villages in the region.

Sights and excursions:
Mühlbach was an important place in the old days, as can be seen in several important old buildings — like the **Ansitz Strasshof**, where once the guardian of the bishopric was housed (the most important government official, in charge of the tolls). Others are **Ansitz Freienthurn**, today cloisters and a

Pustertal/Val Pusteria: the lower valley

school, and **Ansitz Kandlburg**, where the court was once held (today a château-hotel).

The **parish church** is Gothic, with beautiful frescoes dating from the Middle Ages, really worth seeing. Many Roman remains have been uncovered in the late Gothic **Floriani Chapel**, which is open to the public. *Parish museum, with (among other displays) remains from the Floriani Chapel, open Wed/Sat from 10.00-12.00.*

The **Mühlbacher Klause**, dating from 1269, marked the border between the lands of Brixen and the Pustertal (which belonged to the Counts of Görz-Tirol) up until 1500. Mühlbach was the administrative seat at the time; the Kandelburg in the centre of Mühlbach still recalls these days. The building has been restored. *Open Jun-Sep; guided tours or visits upon reservation, with a voluntary contribution.*

● **Walking tip: the Lindenweg**
From Mühlbach the **Lindenweg**, an ancient, probably prehistoric stone-slab track climbs 600m up to Meransen. Allow about 1h30min *to walk down* (waymarked Trail 12, Tabacco 1:25,000 map N° 037). About halfway down, on a flat stretch, you walk below a roof protecting a simple altar and memorial stone with three female figures called the **Jungfernrast**. It depicts the three holy maidens Aubet, Cubet and Cuere (the king's daughters according to legend), who fled the Huns and collapsed half mad with thirst. As they fell to their knees and prayed to God for help, a spring emerged from the rock and a cherry tree sprouted, laden with fruit.

Most visitors ignore the village of **Rodeneck/Rodengo** itself and make straight for the castle, **Burg Rodeneck**. Like all good castles, this one stands on a rock on a steep slope above the Rienz Valley. The setting is charming, the long building with its pre-castle in front most eye-catching. In the 13th century a knight who owned the castle had the '12 Adventures of Iwein' (from the courtly romance better known as 'Yvain, the Knight with the Lion', dating from about 1200) depicted as frescoes. There is also a fresco of one of the knights of King Arthur's Round Table (shown on page 25). These frescoes, one of the earliest examples of non-religious painting in the Alps, were only discovered by chance in 1972. *Open daily ex Sat from May to mid-Oct; guided tours at 11.30, 14.30 (mid-Jul to mid-Aug also 15.30); entry fee 8 €.*

The **Fane Alm**, with its huts, barns and chapel lies on a sunny meadow in the highest reaches of the Valser Tal at 1740 m. The huts are closely packed together; the alm looks like a village, although it's only inhabited in summer. In the past the whole village lived up here, taking care of the cattle and making butter and cheese. There are still cattle, but now you can reach the alm by road. The alm caters for walkers, with hearty snack food at the Gatterer Hut. I heartily recommend **two walks** from the alm up into high alpine terrain (Tabacco 1:25,000 map N° 037): one goes to Lake Grossen and the Wieser Hut, from where you can get back to Vals via the Altfasstal; the other goes way up the Valser Tal to the Brixner Hut, with possibilities of going even further — to Wilde Kreuzspitze (3134m) with its

Pustertal, with the Bruneck basin and Tauferer Tal

fantastic view, or completing a magnificent but very strenuous circuit via Lake Wilden back to the Fane Alm.

Meransen/Meranza

Until a generation ago Meransen was the preserve of local farmers, but tourists are warming to the place. The farms still exist, and on Sunday mornings, when the churchgoers are out in force, you will see Meransen for the the old farming community it still is — despite the lively winter season at the Gitschberg ski area. You can get there by road or lift from Mühlbach (all year round from about 07.00-18.40).

Sights: Meransen's **church** is beautifully situated on the sunny village plateau. The walled-in cemetery is quiet and affords far-off views into the Pustertal and to the Dolomites. A fresco in front of the entrance under the massive tower depicts St Christopher. Nothing outside gives a clue to what lies within: one of the most beautiful rococo interiors in Tyrol — magnificent and bright, with decoration, frescoes, altar paintings and ivory-white wooden sculpture. On the right-hand side altar are late Gothic statues of the three holy maidens mentioned on page 37, to their right a box containing interesting votive offerings.

Vintl/Vandóies and the Pfunderer Tal/Val di Fundres

The Pfunderer Tal runs from Vintl far into the mountains; only a short ridge separates Weisszint (3264m) from the high peaks of the main Alpine ridge. Since there are no lifts in the valley itself, winter is quieter than summer, despite the proximity of the Gitschberg-Jochtal skicircus. But the valley is an **eldorado for walkers** and climbers, as well as really fit mountain bikers. 'Marble' has been quarried in the valley for centuries; it's not real marble, but a green to bright grey serpentine.

Sights and excursions: Vintl: Two churches stand on the hill in Niedervintl, the old parish church and the new one. But the **new**

parish church isn't really so new, it's a true baroque building. The painting is by Josef Anton Zoller (1763), who has a street in the village named after him. On the other hand, the **old parish church** is *really* old; it's referred to as far back as the 14th century when it was already old, having been started in Romanesque style. Inside, 'new' frescoes by Leonhard von Brixen have come to light: they are only about 500 years old.

Pfunders/Fundres lies high in the valley. There is a beautiful view from the church with its late Middle Ages fresco of St Christopher. Pfunders is made up of little hamlets and solitary farms that are attractively dispersed above the valley floor. The farms at **Kammerschien/Camporsino** comprise the highest settlement in Pfunders, at 1520m! Now it is served by a road, but until quite recently it could only be reached on foot (a two-hour ascent). This trail was called the **Kirchweg** (Church Walk), since naturally all the farming families from Kammerschien went to mass on Sundays — half a day's undertaking.

If you go further up the valley, the road ends at a car park beyond the 'Duner Heuschupfe'. From here a private road continues to the outermost farms of **Dun**, the highest in the valley, at 1480 m. There are several signposted **walks** from Dun — to the Edelraute Hut and through the Duner Klamm to Engberg and the Weitenberg alm (5h return; easy to moderate).

Terenten/Terento and Pfalzen/Falzes

The hoteliers up in these villages have been heavy-handed with their hackneyed slogans: 'sunny terrace', 'great view to the Dolomites', etc. But it is an accurate description of the south-facing terraces between Terenten and Pfalzen. Apart from these two villages there are only hamlets and isolated farms. The farms and the large families needed a lot of space and thus settled quite a distance from each other. So there is a large network of tracks joining these old hamlets and single farms. A few have been improved to roads which await your discovery — perhaps by mountain bike, which is the ideal transport up here. But don't be fooled by the road map; between Terenten and Pfalzen it's *not* all flat terrain, although even casual cyclists manage most of the climbs.

Sights and excursions: Thanks to tourism the centre of **Terenten** (stress the first syllable) is heavily built-up today. A bypass road called the 'Pustertaler Sonnenstrasse' avoids the centre, and one can wander round the pedestrian zone undisturbed. The scattered settlements, including those on the hill where the grouped farm buildings stand, date back thousands of years.

The **parish church** has a Gothic choir and tower, but the rest dates from the 19th century. The church cemetery is typical of the Tyrol.

● ***Walking tip: Mills Nature Trail***
Above Terenten the attractive **earthen pyramids** shown overleaf are constantly appearing, due to water erosion. This area lies in the Ternertal and can be reached in about half an hour by following the **Mills Nature Trail**. Some of these old water mills, once used for grinding corn, are still in good condition, and one of them is used for show purposes.

Earthen pyramids above Terenten. You can see them on the Mills Nature Trail.

Between Terenten and Pfalzen, in the hamlet of **Issing**, you can visit the Bergila distillery, which has been distilling herbal oils for over 100 years. Some of the herbs come from gardens around Issing itself. ***Open for visits May-end Oct, Mon-Fri (in Jul/Aug also Sat/Sun) from 08.00-12.00 and 13.00-18.00***.

The houses and extravagant façades in **Pfalzen** are testament to the fact that people once earned a good living here, when court was held in nearby Schloss Schöneck above Issing (private; not open for visits). The baroque **parish church** is very pretty, but of far more interest to art historians is the inside of the little Gothic **Valentinskirche** in the open meadows east of Pfalzen. To get there take the road to the right above the Gasthof and after about 800m turn right to the church. A complete cycle of frescoes painted by Friedrich Pacher in 1487 was discovered on its north wall in 1979/80.

Bruneck/Brunico

Bruneck is certainly worth a visit. But take the lift up **Kronplatz/Plan de Corones** before you explore the town. From up there you have the best view of its position at the confluence of two important valleys.

Old Bruneck is a small town dating from the Middle Ages, really worth seeing. Gates, old village houses, a castle, museum, churches (from Gothic to baroque), a fascinating folk museum in nearby Dietenheim, good places to eat and drink, the best shopping between Brixen and Lienz, theatre — all this brings a lot of visitors. In the evenings the 'Spaziermeile' (Strolling Mile) outside the old town gates is a long open-air café.

The tourist office organises **walks** for all abilities, and can also tell you about special events — like the classical concerts in July and August, the day-long jazz festival in July, street theatre during the first week in September, and various winter events including the Christmas Eve market in the old town, with displays of local crafts.

Transport: There is ample **parking**; the old town is a pedestrianised zone. You can also come by train, with good connections from Brixen, Bolzano and the Hochpustertal, or by bus: the **bus station** is near the **railway station**, and there are connections to all the valleys in eastern South Tyrol.

Sights: You enter the walled old town via the **Ursuline Gate** beside the Gothic **Ursuline**

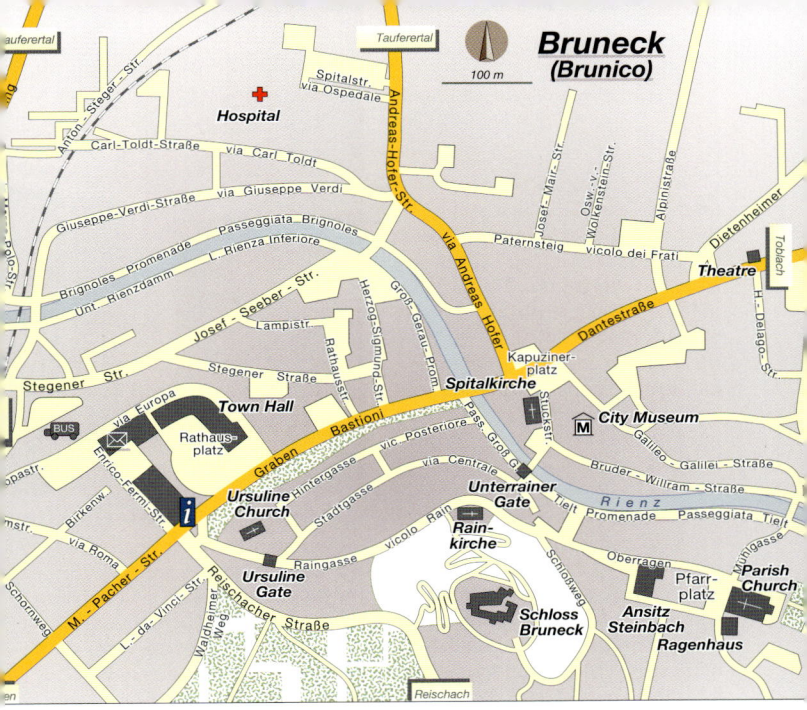

Church. The row of townhouses on **Stadtgasse**, the main thoroughfare, is most attractive. Some of the buildings still have old signs hanging outside; in times past, not only inns, but all business premises had these signs. Walk through the **Unterrainer Gate**, decorated with frescoes, and into **Platz Oberragen**. This is where the craftsmen and civil servants had their premises outside the Middle Ages town. There's a baroque column dedicated to St Mary and, at the end of the square, the **Ansitz Sternbach**, a massive townhouse with bay windows and tower dating from 1664. The neo-Romanesque **parish church** (1855) is one of the first churches built in this style. In Paul von Sternbach Street the Renaissance **Ragenhaus** is worth seeing (today it is a music school).

The **Rainkirche**, dedicated to St Catherine, has a good tower with a two-storey baroque onion dome and a baroque nave. In the little adjacent park there's an open-air bar in summer.

Founded in 1250, the same time as the town, **Schloss Bruneck** has been heavily restored. But it is still an attractive castle, with the coats-of-arms of the Brixen archbishops in the courtyard, and a round tower with a spiral staircase. The rooms are in both the Renaissance and baroque styles; those fitted out in 1500 for Kaiser Maximilian are especially splendid. Part of the castle is now 'Ripa', a **Messner Museum** (see also Kronplatz, page 44): its theme is the development of mountain people on the five continents, and different guests will be invited each year to talk about their homeland. *Open from the 2nd Sun in May to 1 Nov and from end Dec to end April 10.00-18.00, cl. Tue, entry 11 €, concessions 9 €.*

The baroque **Spitalkirche**

Votive offerings in the folk museum testify to St Mary's help.

(1761) has an attractive façade and interior. Part of the altar still has the original marble ornamentation so popular at that time. When you leave the church, take Dantestrasse to leave Kapuzinerplatz and head towards the outside of town. At the first crossing you come to an old shrine-like pillar with crumbled frescoes protected by a roof. These were painted by Hans von Bruneck at the beginning of the 15th century.

Old and new combine to make the **Stadtmuseum für Graphik** a really original attraction. Exhibitions include works by Michael and Friedrich Pacher, Albrecht Dürer, Simon and Veit von Taisten (altar triptych) and modern classics from the likes of Oskar Kokoschka, Alfred Kubin, Paul Klee, Paul Flora, Alfred Hrdlicka and Kurt Moldovan. *Museum open Tue-Fri 15.00-18.00, Sat/Sun 10.00-12.00; in Jul/Aug Tue-Sun 10.00-12.00 and 15.00-18.00, entry 3 €, concessions 2 €.*

On the other side of the valley, at the foot of Kronplatz, **Reischach/Riscone** sits on a sunny terrace with fine views. Today the village forms part of Bruneck. Up here you'll find most of the hotels, *pensions* and rooms to rent. There's also a Gothic church and the huge **Ansitz Angerburg**, dating from the 17th century.

Dietenheim/San Theodone

The **South Tyrol Folk Museum** is located in the village of Dietenheim on the northern edge of the Bruneck basin. It is laid out in the Mair am Hof residence (1690-1700) and three hectares of surrounding land. Just the house itself, with its outbuildings, would have been sufficient for a wide-ranging museum, but the old farmhouses, stables and mills on the open land make the visit even more enjoyable. The buildings have been brought here from all over South Tyrol, balcony by balcony and stone by stone, then carefully reconstructed. The three-story Höfelerhof from Mühlwald is especially impressive. *Museum open from Easter Mon to end Oct, Tue-Sat 10.00-17.00 (Jul/Aug 18.00 and in Aug also Mon), Sun/holidays 14.00-18.00. Entry fee 9 €, families 18 €.*

St Georgen/San Giorgio and Gissbach

The old village of **St Georgen** lies just north of Bruneck in a loop of the Ahr/Aurina. Its presence is thanks to an old ford, where today a bridge crosses the stream over to Gissbach. Romanesque and pre-Romanesque remains have been found beneath the floor of the Gothic **parish church**. The Crucifixion group on the outside wall is probably the work of Hans von Bruneck. The buildings of Gissbach are very impressive: there are two old gabled houses with artistic doors and coats-of-arms (one of which is Schloss Gremsen, now offering rooms with kitchens), as well as many other beautiful old houses.

St Lorenzen/San Lorenzo and Sonnenburg Nunnery

St Lorenzen/San Lorenzo is the oldest settlement in the whole Bruneck basin, as evidenced by the many engravings and the remains of pilgrimage castles in the vicinity. Even the name harks back to ages past, since St Laurentius is a typical saint of late antiquity. The place must also have been founded before the Bavarian land acquisition. It's also known that **Sebatum**, the most important Roman site in the whole Pustertal was located here, and there is a Roman milestone on the road to Sonnenburg. If you walk along that road today it's difficult to take in its original meaning. In the Middle Ages St Lorenzen was the outpost of the Tyrolean prince who held court at the nearby **Michelsburg**, while the Archbishop of Brixen had his seat at Schloss Bruneck. Whoever travelled from Bruneck to St Lorenzen had to pay a toll. The Madonna on the high altar of the **parish church** is the work of Michael Pacher.

The Sonnenburg château-hotel, on a hill, was originally **Sonnenburg Nunnery**. It was an autonomous order with pretty relaxed rules, and the nuns were a law unto themselves. Under the Brixen Archbishop Nikolaus von Kues, who wanted to carry out long-overdue reforms, a conflict arose between Sonnenburg and the bishopric which only ended with the intervention of Prince Sigismund von Tirol, after excommunication and some bloodshed — and even then it was a draw, with the departure of the abbess and the resignation of the bishop. The cloister was half in ruins until 1975, when part of it was rebuilt as an hotel; today of course it is an impressive and well-kept building. During the work the crypt of the earlier collegiate church was uncovered. Later, dynamiting for a new valley road took place just beneath the crypt, causing some damage, so they had to carry on without dynamite.

Cycling tip: from St Lorenzen to Mühlbach/Rio di Pusteria: This easy excursion for the whole family follows the **Pustertal cycle path** — only 18km each way (about 1h15min) and with just 60m of height difference. You can cycle back or take a bus to St Lorenzen or train to nearby Bruneck to start. Several watering holes lie en route. Easy — but not entirely straightforward, so use the 1:25,000 Tabacco map (N° 033) or the 1:50,000 Kompass map (N° 66).

Kiens/Chienes

The parish of Kiens comprises three villages: Kiens, Ehrenburg and St Sigmund, all lying a little above the Pustertal. **Ehrenburg** is known for its eponymous castle, which is a must. There's peaceful walking all around, and canoeing on the Rienz.

Sights: The **parish church** of St Sigmund has a triptych dating from 1480 and the little **pilgrimage chapel** on the road to Vintl some frescoes by Josef Anton Zoller.

Schloss Ehrenburg was the Archbishop of Brixen's castle. It acquired its Renaissance polish in around 1500 when a new section was built with a marvellous three-storey arcaded courtyard. The old Romanesque castle with its

In 2015 'Corones', the sixth, last and highest (2275m) of Reinhold Messner's museums opened on Kronplatz/Plan de Corones (designed by the late Zaha Hadid).

original keep was left untouched. But none of this was good enough for the later baroque princes from Brixen, the bishops. Archbishop Caspar Ignaz Künigl and his brother had the building re-created in the baroque style. Unfortunately the castle is privately owned and closed to the public.

Kronplatz/Plan de Corones

All the winds around Bruneck have their advantage: clouds carrying snow from the north are happy to deposit their white load at the first obstacle south of the main Alpine ridge — like **Plose** (see page 79) and **Kronplatz**. This flat-topped mountain always can be sure of snow, making it the skiing mountain *par excellence*, more developed than any other in the Dolomites. And all that so easily within reach — five minutes by car from Bruneck or by town bus to Reischach and then by lift to the peak. It's even worth driving up in summer; despite the lifts, roads, huts and other features that mar the summer landscape, there are beautiful **walking routes** and even more beautiful mountain bike tours (you can take bikes on the cablw cars).

Olang/Valdaora

Olang comprises four villages on the east side of Kronplatz, with two direct lift connections. The green basin in which these scattered villages lie is bordered in the west by the wooded slopes of Kronplatz and overlooked in the south by sharp Dolomite ridges — like Piz da Peres (2507m) and Maurerkogel (2567m).

Staying in Olang is a good idea if you want to walk in summer (there are over a dozen manned alms in the mountains above) but don't want to be far from the action (Bruneck is just around the corner). It's also fairly quiet in winter, despite its proximity to Kronplatz. Olang rises to the occasion with 28 hotels.

2 HOCHPUSTERTAL/ALTA PUSTERIA

Toblach • Niederdorf • Pragser Tal • Lake Prags • Plätzwiese • Innichen • Sexten • Fischleintal • Sexten Dolomites Nature Park • Helm

Walks: 1-4; *cycling tips:* from Toblach through the Höhlensteintal (page 40); Pustertal cycle path between Mühlbach and Lienz (page 52)
Websites
www.drei-zinnen.info
www.toblach.it
www.niederdorf.it
www.pragsertal.info
www.innichen.it
www.sexten.it
Opening hours: see individual attractions

This area, near the junction of the Rienz and Drau valleys between the Austrian border and Niederdorf/Villabassa, is the setting for some of the most iconic pictures of the Dolomites: the Drei Zinnen/Tre Cime de Lavoredo, Zwölferkofel, Lake Prags/Braies, Innichen/San Candido's baroque church, and the view from the Sennesalpe to Monte Cristallo.

Sexten/Sesto, Innichen, Toblach/Dobbiaco, Niederdorf and Prags offer plenty of beds for the visitor returning from a long walk, a strenuous day on the mountain bike or a car tour along the endless hairpin curves. You may even be glad to sink into bed after a hard day lazing about — like swimming in one of the icy mountain lakes (Prags, Dürren/Landro or Toblach). Or there's always Aquafun in Innichen for the odd rainy day.

Three valleys stretch south from the Hochpustertal. From Niederdorf the Pragser Tal/Val di Braies reaches far into the Dolomites. From Toblach the narrow Höhlensteintal/Val di Landro, hemmed in by high walls, runs to romantic Lake Dürren. In Innichen — historically the most important of all these villages — yet another valley branches off: the Sextental. On its south side are the Sexten Dolomites and the Drei Zinnen; to the north the Carnic Alps delineate the Austrian border.

Transport: The road through the Pustertal bypasses Niederdorf, Toblach and Innichen, all of which have plenty of **car parks**. There's a relatively good **bus service** in the valley ('Corriera'), which also serves Cortina d'Ampezzo. By **train** there are connections to Franzensfeste/Fortezza, Innsbruck and Bolzano as well as to Lienz in Austria.

Events: Some events are organised by the whole Hochpustertal area, among them the **International Choir Festival** in the last week of June (www.festivalpusteria.org). There are performances in all five parishes, including open-air concerts near the Haunold Hut or the restaurant on Helm, etc. Programmes include hymns, folk, spirituals, jazz...

Also common to the whole valley is the **'3 Zinnen Mountain Card'**, a summer pass covering the lifts up Haunold, Rotwand, Helm, Stiergarten and Col d'la Tenda (including bikes): 1 day 36 €, 3 in 4 days (up and down) 48 €, 5 in 7 days 62.50 €.

Dolomiti SuperSummer offers two kinds of **lift passes**: the **Super Summer Card** lets you use

The baroque parish church at Toblach/Dobbiaco is a gem.

100 lifts, including with bike: 1 day 47 €, 3 in 4 days 110 €, 5 in 7 days 147 €.

The **Holiday Pass** is given free to hotel guests and offers unlimited use of public transport, walking and skiing buses.

Toblach/Dobbiaco

Toblach lies at the point where the 'Alemagna' — the old trading route from Venice to southern Germany — meets the Pustertal.

The little village centre, with its magnificent late baroque church, is now surrounded by a host of new buildings — hotels, *pensions* and apartments. Toblach is one of the most important holiday bases in South Tyrol.

And has been for a long time: even in the 19th century there were hotels like the Grand in **Neutoblach/Dobbiaco Nuovo**, at that time a 'new' settlement, as the name implies. During the First World War Toblach lay in the firing line of the Italian emplacements on Mt Cristallino, and Neutoblach — except for the Grand Hotel, which was in a well-sheltered area — went up in flames; even the parish church was hit. The one-time enemy is now the most important visitor in August, at Christmas/New Year and in February — and of course during these times the people of Dobbiaco (as the place was christened in 1919) naturally speak Italian.

But it is for Toblach's setting that people come. Top of the list of course are the Drei Zinnen in the background (they can be seen from the higher village of Wahlen), but there is also the Höhlensteintal with Lake Toblach and Lake Dürren. The 'Alemagna' runs the whole length of the Höhlensteintal towards Cortina, which is under an hour's drive away. Toblach is well situated not only for Cortina; Innichen, Bruneck and Lienz in Austria are easily reached by bus or train. At Toblach there are **hikes and strolls** on your doorstep.

Transport: There is a large **car park** on Mittelweg, the **bus station** is Johannesstrasse (a continuation of Dolomitenstrasse), and the **railway station** is in Neutoblach (it's not manned, so there is an automatic ticket dispenser).

Events: Among the most popular events are the **Gustav Mahler Weeks** (www.gustav-mahler.it) and the **Festspiele Südtirol** (www.festspiele-suedtirol.it) with concerts by regional and international orchestras and ensembles, conferences and seminars.

For winter visitors, St Nicholas Day (6 Dec) or the day before ('Krampustag', 5 Dec), sees

St Nic's black companion, the '**Krampus**', making his rounds in Toblach and many other towns in South Tyrol. The Krampus impersonators, wearing masks and dressed as the Devil, gather for the large 'Krampus Run', which takes place throughout the entire 'Krampuszone' of the German-speaking areas. Participants come from all over South Tyrol, North Tyrol, Carinthia, Salzburg, southern Bavaria and German-speaking Switzerland. If you're frightened by the Krampuses, who carry huge brooms, then find a safe spot in one of the roped-off areas and enjoy your *glühwein* in peace.

Sights and excursions: Restored after the damage caused during the First World War, Toblach's **parish church, shown opposite,** is a splendid example of late baroque. The ceiling paintings (the Life of St John the Baptist) and those on the altar are the work of Franz Anton Zeiller. Everything is decorated with plaster and gilded, but not excessively so.

The **Calvary** along Maximilianstrasse (which runs to the church and cemetery) is the oldest in Tyrol, dating from 1519; five Stations are still in good condition. Together with the old Gorizian chapel in the parish church and the round hilltop chapel at the eastern exit from the village they make a complete 'sacred mountain', as was the vogue in northern Italy at that time.

The **Naturparkhaus** is located in the Cultural Centre of the old Grand Hotel in Neutoblach. This is a visitors' centre for the two parks bordering Toblach, which make up a large part of the Dolomites — the **Sexten Dolomites Nature Park** and the **Fanes-Sennes-Prags Nature Park**. Nature and culture, geology and fauna, plants and Alpine farming are presented in a modern setting. *Park House open 1 Jan to Mar and 1 May-31 Oct, Tue-Sat from 09.30-12.30, 14.30-18.00, Thu until 22.00; in high season also open Sun. Entry free.*

The farming village of **Wahlen/Valle San Silvestro** lies on sunny slopes where the Silvestertal comes into Toblach. There are a few *pensions* and large farm houses. From the village a wide level track (closed to motor traffic) runs out of the valley: in five minutes one comes to a **chapel** with a breathtaking view to the Sexten Dolomites including the Drei Zinnen. The village church, dedicated to **St Nicholas**, is worth seeing for its beautiful late Gothic net vault and the fresco near the door depicting the Poor Souls in Purgatory.

Aufkirchen/Santa Maria lies in a sunny spot high up between Toblach and Niederdorf. The village is dominated by the pilgrimage church of St Mary (**Marienwallfahrtskirche**), built in late Gothic style (1475) on the site of an older church which had become too small for the congregation. One can't miss the outsized fresco on the south wall, attributed to Simon von Taisten. It's a beautiful view for St Christopher and the Christ Child — and for us as well. From St Mary's you can follow the 'Meditation Path' (Besinnungsweg) with its seven Stations of the Cross to the little church of **St Peter im Kofl**. At a height of 1450 m, this is reputed to be the oldest church in the Pustertal.

The **Mahler Festival** in Toblach is a reminder of the three summer visits the composer made to the village. As the very busy Director of the Vienna State Opera, he escaped to the Trenkerhof in **Altschluderbach**, where he worked simultaneously on his Ninth and unfinished Tenth symphonies, as well as the 'Lied von der Erde'. In the adjacent '**Wildpark**' (game park) there's a small wooden house that Mahler had built, so he could work undisturbed. *Access is via Rienz (from the road into the Höhlensteintal turn right on a small road just past the railway overpass). Park open daily, Jun to Sep from 09.00-17.00, Fri-Wed, Oct to May from 10.00-16.00. Mahler's room in the Trenkerhof can no longer be visited, unfortunately.*

Niederdorf/Villabassa

The Pustertal road towards Toblach is referred to in the Niederdorf region as 'Frau Emma Strasse'. Frau Emma was Emerentia Hausbacher (1817-1904) and widely known throughout Tyrol: together with her husband, who came from Niederdorf, she built up an early hotel empire. The 'Schwarze Adler' in the Rathausplatz was the first step; next was a hotel at Lake Prags, then hotels in Meran, Innsbruck and the Vinschgau. Her cooking was as famous as her hospitality. One anecdote tells of an American who sent her a letter addressed simply to 'Frau Emma in Europe, Austria' — it was delivered, no problem! The **Hochpustertal Tourist Board Museum** between Niederdorf and Sexten, with its displays about early tourism in the area, was probably set up here because of her. It's housed in the late Middle Ages **Haus Wassermann**, with its beautiful coffered ceilings, old panelling and tiled fireplaces. *Museum open Jun-Oct daily (ex Mon) from 16.00-19.00; entry fee 5 €, concessions 3 €.*

Sights: Apart from the attractive houses in the town hall square (Von-Kurz-Platz) with the courthouse and church (Spitalkirche), it's worth crossing to the other side of the Rienz, to visit the **parish church** with its chapel dedicated to St Anna as well as the somewhat higher church of **St Magdalena im Moos** (open May to end Sep, Sun 14.00-18.00), where there are occasional concerts. This church was founded in 1491 and holds frescoes dating back to the period of Simon von Taisten.

Pragser Tal/Val di Braies

The Pragser Tal has a really flat area lower down (called **Ausserprags**), then the valley forks at **Schmieden/Ferrara**: the branch to

The Rienz River at Niederdorf/Villabassa

Dolomiti Superbike
One of the classic mountain bike races, the Dolomiti Superbike, begins in Niederdorf. It's been run on the first weekend in July since 1995. Experts and trained amateurs compete on the routes: 111km with 3000m height gain or 59 km/1500m height gain. Even beginners can enter the short race (25 km/800m height gain). The race mostly uses forestry roads and tracks, via Toblach, Innichen, Sexten and Prags. See www.dolomitisuperbike.com.

the left leads towards Plätzwiese, the one to the right to Lake Prags. First taking the branch to the right, you come to **Innerprags/ Braies**, where farmhouses lie on the sunny slopes — some grouped together, others singly. Early tourism to the area (to Frau Emma's hotel at Lake Prags) meant that hotels and guest houses sprang up in the valley, especially alongside the road to the lake.

Lake Prags
The **Pragser Wildsee/Lago di Braies** is one of the jewels of the Dolomites: it's 36m deep and lies at an altitude of 1489m, below the massive north wall of Seekofel (2810m), the most northerly of the Fanes peaks. The water changes colour constantly — sometimes emerald, then blue and somewhat milky, sometimes black — and so clear that you can see the bottom. And cold, cold, *cold*. Just right for trout and the delicious char.

You can hire boats at the Hotel Pragser Wildsee boathouse and row to the south end of the lake, where there's a lovely pebble beach. Or you can circle the lake on foot — see the short version of Walk 1 on page 55.

Plätzwiese/Prato Piazza
At the top end of the other fork in Schmieden is **Plätzwiese**, huge undulating alm meadows between the Prags and Höhlenstein valleys. The Plätzwiese Hut offers refreshments all year round. With its wind-tousled Arolla pines, the place is a panoramic balcony.

Transport: Up to 15 buses a day come up here from Prags from 10 Jul-20 Sep, and during this period private cars can only use the road before 10.00 and after 16.00 (maximum 100 cars a day; toll 9 €).

The **Fanes group** is to the right, with Hohe Gaisl; the **Cristallo group** is straight ahead (so close that you can see every little glacier and *névé*); to the left, alms rise up to **Dürrenstein**. The cattle up here graze on common alms, in contrast to other places in South Tyrol and the Dolomites. Farmers don't go to the alm, but entrust their animals to paid shepherds.

From Plätzwiese there's an old military road down to the main Toblach–Cortina road, popular with mountain bikers.

Cycling tip: from Toblach through the Höhlensteintal/Valle di Landro
Time/length: 3h with ease; 32km
Grade: 300m ascent between Toblach and the Gemärk Pass, then descent of 300m to Cortina. The cycle path is in very good condition. *An excellent day out for the whole family;* take a bus back from Cortina.

The deeply-etched Höhlensteintal south of Toblach was scraped out by glacial action. The route runs over a small pass called **Im Gemärk/Passo di Cimabanche** to the Ladin area and Cortina (described in Book 2). The mountain giants on both sides — Dürrenstein, Drei Zinnen, Cristallo — are too steep for normal walkers. Up until the 1960s a branch railway ran through the valley to Cortina and on to the Cadore. Now the old line is a pleasant and easy **cycle path** through one of the most beautiful landscapes in the Dolomites.

Starting just south of the railway line at **Neutoblach**, almost at once you pass **Lake Toblach**, covering an area of 14.3ha (but only 3.5m deep). It's a protected area; its southern, silted-up banks are an important habitat for amphibians and birds. The route runs almost flat to a signposted **Austrian military cemetery** on a slope to the right (**car park**).

Lake **Dürren** announces itself with the Drei Zinnen Hotel and the **car park** for the viewpoint. The Italian name for the lake is Lago di Landro, and that was the name of the hotel that preceded the current one; it was shot to pieces in the First World War. The lake is very shallow and in autumn often only half as large as in spring when it's full of melt-water. Just to the south is mighty **Monte Cristallo** (3216m); the canons of the Italian emplacements on Monte Cristallino (2786m) to its left were those that left Neutoblach in debris and ashes. The wild mountain flanks on the east side of the lake belong to **Monte Piana**, most of which lies in Belluno. Piana also saw heavy fighting in 1915-17, and there are still many emplacements which have been made into an open-air museum. A farmer called Ploner from Alt-Schluderbach near Toblach once built a guest house in **Schluderbach**; today the site is the Hotel Ploner, with apartments and a restaurant. An old military road (closed to motor traffic) runs from Schluderbach up to **Plätzwiese** — great for mountain bikers (mentioned on page 49).

The top of the route is **Im Gemärk**. The mountain half-right above this pass is **Hohe Gaisl** (3146m), called '**Croda Rossa**' by the Italians on account of its red-coloured rock.

Descending, one passes the **Ospitale**, an old hospice on the 'Alemagna', of which only the small Gothic chapel on the other side of the road remains. From the hairpin bend 3km down from the pass there is a panoramic view to the **Fanes group**.

Excursion to the Drei Zinnen via Lake Misurina

A good but steep road (11%) runs from **Schluderbach** over a low pass to famous **Lake Misurina** in the Cadore (Belluno Province). The view from the car park on the north shore across the lake to the Sorapis group (3205m) is one of the finest not only in the Dolomites, but all the Alps. The fashionable Grand Hotel on the south bank is one of the oldest in the whole region.

A toll road runs from the north shore towards the **Drei Zinnen** and ends at a large car park below the Auronzo Hut. Anyone can walk from here to the Drei Zinnen Hut along the motorable track, but if you want to make the most of the excursion, see Walk 30 in Book 2.

Innichen/San Candido

For the whole length of the Pustertal, Innichen is rivalled only by Bruneck and Lienz; in the Hochpustertal there's no

Hochpustertal/Alta Pusteria 51

Collegiate church at Innichen/ San Candido

competition. Only Innichen has a town-like atmosphere and can live without tourism — although it's quite happy to profit from it all the same.

History books record that the coming of Christianity to the Pustertal began with the building of Innichen's collegiate church. In the dark interior of this Romanesque church the past comes alive, and you can almost feel yourself back in the times when the little settlement was surrounded by thick woods full of bears, wolves and lynx. The building of this church, in a total wilderness, must have been an epoch-making event for the few Slav settlers in the valley, all of them heathens.

The huge water park, Acquafun, is today's most impressive bit of infrastructure, together with the two mountain railways, the chair lifts to Haunold/Rocca dei Baranci (the town's local mountain), and the lifts from Vierschach/Versciaco to Helm/ Monte Elmo on the main ridge of the Carnic Dolomites.

Transport: There are free **car parking** places by the side of the road at the south end of Freisingerstrasse, a **railway station**, and **bus station** on Mantingerstrasse at the west end of P P Rainerstrasse, above the bridge over the Drau (but some buses set off from the area in front of the station). Good direct connections with Bruneck, Brixen, Sexten.

Sights and excursions: The collegiate church (**Stiftskirche**) is on busy Pflegplatz, but separated from it by the cemetery. In 769 Duke Tassilo III of Bavaria gave Abbot Atto von Scharnitz a large area around what is today Innichen, to found a monastery. The present church is the third building on this spot. The first church was replaced in 1000 by a larger building, of which the crypt is still preserved under what is today the choir. Both the village and the church burned down in 1200, making way for a third church. This was built in Romanesque style and dedicated in 1284 — today's collegiate church. The south door, entered from Pflegplatz, is deeply recessed, with a magnificent relief in the tympanum. Above the doorway is a still fresh-looking fresco by Michael Pacher. The interior of the church has three naves in a most attractive Romanesque style. The middle nave is wide; a wooden Crucifixion group dating from 1240 draws the attention. The choir is raised, with the crypt below, accessible from both sides.

The church museum (**Stiftsmuseum**) is reached from Attostrasse; the collection comprises the cathedral treasures, sacred art and manuscripts. The rooms are as spectacular as the exhibits: in the 'Kapitelsaal', where the cathedral treasures are exhibited, frescoes depict the coats of arms of the canons, and the choirboys' schoolroom (Schulstube), with panelling and a huge green-tiled fireplace (dating from about 1550) is a real eye-opener. *Museum open Jul to mid-Sep, Tue-Sat from 14.00-19.00. Entry 7 €, concessions 4 €.*

Squeezed between the road and the railway line, and deep below today's street level, is a curious, unique complex. Three little towers signal the three adjacent churches within. Inside, the complex consists of an octagonal building with tower (the **Altöttinger Chapel**), the adjacent nave with a little tower (the **Passionskapelle**), and a round building with a little tower and the Holy Sepulchre Chapel (the **Heiliggrabkapelle**). The complex dates from between 1633 and 1653. The donor was a religious man of Innichen, who made many pilgrimages. From the shrine of Altötting (near Munich) he brought a copy of the statue of St Mary and a plan of the church housing it, which he had copied here in miniature. From Jerusalem he brought the plan of the Church of the Holy Sepulchre, which was also copied. In niches and on pillars there are statues and even whole scenes — like the Life of Mary in the Altöttinger Chapel and a wooden statue of the dead Christ in the Holy Sepulchre Chapel. Truly striking! *Museum open Jul to mid-Sep, Wed-Sun from 10.00-12.00 and from 16.00-18.00; in Jun only on weekends; donations welcome.*

The yellow-painted **Franciscan church** takes up a large flat area in the western part of the old town. The church is plain, but the altar is baroque, with a very good painting by Christoph Unterberger dating from 1764, depicting the Holy Mother and Child with St Francis and St Leopold of Austria kneeling before her. The cloister was also decorated in the baroque style by a naive painter, with more than 70 scenes from the life of St Francis. It is interesting to see how he depicts the reality of his own era (around 1700) — the contemporary dress the women are wearing and the décor. *Church open daily 07.30-18.30; cloister only open on request.*

Mt Haunold/Rocca dei Baranci: Wooded Mt Haunold at Innichen is fairly unimpressive. But in winter you can ski down the north side all the way to Innichen, and for summer there are many pleasant, **easy walks**. There are two huts at the top, the Haunold and the Jora. And young people particularly like the 1.7km-long bobsled run that begins at the mountain station and can reach speeds of 36km/h. The 4-seater chair lift to the upper station (1500m) runs from Jun to mid-Oct from 09.00-17.30, in high season until 18.30; one way 11 €, up and back 17 € (children one way 7.50 €, up and back 12 €). www.dreizinnen.com.

Cycling tip: Pustertal cycle path between Mühlbach and Lienz

The cycle path beside the river Drau from Toblach to Lienz, is very popular in summer. You can pedal along the river, then let the

Austrian Railways (which have cycle wagons just for this purpose) take you back to Toblach or Innichen in the evening.

This section (44 km) is just the eastern part of a long cycle path through the whole valley from Franzensfeste in the west, where it forks off from the Eisacktal cycle path, to the main European watershed at Toblach (where the Rienz flows west to the Etsch and Adriatic and the Drau flows east to the Donau and Black Sea and across the border to Lienz, where the Pustertal ends).

The path is mostly asphalted and very well signposted. Since the Pustertal is served by bus and train, you can break off at any point. Better still, you can rent bikes in many centres and, for a small additional cost, leave them somewhere else.

Sexten/Sesto

Sexten, home to mountain guides and climbers, lies in a wide green valley between the gentle slopes of the Carnic Alps and the rough walls of the Sexten Dolomites.

From Sexten and Moos/San Giuseppe, a bit higher up the valley, the Fischleintal runs right into the Dolomites, at the foot of Zwölferkogel and the Drei Zinnen. Sexten's mountain guide dynasty, the Innerkoflers, used to take climbers from England, Germany and Austria up to these peaks. Sexten was destroyed in the First World War — the Italian artillery was encamped at the nearby Kreuzberg Pass. Today's pseudo-Tyrolean houses are often less than 50 years old. But people don't come to Sexten for the architecture!

Transport: There is a large **car park** by Congress House at the valley station of the Helm lift; good **bus connections** to Innichen and Toblach and all year round to the Kreuzberg Pass (but no buses from there into the Cadore!).

Fischleintal/Val Fiscalina

From Sexten and Moos the best way to visit the deeply-cut Fischleintal is by going up the left-hand side of the valley, past meadows loosely scattered with old larches. From the Hotel Dolomitenhof there is a lovely view to the wreath of peaks called the **Sextener Sonnenuhr** (Sexten Sundial). People in Sexten have always been able to read the time by looking to see where the sun is on the Elfer, Zwölfer, and Einserkofel (the 11th, 12th and 1st summits). Only dirt roads run to the hut at the end of this valley, from where there are **various walking routes** (see Walk 2).

A 6-seater **cable car** runs from **Bad Moos/Bagni di San Giuseppe** at the entrance to the Fischleintal up to the meadows of **Rotwand** at 1921m: early Jun to mid-Oct 08.30-17.30; in high season from 08.00; one way 16 €, up and back 21 €.

At the top there are fantastic views, several **walking routes**, ski runs — and two huts with good cooking: the Rotwandwiesen Hut and the Rudi Hut. In most cases those who want to go higher will have problems, unless they are experienced and well-equipped climbers. There is just one quite straightforward protected ascent (Alternative walk 3 on page 59).

Sexten Dolomites Nature Park

This park encompasses one of the most important areas in the whole Dolomites: the **Sonnenuhr** around Sexten, between **Rotwand, Elferkofel, Zwölferkofel** (3094m) and **Einserkofel**, the isolated **Dreischusterspitze** (3145m), the world-famous **Drei Zinnen** (up to 2999m) and the **Haunold massif** (2966m).

From the Kreuzberg Pass to Lake Dürren the park boundary follows the boundary with the province of Belluno. Wild rock walls like the 'Zwölfers' and the Drei Zinnen, and jagged rock towers like those on Rotwand are just one side of this mountain landscape. The other is the alm landscape between the Drei Zinnen and the Toblingerknoten and between the Toblingerknoten and the Büllelejoch: little lakes, green meadows, rhododendrons…

Around the Fischleintal and Drei Zinnen the park is well served with tracks and huts; in contrast the northwestern stretch between Bullköpfe and Neunerkofel is quite empty. During the First World War, the Front ran right through this area, via Monte Piana, the Toblingerknoten north of the Drei Zinnen, the Büllelejoch Hut, upper Fischleintal and Rotwand. The emplacements are still there today, just by the trails.

Many rare flora can be seen in the park, like the alpine Rhaetian poppy, with its bright yellow- to orange-coloured blooms, which proliferate for instance on the scree slopes between Büllelejoch and the Drei Zinnen Hut.

For information about the park visit the Park House (see page 47).

Kreuzbergpass/Passo Montecroce Comelico

It's just a few minutes from Bad Moos to the **Kreuzbergpass** (1696m), which links to the Cadore. There's a good hotel at the pass and **walking routes** on both sides. One of the most attractive **walks** is to the **Rifugio al Popera A Berti** at 1950m — Trail 124, which begins at the hotel car park (2h30min up, 1h30min back). From the hut there's a very unusual (but equally appealing) view to the Sextener Rotwand and 'Elfer' (the eleventh summit, see page 53) — from its southeast side.

From the north side of the pass the **Malga Coltrondo** makes a good **walk**. Take Trail 149, about 1.2km past the pass towards Auronzo (ascent about 300m; up 2h, back down 1h30min). Or you can drive there: the access road turns off left after about 5km. This alm has real mountain cooking. The area near the *malga* saw fierce trench warfare between Italians and Austrians from 1915 to 1917.

Helm/Monte Elmo

The Carnic Alps stretch from Sexten to Tarvis, forming the border between Austria and Italy.

Only the far western stretch of the massif, with **Helm**, lies within the area of this book. **Three lifts** run up to the alms beneath this peak with its far-reaching views (and ruined hut): a cable car from Vierschach/Innichen and two more direct from Sexten. All run from 08.30-17.30 and all cost 16 €, up and back 21 €. **Helm cable car** (from Sexten) end Jun to mid-Oct; **Drei Zinnen cable car** (Stiergarten): Jun-Oct; **Vierschach cable car**: end Jun to mid-Oct. Also: **chair lift** Col d'la Tenda, end Jul to early Sep, 09.00-17.00; www.dreizinnen.com. (Controversy surrounded installation of the new cable cars, and one of the lifts was rerouted to avoid the habitat of the protected tamarisk, *Myricaria germanica*.)

Walk 1: FROM LAKE PRAGS/LAGO DI BRAIES TO THE SEEKOFEL HUT/RIFUGIO BIELLA

Distance/time: about 13km/7.8mi; 5h30min
Grade: ● ❗ moderate-strenuous, with an ascent/descent of almost 900m/3000ft; quite a steep mountain hike; several cable-protected places higher up, but they are not very difficult.

Tip: You may well spot ibex in the Seekofel area!

Waymarking: red/white; all Trail 1 (Dolomites High Route 1)
Equipment: walking boots, sun protection, walking poles
Refreshments: available at the Seekofel Hut/Rifugio Biella (open from end Jun to Sep)
Walking map: Tabacco 031, Pragser Dolomiten/Dolomiti di Braies, 1:25,000

Transport: 🚗 to the large, paying car park at the Hotel Pragser Wildsee (46° 42.009'N, 12° 5.087'E). Or 🚌 442 from Toblach/Dobbiaco, which stops in the car park (daily from mid-Jun to mid-Sep; out of season the bus only goes as far as St Veit/San Vito, 3km down the road).

Short walk: Circle the lake
(● ; 3.6km/2.2mi; 1h). Start out by following the main walk on a wide track closed to motor traffic, but leave it at **3**, for a 'balcony' path, sometimes on log steps, beside almost vertical edges dropping 30m/100ft to the lake (protected with fencing at all exposed points). You pass a jetty with rowing boats for hire before coming back to the start.

This walk features what many consider the most beautiful lake in the Dolomites; you can see it from all angles whether you do the main walk or simply circle the emerald-green mirror — a focal point for landscape photographers.

Sunrise: returning to the hotel on the log-stepped path at east side of the lake; the quite sheer drops are protected at all exposed points.

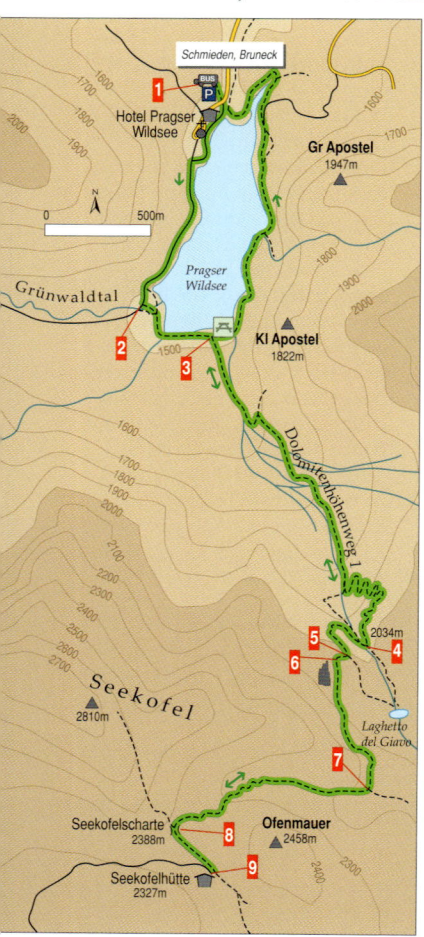

Start the walk from the car park and bus stop at the **Hotel Pragser Wildsee** (**1**). Take the wide track (signposted Trails 1 and 4) to the right, past a chapel, and walk along the western shore of the lake. Ignore a turn-off right (**2**) up the Grünwaldtal/Val di Foresta; keep left on Trail 1 (also Dolomites High Route 1) which you will follow all the way to the hut more than 800m/2600ft higher up.

On the south side of the lake, you come to a fork (**3**; **30min**) and turn up right with Trail 1 for 'Seekofel/Seekofelhütte'), ignoring Trail 4 off to the left (your return route). *But the Short walk turns left here.*

Follow Trail 1 uphill over loose scree flows, through dwarf mountain pines and rhododendron. As the valley that you're following gets narrower, the way bears right and climbs in zigzags to a rocky spine (benches before and after). Go right here, slightly downhill, back to the bed of the stream you you followed at the start of the walk and cross it (**4**; **2h**). There follows a very short section on wooden 'steps', cable assisted, as you round a crumbling rock face.

Shortly after, at a junction (**5**), keep right on Trail 1 ('Seekofelhütte 1.30 Std'), leaving Trail 4 off to the left. From here the way climbs the steep slope and heads left below a steep rock wall (**6**).

Beyond here you're in a high valley, surrounded by larch, mountain pines and stone pines through which you climb in tight zigzags. These are again cable-protected, but they are longer stretches this time — *take care!*

Ignore Trail 3 off to the left (**7**) and keep climbing — to emerge eventually at the **Seekofelscharte/Forcella Sora Forno** (2388m; **8**). The **Seekofel Hut/Rifugio Biella** lies not far below to the left (**9**; **3h30min**).

Return the same way and complete the circuit of Lake Prags by following the eastern shore — sometimes high above it — as you can see in the photo on page 55. You'll be back at the hotel car park/bus stop in **5h30min**.

Walk 2: TO THE DREI ZINNEN/TRE CIME DI LAVAREDO

Distance/time: about 15.6km/ 9.7mi; 7h
Grade: ● quite strenuous, with an ascent/descent of about 1100m/ 3600ft; a straightforward hike on mostly good mountain paths, but you must be fit — it's quite tiring. Or split it, as suggested in the intro.

Tip: *For an easier walk round the Drei Zinnen, see Walk 30 in Book 2.*

Waymarking: red/white; Trails 102/103 from **1** to **2**; Trail 102 to **3**; 101 to **7** and 103 to the end
Equipment: walking boots, sun protection, walking poles
Refreshments: available at the Büllelejoch Hut/Rifugio Pian di Cengia, Zsigmondy Hut/Rifugio Comici, Drei Zinnen Hut/Rifugio Locatelli. The tiny Büllelejoch Hut (just 11 bunks) is served by helicopter and mini-tractor. It's a magnificent place to spend a night in the mountains, with Tyrolean cooking and the chance to watch the sun set on the Drei Zinnen.
Walking map: Tabacco 010, Sextener Dolomiten/Dolomiti di Sesto, 1:25,000
Transport: 🚗 to the large (paid) car park at the end of the road in the Fischleintal (Hotel Dolomitenhof; 46° 40.011'N, 12° 21.211'E). Or 🚌 446 from Toblach/Dobbiaco (stops at the car park, daily from mid-Jun to mid-Oct). From here take one of the horse-drawn carriages to the Talschluss Hut/ Rifugio Fondo Valle at the end of the valley (shuttle service from the Hotel Dolomitenhof) — or walk.

Of all the motifs associated with the Dolomites, the Drei Zinnen/Tre Cime di Lavaredo is the most famous. This walk is pretty tough, but terrifically rewarding. You could do it in two parts by climbing east to the Zsigmondy Hut or west to the Drei Zinnen Hut (each about 4h out-and-back).

Start the walk at the **Talschluss Hut/Rifugio Fondo Valle** (**1**) at the end of the **Fischleintal/Val Fiscalina**, where the north wall of Einserkofel/Cima Una dominates the view. Follow Trails 102/103 (Dolomites High Route 5) diagonally to the right uphill, to a fork (**2**) just short of a stream: go right uphill here on Trail 102 (to the left is your return route).

At first you rise alongside the stream, then you curve to the right and the terrain is steeper. When the route flattens out again you reach the **Bödenalm** with its little lake; a little higher up is the **Drei Zinnen Hut/ Rifugio Locatelli** (**3**; **3h**). It's all happening here, with lots of people coming from the nearby Auronzo Hut, where the road from Misurina in the south ends (see Walk 30 in Book 2). There is a fantastic

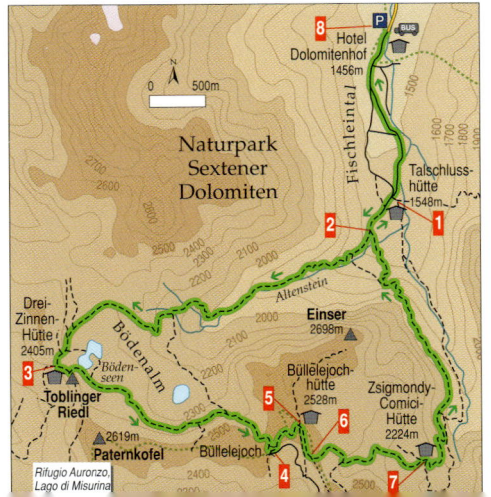

view to the Drei Zinnen and Paternkofel/Monte Paterno, which was so bitterly contested during the First World War.

From the hut follow sign-posting to the 'Büllelejochhütte 1h' now on Trail 101, heading back across the Bödenalm above the lakes (**Bödenseen/Laghi dei Piani**). After crossing several scree gullies you reach the **Büllelejoch/Forcella Pian di Cengia** (**4**). Contour left from this pass to the nearby **Büllelejoch Hut/Rifugio Pian di Cengia** (**5**; **4h15min**) and then on to the **Obernbacher Joch/Passo Fiscalino** (**6**). From here you look down to the end of the valley below Zwölfer-kofel/Croda dei Toni (right) and Hochbrunnerschneid/Monte Popera (ahead).

Now descend in zigzags. Take a break at the **Zsigmondy Hut** (**7**; **5h**), then continue out of the valley on Trail 103 (Dolomites High Route 5). After crossing the Altenstein Stream you reach your outward route at **2** and quickly regain the **Talschluss Hut** (**1**; **6h30min**) and the **Hotel Dolomitenhof** (**8**; **7h**).

The Drei Zinnen/Tre Cime di Lavaredo from the north

Walk 3: CIRCUIT UNDER ROTWAND/CRODA ROSSA DI SESTO

Distance/time: about 11km/ 6.9mi; 4h30min
Grade: ● easy-moderate descent of 320m/1050ft, followed by a similar ascent.
Waymarking: red/white; Trail 15 from **1** to **3**, then Trail 15a to **6**, and Trail 18 back to the start
Equipment: walking shoes or boots, sun protection
Refreshments: available at the Rotwandwiesen Hut/Rifugio Prati di Croda Rossa and Rudi Hut at the start/end, and at the Kreuzbergpass Hotel midway
Walking map: Tabacco 010, Sextener Dolomiten/Dolomiti di Sesto, 1:25,000
Transport: 🚗 to Bad Moos/Bagni di Moso in the Fischleintal; park at the car park for the cable car to Rotwand (46° 40.899'N, 12° 21.862'E). Or 🚌 446 from Toblach/Dobbiaco, which stops at the car park (daily from early Jun to mid-Oct, every 2 hours, in high season half-hourly). From here take the cable car to Rotwand (early Jun to mid-Oct, 08.30-12.30 and 13.30-17.00, in high season no midday break; one way 16.50 €, up and back 21.50 €)

Short walk: Kreuzberg Pass/Passo Montecroce Comelico. ● easy descent of 320m/1050ft; 2h15min. Just do the first half of the walk and return to Moos on 🚌 446.

Alternative walk: Rotwand/Croda Rossa di Sesto summit. 8.4km/5.2mi; 6h; ●❗; ascent/descent 1100m/3600ft. Very strenuous but 'easy' *via ferrata* for those with the *the right experience and equipment*.

> **Sextener Rotwand/Croda Rossa di Sesto**
> This mountain, with its five summits, was one of the most bitterly contested during the First World War, and still holds dugouts, trenches and ladders put in place by the Alpine troops who were sacrificed in those sad years. The Austrians, who had the easiest northerly access — the route from the Fischleintal suggested for the Alternative walk — held the summit throughout.

Descending to the pass on Trail 15a

The first part of this walk is a wonderful traverse down to a grassy pass which marks the border between German-speaking South Tyrol and Italian-speaking Belluno. If you prefer to climb at the start of your walk, do the hike in reverse; there's parking and a bus stop at the Kreuzberg Pass.

Start the walk from the **top station** of the **Rotwand lift** (**1**). Go down past the **Rudi Hut** (on your right). Just past it, at a crossroads, ignore Trail 15 off right (to the Rotwandwiesen Hut); walk straight ahead across the lovely Rotwand meadows to a **3-way junction** (**2**) where you go straight ahead, following sign-posting to the 'Burgstall/Castelliere'. (You will return from the left, and the Alternative walk goes right here.)

At the next fork (**3**), *keep left* on Trail 15a, descending slightly at first, then rising to round the northern side of the spiky Burgstall/Castelliere outcrop. The path drops a little once more, and after a little under 2km Route 15b (a more difficult path which *crosses* the Burgstall and demands agility and a head for heights) comes in from the right (**4**).

Now Trail 15a easily traverses below the mighty Sextener Rotwand, across a river of scree and a wild landscape of fallen blocks of rock.

At the next junction (**5**), below Arzalpenkopf/Croda Sora i Colesei, follow Route 15a to the left, gently downhill, heading northeast through light conifer woods in an area punctuated by First World War fortifications — mostly concrete bunkers.

Meeting a track, follow it to a junction by a ski lift and a large bunker (**6**), where you turn left, still on Route 15a, to the hotel/bus stop at the **Kreuzberg Pass/Passo Montecroce Comelico** (**7**; **2h15min**). The short walk ends here at the bus stop.

Those continuing the main walk should follow the SS52 to the left, after less than 200m turning left on Route 15 and almost immediately right on Route 18 (**8**). This track crosses the **Weissbach** (**9**) and runs gently uphill, back to the **3-way junction** (**2**). Retrace your steps to the **Rotwand lift** (**1**; **4h30min**).

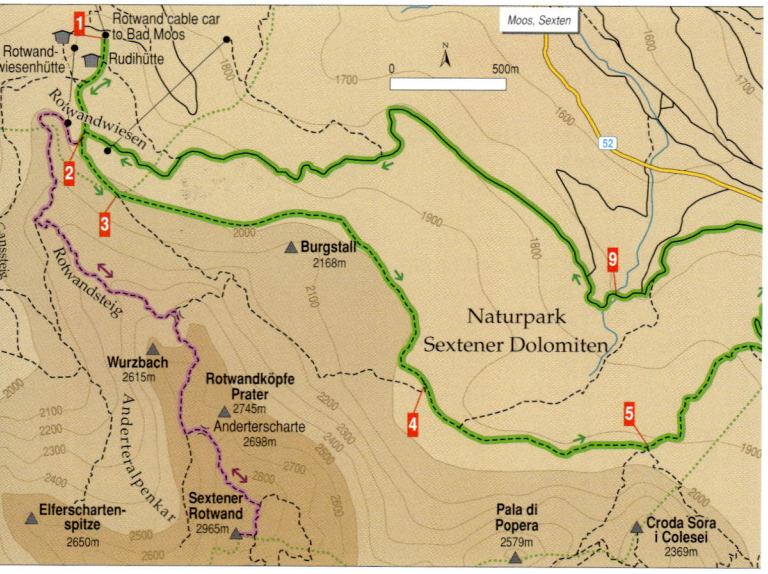

Walk 4: TO HELM/MONTE ELMO AND THE SILLIANER HUT

Distance/time: about 8.8km/ 5.5mi; 3h15min
Grade: 🔵 easy-moderate mountain walk, with an ascent/descent of 450m/1475ft; good paths and tracks underfoot
Waymarking: red/white; Trail 20 to **7** (except for a short section on an unmarked path after **2**); Trail 4 from **7** to **9** and back; the track from the Sillianer Hut back to the start is 20, but also partly 3, 4
Equipment: walking shoes or boots, sun protection
Refreshments: available at the Helm restaurant, the Sillianer Hut and the Hahnspielhütte
Walking map: Tabacco 010, Sextener Dolomiten/Dolomiti di Sesto, 1:25,000
Transport: 🚗 to the large car parks at the valley stations for the Helm lifts at Sexten/Sesto (46° 41.831'N, 12° 21.418'E) or Vierschach/Versciaco (46° 43.915'N, 12° 19.764'E). 🚌 446 from Toblach/Dobbiaco to the Sexten valley station (daily, hourly, in high season half-hourly), 🚌 447 from Toblach/Dobbiaco to the Vierschach valley station (daily, hourly, in high season half-hourly). From either valley station take the Helm cable car (early Jun to end Oct, 08.30-17.30; one way 16.50 €, up and back 21.50 €)

In and out of Austria, this walk along the Carnic Ridge separating the two countries offers spectacular views to the Sexten/Sesto Dolomites. Of course the ridge saw very heavy fighting during the First World War. In 1953 an international group of european boy scouts built a cross at the top of Helm (the most westerly summit on the ridge), in the hope that history will never repeat itself.

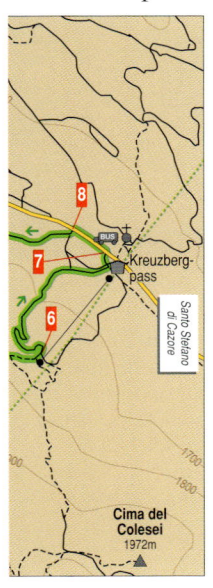

The walk starts from the **top station of either Helm lift**. You can't really start before you take in the fantastic panorama of the Sexten Dolomites from here! From the top station of either lift, follow signposting to 'Hüttensteig' (Trail 20), which begins between the two lift stations (**1**). It runs on the north side of the ridge; after a short climb the way levels out in high alm terrain.

After 20 minutes, *leave* Route 20 (**2**): go right on an unmarked but well-trodden path, coming to the main ridge of the **Carnic Alps** (**3**). Heading steeply up to the left, you meet Trail 20 again (**4**), pass ruined barracks and rise to the summit of **Helm** (2434 m; **5**), with its closed, ruined hut and a wonderful panorama. The hut was built in 1891 by Alpine clubs in Italy and Austria and it survived until 1915 and World War I. There has been talk of rebuilding it.

Continue along the crest, sometimes crossing the border into Austria. Keep left at a fork (**6**) and come back onto the motorable

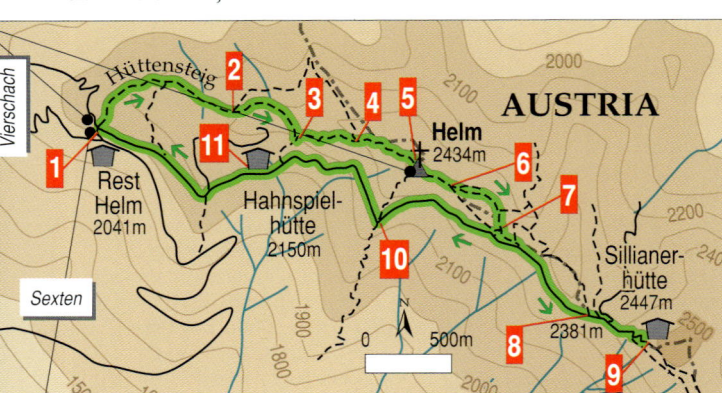

View to the Sillianer Hut and Helm/Monte Elmo

track (7) at a signpost. Follow this to a gap (8) below the **Sillianer Hut** and climb up to it (9; **2h**). East Tyrolean (Austrian) cooking awaits you here — not very different from the cuisine in South Tyrol.

Return along the wide main route on the Italian side of the ridge, keeping left at the fork in the gap (8). You pass a turn-off to Helm (10) and walk to the left of the manned Hahnspiel Hut/Rifugio Gallo Cedrone (11) and back to the **top lift stations** (1; **3h15min**).

3 TAUFERER TAL AND AHRNTAL/VAL DI TURES AND VALLE AURINA

Sand in Taufers • Mühlen • Reintal • Rieserferner-Ahrn Nature Park • Ahrntal • Luttach • St Johann • Steinhaus • Prettau • Kasern

Walks: 5; *walking tips:* Kofler zwischen den Wänden (page 65); St Francis meditation path (page 66); Lake Klaus/Chiusetta (page 68); Kehreralm (page 69); Krimmler Tauern (page 71); *cycling tip:* from Bruneck to Sand in Taufers (page 64)

Websites
www.pustertal.org
www.taufers.com
www.kofler-zd-waenden.com
www.ahrntal.it
www.mineralienmuseum.com
www.bergbaumuseum.it

Opening hours: see individual attractions

The long axis of the Tauferer and Ahr valleys runs from Bruneck/Brunico in the Pustertal to the high Alpine ridge and the northernmost part of Italy. Here, and in the two neighbouring valleys (Reintal and Mühlwalder Tal) walking and mountain climbing are the main attractions.

Bruneck lies at a height of 835m; Grosser Möseler in the Zillertal Alps reaches up to 3478m, and Hochgall on the border with East Tyrol attains 3495m. In between these landmarks nature is at its finest, with green meadows, alms, woods and high alpine pastures, glaciers and a couple of pretty old places like Sand in Taufers/Campo Tures.

Bring your mountain bike — or rent one! Every alm and every farm has its own lane (while in contrast the trails between the isolated high farms and alms are often so steep and exposed that they are only accessible to experienced mountain climbers). But you will also find castles, old stately homes, a mining museum with old tunnels, and rustic cooking in even more rustic local inns. And it's also possible to experience the age-old way of life on farmhouse holidays.

Sand in Taufers/Campo Tures

Sand in Taufers lies just where the almost-flat Tauferer Tal suddenly forks and, after a steep gorge section in the Ahr/Aurina and Rein/Riva valleys gets much narrower and far from flat!

In the past, whoever wanted to cross the mountains to the Salzburg area had to go through Sand. For merchants it was a necessity. Wine from Bolzano was taken over the Krimmler Tauern Pass to the north, where it was needed for communion wine. Salt from Hallein and other salt-producing places was taken south (where it was in equally heavy demand) on the same route. Sand profited from all this trade and, just where the Ahrntal begins, an early castle rose to protect the route — spectacular **Schloss Taufers**. The view is impressive, unforgettable: from the meadows by Sand you look out to the Neumelans estate with its mighty hipped roof and delicate bay windows, Schloss Taufers above it, surrounded by woods ... and all that crowned by the snow- and ice-

Pseudo-Tyrolean architecture in Sand, with Schloss Taufers in the background

capped peaks of the high Alpine ridge.

Transport: There is a large **car park** in the southern part of Sand. Parking on the road in the Ahrntal is not allowed. There are up to 25 **buses** a day to/from Bruneck and either Kasern or Prettau.

Cycling tip: from Bruneck to Sand in Taufers: The cycle route between Bruneck and Sand (Tabacco 1:25,000 map N° 036) is well marked and family-friendly, thanks to the very limited ascents. For most of the way this is a wide asphalted cycle path built over an old railway line. There are benches en route where you can take a break. The only time you might get lost is when you leave Bruneck, and for that you have two choices. You *can* take the main road into the Tauferer Tal, but as soon as you reach the beginning of St Georgen, take the first road to the right — *watch for the sign!* But it is prettier to start out along the road to Dietenheim and from there take the road to Aufhofen and St Georgen. As you reach St Georgen via this route, the cycle path crosses and you can join it. Allow 2-3 hours return.

Sights and excursions: While Sand is small, it has an excellent infrastructure, in fact it's the shopping centre for several valleys. Most of the shops are on Ahrntaler Street, on the western edge of town. The old town is partly pedestrianised, its centre lying around Josef Jungmann Street; here's where you'll find the town hall, post office, bank, tourist office, bookshops and the **Naturparkhaus Rieserferner-Ahrn**. It has a very good multi-media presentation about the nature park (see page 66) — you may never get past the entrance hall with its film taken from a helicopter! *Park House open from May to end Oct and from end Dec to end Mar, Tue-Sat 09.30-12.30 and 14.30-18.00; also Sun in Jul/Aug (same hours). Entry free.*

The **parish museum** displays sacred art from the churches and chapels around Sand. Many of their treasures had to be brought here for protection in the 1960s and 70s, when there were a great number of thefts. *Museum open Wed-Sat from 16.00-18.00; Sun (10.00-12.00). No entry fee; donations welcome.*

South of Sand (towards Bruneck) is the impressive **Ansitz Neumelans**, already mentioned, in its own park. The building was commissioned by the lord of the manor, Hans Fieger, in 1582 and finished in just 12 months. It must have been more comfortable down here than up in the drafty castle.

The difference in height between the Ahrntal and the Tauferer Tal in the gorge above Sand is almost 100m, and the Almbach breaches the drop in cascades. The gorge is so narrow that only in modern times were the road builders able to blast a way through the rock. Before that the route through the gorge went just past the perched castle, **Schloss Taufers**. The castle's mighty grey granite walls and high keep make a deep impression even today. The Taufers, a noble family, had it built in the 13th century as their base, so it is an early Middle Ages building. The Taufers were a very important family, for quite a long time able to measure up to the Counts of Tyrol and the House of Andechs (forerunners of the well-known German brewery).

During your visit you will see the Romanesque chapel; its frescoes were uncovered during restoration. They are among Michael Pacher's masterpieces; the Byzantine Christ is majestic. The dining room, with the large tiled oven, the courtroom, the war chamber with Middle Ages and Early Modern arms and armour, the knights' room with portraits of noblemen, and the lovely library can all be visited — as can the private quarters of Margarete von Taufers, a beautifully panelled Renaissance room. It is said that her husband was killed on their wedding day, and so she shut herself away in this room (just fiction, but a pretty story). *Castle open daily from Easter to 31 Oct from 10.00-12.00 and 14.00-17.00; entry fee (includes guiding) 8-10 €, concessions 5-7/3-5 €. www.burgen institut.com.*

Sand's **late Gothic parish church** is not in the village, but south of **Taufers**, a hamlet comprising just a few houses. It was completed in 1527. The ensemble makes a very impressive picture: the church, the cemetery chapel (also late Gothic) and the sexton's house on the other side of the square, with its beautiful entrance gate and bay window.

● *Walking tip: visit to Kofler zwischen den Wänden.* The area of scattered isolated farms on the sunny slopes above Sand is called **Ahornach**. Today the farms are all joined by roads, but just a generation ago they were only accessible by tracks and trails. East of Ahornach, on cliffs high in the Rein/Riva Valley, is one of the most isolated alms in South Tyrol, **Kofler zwischen den Wänden** ('between the walls').

The steep trail that rises from just below (today no longer an official route), involves ladders. But a flatter access track (in the past extremely narrow and dangerous) has been widened and protected. You can reach the alm today by one of three routes (see Tabacco 1:25,000 map N° 035): Route 5 from Ahornach is a straightforward walk of about 1h (road as far as the Stockner Hof); Route 5 from Tobl in the Reintal, at the junction with the road to Ahornach, is a steep ascent of 1h30min; Route 10 from Rein follows a motorable track, then Route 65 — all well-waymarked and taking about 2h.

But though access is now easier (there is even a drive to the alm *for overnight guests only*), the setting — on a small flat meadow between steep cliffs (the 'walls') — will still astonish you, as you enjoy some fantastic local cooking.

Mühlen/Molini di Tures

Mühlen, south of Sand, is named for the many mills in the area, driven by its stream. There's a lovely drive from here up the **Mühlwalder Tal**, a valley which attracts both walkers and climbers. You go via **Mühlwald/Selva dei Molini** with its impressively sited parish church to **Lappach/Lappago**, the highest village in the valley at 1436m. From here a motorable track, closed to private cars, runs to the **Neves Reservoir**.

This beautifully located lake is the starting point for two interesting **mountain walks**. To the west you can reach Pfunders (see page 39) via the Eisbruggjoch; to the east you can climb to the Chemnitzer Hut on the Nevesjoch and then go down to Weissenbach, where you'd meet the Ahrntal road. From Mühlwald itself two hours of steep climbing would take you to idyllic Wenger Lake, in a corrie surrounded by larches and Arolla pines (but no hut/refreshments).

Reintal/Valle di Riva

A minor road leads from Sand along the **Rein/Riva Valley**.

● **Walking tip: Franziscusweg.** Under 2km along, park at the Toblhof (inn), to see one of South Tyrol's most spectacular waterfalls, the three-tiered **Reinbachfälle**. You reach it on a meditation path dedicated to St Francis (the '**Franziskusweg**'; ascent of 160m; allow 1h return). On your return, take some refreshment at the inn.

Higher up, the Reintal widens out a bit and, after some fine new views to the surrounding 3000m-high peaks, you come to **Rein in Taufers/Riva di Tures** (1595m), the main village in the valley. Rein is far from the highest settlement in the valley, since mountain farms like Hirber (1674m) and Eppacher (1687m) lie even higher up. Meadows, old tracks and trails, unspoilt farmhouses, alms and the isolated mountain world are the strong points of this area.

The **Rieserferner-Ahrn Nature Park** completely encloses the settled and farmed parts of the village. This nature park is probably the most isolated and untouched in all South Tyrol. A straightforward but **magnificent ascent** (Route 3, the 'Erlanger Weg') leads from south of Rein to the Rieserferner Hut on the main ridge of the range; it's an ascent of some 1280 m, for which you should allow *at least* 8h return.

Rieserferner-Ahrn Nature Park

The Rieserferner group almost met the same fate as so many other mountain ranges with a lot of water and steep declivities. Plans were in place for reservoirs, power stations, tracks and roads, with plenty of ski lifts for good measure. But all this was vetoed by the South Tyrol provincial government, so that today we have a nature park of national interest — and of international significance, because it is virtually untouched.

The terrain in the park is composed of impermeable prehistoric rock and slate, and a lot of rain falls here. So there is plenty of water in the streams. Ice Age glaciers scoured the whole area, carving steep valleys topped by the flat terraces that are today dotted with alms. From these terraces with their little lakes the streams bounce down into the valley as noisy waterfalls. It's true that the

A cemetery like a garden — in the Ahrntal nature is never far away.

glaciers here are contracting at a great rate, but if you look up to Dreiherrenspitze (3499m) or Hochgall (3436m), you'll find that they still look quite impressive.

Ahrntal/Valle Aurina

People staying at the bottom of the Ahrntal are often disappointed to learn that the holiday area lies further uphill. But it doesn't take long to drive the 30km of good road between Sand in Taufers at 870m and Kasern/Casere at 1600m.

Transport: There are also **bus** connections: up to 15 buses a day ply the route from Bruneck via Sand to Kasern in the upper valley, although some end at Prettau.

From a car, the bottom of the valley is a rushed haze of unsightly buildings. But doing the road by bike you notice the little wayside chapels, the barns, old farm buildings and farm gardens with pear trees on the south-facing walls. Only **walkers** and mountain bikers experience the upper reaches: beyond the zone of the mountain farms there is an almost unbroken forest belt. It's not old forest, however, since it took a lot of wood to build all the hotels down in the valley! And what wasn't used for the hotels went to the furnaces: there is still a half-ruined chimney stack visible on the road above Prettau. Going up even higher you come to the alms, where the farmers took their cattle to graze in summer and cut hay to provide for both the animals and themselves during the long winter. Even further up sheep and goats graze around the lakes in the mountain corries — lakes Griessbach, Waldner, and Klaus (the latter can be reached by lift; see overleaf). Above all this shine the ice-capped peaks — territory only accessible to experienced, properly equipped climbers.

Luttach/Lutago

This old village has been transformed by the Speikboden ski area on the doorstep and the typical Italian industrial and trading estate alongside the road. The new wooden buildings can't make much impact on that. The lovely private two-storey **Maranatha Museum** is worth a visit (cribs and folk art). *Museum open all year, Mon-Sat from 09.00-12.00 and 14.00-18.00, Sun from 14.00-17.00; entry fee 5 €, concessions 2 €, families 12 €.*

A **cable car** runs from Luttach up to **Speikboden/Monte Spico** (early Jun-early Oct 08.30-12.00/13.00-16.30; 17 € one way, up and back 21 €). In summer the peak (2523m) is a goal for **walkers**, reached from the top station (1974m) via meadows full of rhododendrons in about 1h30min (2h45min return). The onward route via the Kellerbauerweg to the Chemnitzer Hut (Nevesjoch Hut) is only recommended for experts and only in fine weather.

St Johann in Ahrn/ San Giovanni

The old main village street still has a couple of lovely façades, due to the fact that there is a bypass road.

Sights: The **parish church of St Johann**, which towers above all the other buildings, has beautiful and well-preserved baroque frescoes; the whole impression is colourful and cheerful. The church dates from 1783-1785; it was built on high ground, as the whole valley was subject to flooding.

St Johann's **Kirchler Mineral Museum** houses the beautiful collection of a private donor; the displays are from the Ahrntal mines. This is really worth seeing, as it gives a good grounding in the colourful mineral world of the valley. There is also a sales room with local, regional and international objects. *Museum open Apr-Oct daily from 09.30-12.00 and 14.00-18.30 (Nov-Mar 15.00-18.00); entry fee 4 €, concessions 2.50 €.*

Steinhaus/Cadipietra

Steinhaus is the only really self-contained village in the valley. The administration and stores of the mining area were once located here in the **Ansitz Gassegg**. The houses are imposing, but lack outbuildings, since they were not built as farms.

The **Bergbaumuseum** (Mining Museum) is located in the 'Kornstadel', the former mining stores. It is extremely interesting — one of five establishments which together make up the South Tyrolean Mining Museum (others are the show mine in Prettau and museums in Sterzing, St Leonhard im Passeier and Ridnaun). The collections are housed in their original setting, which has been beautifully restored. There are multi-media displays (PCs with good reference programs on the top floor). What comes over most forcefully is the everyday life and the harsh working conditions of these miners. There are special exhibitions on the ground floor. *Museum open Apr-end Oct daily (ex Mon) from 10.00-17.00; entry fee 4 €, children 2.50 €; combination ticket giving also entry to the show mine at Prettau 10/4 €. (www. bergbaumuseum/it/en)*

● **Walking tip: Lake Klaus/ Chiusetta.** The fact that the cable car from Steinhaus up **Klausberg** only goes up to 1600m keeps the number of people visiting the wild mountain corrie holding **Lake Klaus** at 2162m to a minimum, so if you go there, you won't be overwhelmed by tourists. The **cable car** operates daily from mid-May to mid-Oct, 08.30-12.20 and 13.00-17.15 (one way 17 €, up and back 21 €; children 10.50/ 12.50 €). There is a large **car park** at the bottom station. The Berggasthof Kristallalm, up by the top station, is open all year and offers excellent Tyrolean cooking, as well as snacks and cakes.

A good trail (Route 33; Tabacco 1:25,000 map N° 035) rises 120m from here via the Moareggalm to the Speckalm. A lot of people manage this. But then the route hairpins up another 450m to the lake, and this is a very effective filter … as is the fact that there's nowhere at the lake for refreshments! So despite the lift, the peak itself, like Durreck (3135m), rightly belongs to the unspoilt Rieserferner-Ahrn Nature Park. Allow 2h30min-3h return.

Prettau/Predoi

Up at the old farming village of Prettau it's noticeably cooler than down in the lower valley; larch and birch are among the trees lining the road.

Sights and excursions: The show mine of the South Tyrolean Mining Museum *(www.bergbaumuseum/it/en)* is a must; it's reached by taking a short minor road off the main valley road (**car park**). Since the temperature will be only about 7-8 °C, dress warmly (no sandals)! Copper mining here dates back 4000 years, until the mining industry proper was established in the 20th century. Prettau copper was much sought after and expensive.

You board a pit train and travel through one of the many tunnels (protective clothing is provided), then follow a circuit on the ground, 6m below the level of the gallery. Down here you'll see working techniques depicted by models and machines. *Museum open Apr-Oct daily (except Mon) from 09.30-16.30; in high season be sure to book ahead. Entry fee 10 €, children 5 €, families 20 €; combi-ticket also giving access to the Steinhaus Mining Museum 14/8 €.*

A mining **'teaching' trail** that runs up into the high mountains is a good continuation of the trip into the galleries, but only recommended for strong walkers. There are information panels along the way.

As mining fell into crisis at the end of the 19th century, the situation was dire for many families. One of the parish priests had the idea of starting a **lace-making** business to help the economy. The village women learned fast. In summer you'll see women working on the lace pillows. Another source of income is the carving of wooden masks, usually carried out by the men; it's an older trade than lace-making, but cannot compete with the mask carving of Gröden (Book 2).

Kasern/Casere

The hamlet of Kasern is just a handful of houses, an information kiosk for the **Rieserferner-Ahrn Nature Park**, a snack-bar, three hotels and a large car park. *Park house open May-end Oct and end Dec-end Mar; Tue-Sat from 09.30-12.30/14.30-18.00; entry free.*

● **Walking tip: Kehreralm.** From Kasern a road (closed to traffic) runs 5km to the **Kehreralm** (1842m; see map overleaf), where it ends. With an ascent of little more than 200m, this is a popular route for those who won't want to tackle Walk 5. On the way you can visit the late Gothic **pilgrimage church of the Holy Ghost** (always open), just 1km from the Prastmann Snack Bar at Kasern; it's on the other side of the stream and was once a votive chapel for the mountain people of Prettau. The setting is shown overleaf — this is the first part of Walk 5.

Walk 5: FROM KASERN/CASERE TO THE BIRNLÜCKEN HUT/RIFUGIO TRIDENTINA

Distance/time: about 15.2km/ 9.4mi; 5h
Grade: 🔴 moderate-strenuous, with an ascent/descent of 850m/ 2800ft
Waymarking: red/white; Trail 13
Equipment: walking shoes or boots, sun protection
Refreshments: available at the Birnlücken Hut, open Jun to early Oct; food, beds and bunks

Walking map: Tabacco 035, Ahrntal/Valle Aurina, 1:25,000
Transport: 🚗 to the large car park at the end of the road in Kasern/ Casere (47° 3.086'N, 12° 7.763'E). 🚌 450 from Bruneck/Brunico to Kasern (daily, hourly, in high season half-hourly). From the bus stop, walk the short way to the end of the road in front of the Naturparkhaus Riesenferner-Ahrn

We climb beside the bounding Ahr/Aurina Stream towards its source on the heights. On the right is the Dreiherrenspitze/Picco dei Tre Signore — a summit draped in glaciers. Our goal, the Birnlücken Hut, is the base for the few climbers who will scale that peak — and walkers who will continue up to the Birnlücke and then continue on Trail 13 or go over into the valley of the Krimmler Ache in Austria.

From the car park in **Kasern/ Casere** (**1**) follow the good road, closed to traffic, further into the valley towards Prastmann and the Heilig Geist church. Beyond the hamlet of Prastmann you pass the church of the **Holy Spirit** on the far side of the **Ahr/Aurina Stream** in the setting shown opposite.

When the road ends at the **Kehrer Alm** (**2**; 1h30min), go right, over the stream on Trail 13, winding up to the **Lahneralm** (**3**; 2h; refreshments). The floor of this alm is flat as a pancake; it's an old dried-up lake. It's a peaceful place in the middle of a wild landscape — to the north are the frightening flanks of the Zillertal Alps with their sheer ridges and boulder-filled corries, in the east and southeast are glaciers surrounding the Dreiherrenspitze. Between these peaks is the Birnlücke, the only gap in this wilderness.

From the end of the lake floor Trail 13 hairpins up to a higher flat area in glacier terrain, where you come to the **Birnlücken Hut/ Rifugio Tridentina** with its panoramic views (**4**; 3h). From here the view to the glaciers on Dreiherrenspitze (3498m) is magnificent.

If you decide, after a refreshment break, to climb another 200m to the **Birnlücke**, it's likely that the pass will covered by a snow field. But the main walk ends at the hut: retrace your route back to **Kasern** (**1**; 5h).

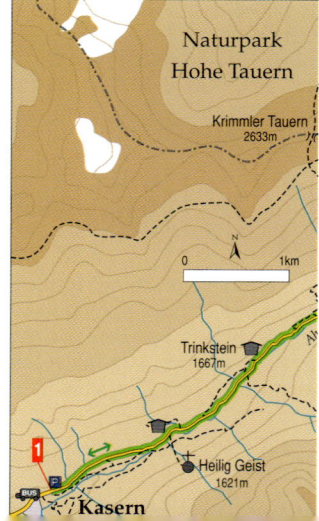

70

Walk 5: From Kasern to the Birnlücken Hut

Krimmler Tauern

A straightforward but strenuous route rises from Kasern to the Krimmler Tauern (Route 14; see map below) — the old Tauernweg, which was used for trade back in the Middle Ages. You can still see the slabs of the old cobbled route. There is no hut on Tauern, so for this 5h round trip you would need to take plenty of sustenance! The route is still used twice a year by the Ahrntal cattle farmers who own alms high up in the Austrian Krimmler Tauerntal. In spring this means that they must cross large *névés*, since the pass lies at 2633m!

The bounding Ahr/Aurina outside Kasern/Casere, with the church of the Holy Spirit on the far side of the stream

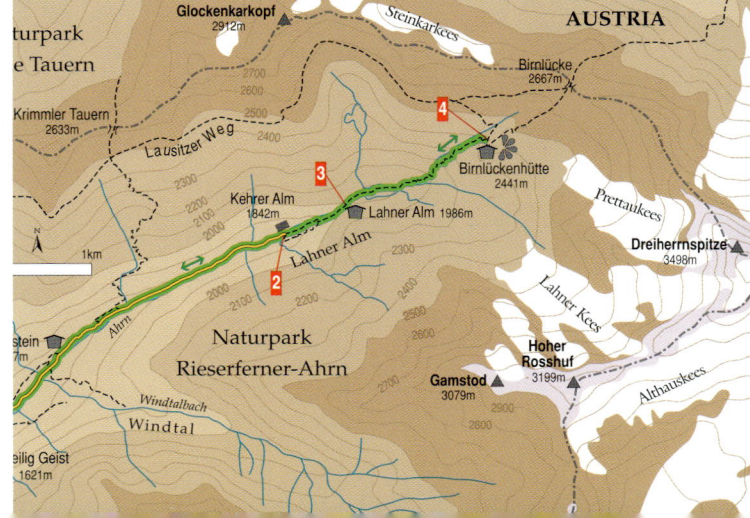

4 ANTHOLZER TAL AND GSIESER TAL/ VAL DI ANTERSELVA AND VALLE DI CASIES

Rasen • Mittertal • Lake Antholz • Welsberg • Gsieser Tal • Taisten

Walks: none; *walking tips:* Grentealm and Kumpfleralm (page 73); Lake Antholz (page 74)
Websites: www.rasen.it
www.antholz.com
www.gsieser-tal.com
www.welsberg.com
www.taisten.com
Opening hours: see individual attractions

These are two of the least-developed valleys in eastern South Tyrol, outside the Dolomites proper, but ideal for anyone who wants a peaceful holiday — to relax, do a little sport (nothing too ambitious) and get to learn about the farming culture of the area (perhaps at an *agriturismo*).

The Antholzer Tal/Val di Anterselva strikes off from the road in the Pustertal/Val Pusteria at Niederrasen/Rasun di Sotto and climbs 1050m over 23km to the Stallersattel/Passo di Stalle on the boundary with Austria. That sounds steeper than it really is. The last 450m, from Lake Antholz to the saddle are covered in under 3km as the bird flies (but with corresponding hairpins, 10% gradient, one-way traffic … with waits of up to 45 minutes … and closed to caravans). It's an ideal area for short walks and long-distance skiing.

The Antholzer Tal/Val di Anterselva is the best valley in the Dolomites for long-distance and biathlon runners and the goal of the Pustertal Cross-Country Ski Marathon which starts in Innichen. To quench the thirst and stave off the hunger pangs of the brave walkers who are making long sweaty treks in the Rieserferner

Antholz Mittertal: the Rieserferner group/Vedretta di Ries rises above the village

Nature Park or the mountains around Rote Wand in the south, there's a whole array of alms and mountain huts taking guests. Some of these have every modern convenience and are as comfortable as can be. It's worth while, too, taking your bicycle if you're travelling by car — there's little traffic on the road and you can pedal up and whiz down; there's also a plethora of forestry roads and drives leading from the valley floor up to alms on the slopes.

Transport: There are up to 18 **buses** a day *(Sundays only 4!)* between Bruneck, Olang and Antholz Mittertal; about 5-6 a day run up to Obertal.

At the top end of the valley is the Stallersattel. If you plan to cross the border with Austria here, the pass should be open *during daylight hours* from mid-May to end Oct. Take passports for the border crossing. Despite the one-way traffic (uphill in the third quarter of every hour, down in the first quarter), this pass draws both motorists and cyclists. Because of the hairpin bends the buses can't handle it, but once at the pass, there is an Austrian bus (summer only) which you could take to Lienz.

Rasen/Rasun

Rasen is the first settlement in the Antholzer Tal. An eye-catching row of really stately farm houses runs from the chapel in **Niederrasen** at the valley exit to the church at Oberrasen. **Oberrasen** is the more important village, where the upper-crust lived — in what is today the **Neurasen castle ruins** on a wooded rocky spur above the road.

Heading up to Oberrasen you'll see a very impressive castle-like building with towers and bay windows on the right, the **Ansitz Heufler**. The Heuflers of Rasen (they had already been here for several generations) had this built in 1580 in what was then the modern Renaissance style. The property is not the only one of its kind in South Tyrol, but certainly one of the most beautiful; today it's a château-hotel. The three-storey building is square and completely symmetrical, with diagonally placed corner towers. The first floor contains some representative decoration and beams, especially in the 'Herrnstube', which is one of the most magnificent rooms in Tyrol.

● **Walking tip: Grentealm (and Kumpfleralm)**. You can get to the **Grentealm** and its two manned huts from Antholz Niedertal on a delightful walk: turn left off the main road, signposted for 'Kaltenhauserhof Appartments' and then take Trail 6; Tabacco 1:25,000 map N° 032). This hairpins up through woods to 2002m. The Messnerwirt is manned from 20 Jun to 5 Oct, the Pfaffing from end Jun to end Sep; both offer typical rustic alm cooking — try the *graukäs* (grey cheese)!

From the Grentealm other routes run to the **Kumpfleralm** and Mittertal. Allow 3h30min-4h up to the panoramic Grentealm and back down the same way; if you come down via the Kumpfleralm, allow 4h-4h30min. Both routes involve an ascent/descent of 750m/2500ft.

Antholz Mittertal/Anterselva di Mezzo

Just a generation ago Mittertal was a strung-out settlement with a church, but today it's a compact village with guest houses, mini-markets, bakery and butcher. Above the village are two alms in panoramic settings: Grentealm and Kumpfleralm.

● **Walking tip: Lake Antholz/Lago di Anterselva.** Lake Antholz is often referred to as the Lower Lake, since there is another lake by the Stallersattel called the Upper Lake (Obersee), although today that lies in Austria. While the southern stretch of Lake Antholz is a bit spoiled by the nearby road with its hotels and restaurants, the northern part lies in the nature park and is still pristine, so it's worth doing the circuit (1h-1h30min).

Leave your car at the large **car park** at the **Huberalm** in Antholz Mittertal (or take the bus to the next, **smaller car park** by the lake) and walk in a counter-clockwise direction around the lake, leaving the best part till last. The road which you have to follow at first sees little traffic, since most people stop at the large car park. Marvellous views await you: first you see mighty Hochgall (3436m) and Wildgall (3273m), and later the Rote Wand (2818m).

Welsberg/Monguelfo

The road between Olang and Welsberg has to make a long climb, since the electricity works have used the wide part of the valley for a reservoir. **Welsberg** is a lovely, well-knit place, almost looking like a town. Beautifully kept Welsberg Castle stands above the mouth of the Pieding Stream which opens out from the Gsiesertal.

Transport: The narrow road through the village, which used to be subject to kilometre-long hold-ups, has been bypassed. There is a good **bus** service: Welsberg is on the Bruneck/Innichen route, with up to 15 buses a day). There is also a **railway** station.

Sights and excursions: A stroll around Welsberg should first take in the **parish church of St Magdalena**, with its high- and side-altar paintings by the baroque artist Paul Troger (1698-1762), who was born in the village. The church was newly built in the baroque style.

A **large shrine-like pillar**, with frescoes by the great Michael Pacher, stands on the square near the main road; unfortunately the frescoes were almost completely destroyed by high water in 1882.

Beautiful properties attest to Welsberg's past, when court was held here — like **Ansitz Zellheim** on the main through road, with its gables, double-arched window and splendid wrought-iron gates.

On a hill somewhat outside the village towards Toblach/Dobbiaco is the **Rainkirche** — today the cemetery church. A beautiful net vault in the choir and Gothic frescoes adorn the otherwise baroque embellishments of the church.

A road runs from the village to **Schloss Welsperg**, the oldest castle in the upper Pustertal/Val di Pusteria between Bruneck/Brunico and Lienz in Austria. It retains its old, very high keep. At that time (1126-1140) the castle was the seat of the House of Welsberg (later Counts and Princes of the Realm), who ran their extensive holdings from here. The castle was rebuilt and extended at a later date, but partly burned in 1764; it has been completely restored only fairly recently. *Castle open end Jun to mid-Sep, Mon-Fri from 10.00-16.00, Sun from 15.00-18.00;*

Welsberg and the lower Gsiesertal from the path to Olang

closed Sat. Open from mid Sep to end Oct, Thu from 14.00-16.00. Entry fee 4 €, concessions 3 €. Also open for occasional concerts: see www.schlosswelsperg.com.

Gsieser Tal/Valle di Casies
If you follow this still-pastoral valley, mainly frequented by walkers and a few tourists, you'll be on an old smugglers' route; they used it to take their goods over the Gsieser Törl (2205m) to Austria.

The valley begins with a small climb via Taisten, a mecca for art lovers. Further up are Durnwald, Unterplanken, Pichl, Oberplanken, Preindl, St Martin and St Magdalena; only these last two have any 'character'. There are about 15 **buses** a day from Welsberg to St Magdalena (no Sunday service).

Although most **alm huts** open at the end of June at the earliest, those in the Gsieser Tal open from mid-May — a boon for walkers and enthusiasts of alm cooking! Ask the tourist office to tell you which will be open.

St Martin/San Martino is the setting for an annual 'Alm Hut Festival' in the middle of September (exact dates from the tourist office), with brass bands and a two-hour procession from alm to alm, with each serving up its culinary speciality.

Another plus point: quite a few **winter walking** routes are open, so if you enjoy winter holidays but don't like skiing, you can still commune with nature. These routes link the valley floor with various alms — which are also open in winter (addresses from the tourist board).

Taisten/Tésido
Two churches, a chapel and a shrine-like pillar attract art lovers to **Taisten**: the original Romanesque church of St George, the baroque parish church, the cemetery chapel and the Gothic pillar at the entrance to the village. Simon von Taisten (about 1460-1530), an important painter of the late Middle Ages, came from Taisten and painted the frescoes in the **Jakobskapelle** at the cemetery. The baroque **parish church** was decorated by Franz Anton Zeiller, whose frescoes also adorn the parish church in Toblach. Even Michael Pacher is represented, with his Madonna in the arch of the gothic **Welsbergkapelle** adjacent to the parish church.

> **Smuggling in the Gsieser Tal**
> Except for a handful of farmers, valley people were poor and most had to take lowly jobs like stable-boy, maid or shepherd — badly paid, or not paid at all, but given food and 'lodgings' in a covered haystack. Food was at best ham, noodle and milk soup. No wonder smuggling flourished once the crossing into the Defreggental suddenly became the Austrian border in 1919. Today you can still see the Italian toll watch hut at the Gsieser Jöchl/Forcella di Casies (somewhat hidden, so it can't be seen from the Austrian side).

5 EISACKTAL/VALLE ISARCO

Brixen • Neustift Monastery • Plose • Lüsner Tal • Klausen • Lajen • Waidbruck • Villnösstal • Puez-Geisler Nature Park

Walks: 6-14; *walking tips:* guided walks run by various tourist boards; *cycling tips:* three good cycle paths start in Brixen: to Innichen via the Pustertal; to Sterzing via the Wipptal and then on to the Brenner Pass; along the Etsch/Adige to Bozen, Salurn and Trient

Websites
www.eisacktal.info
www.brixen.org
www.luesen.com
www.klausen.it
www.lajen.info
www.villnoess.com

Opening hours: see individual attractions

F rom the Brenner Pass it's an easy ride to Bozen/Bolzano, and that's all most people see of the Eisack/Isarco Valley. They race along the motorway or take the fast EuroCity trains through the narrow valley between Brixen and Bozen without any view of the Dolomites — the wild peaks of Geisler/Odle and Schlern/Sciliar can only be glimpsed at a couple of points. Pity. It's also a pity because Brixen, Klausen and Bozen are beautiful old towns to explore — to say nothing of the many little villages with their slender church spires, culinary surprises and delicious 'Eisacktaler', the valley's dry white wine.

Brixen/Bressanone

The town (there is a town plan overleaf) lies somewhat apart from the Dolomites, but this bishop's seat is worth a stop en route, or even a longer excursion.

It's only around Brixen that the valley opens up enough to make room for the town. In the old town, near the cathedral (which can be seen on the approach from the motorway or train), there is a well-kept centre with shops, restaurants and good hotels.

Plose, a mountain with many **walking routes** and ski runs, rises behind the city, surrounded by vineyards — a most attractive picture.

Transport: All **trains** between the Brenner Pass and Bozen stop here, and it's the hub for **buses** to Bozen, Bruneck, Innichen and most of the valleys in the area. The centre is closed to cars, but there is a paid **car park** north of the old town on the Brenner Pass road.

Sights: The façade of the **cathedral** (**Dom**) dominates the large **Domplatz**. The original building is only partially preserved. The lower parts of the towers are Romanesque and the high chancel Gothic. Today's magnificent baroque edifice was built in 1745. In the cloisters there are wonderful frescoes from the late Middle Ages. *Dom and cloisters open daily from 07.00-18.00, in Nov and from 7 Jan to Holy Week closed 12.00-15.00.*

There are interesting gravestones in the arcades of the old cemetery (**Alter Friedhof**, left from the front of the cathedral). The adjacent church of St Michael (**Michaelskirche**) is very old, but has been completely given over to the baroque. *Cemetery always* *open, St Michael's about 08.00-19.00.*

The **Priesterseminar** is a late, restrained baroque building dating from between 1764 and 1771, with frescoes by Franz Anton Zeiller. The library hall, two stories high, is a real baroque jewel. *In term time limited access, no fixed opening times.*

Two arcaded streets, the **Grosse and Kleine Lauben**, which meet at a right angle, were laid out in the original 11th-century town plans. Don't miss the **Pfaundlerhaus** (1581).

The old city trench (**Grosser Graben**) was filled in long ago; today it's a street. The **Säbenertor** (gate), with its high tower, breaks up the straight line of the adjacent façades.

The seat of the bishops of Brixen (**Hofburg**) is a Renaissance castle. The courtyard, with black statues on a yellow ground, is especially attractive. The **Diocesan Museum** is certainly worth a visit, with its huge collection of cribs, wood-carvings, altar triptychs, and wall paintings. *Hofburg and museum open from 15.3-31.10 daily (except Mon), 10.00-17.00; from 1.12-31.1 (except 24/25 Dec) daily, 10.00-17.00. Entry fee 8 €. www.hofburg.it.*

Neustift Monastery/ Novacella Abbey

This huge complex, with several courtyards, large church, towers and well-maintained outer walls lies just 2.5km from Brixen, surrounded by its own vineyards. It was founded by Augustinians in 1142, and today only monks of this order live here. The ground floor of the present building postdates a fire in 1190 and was

View from the Hofburgplatz to the Domplatz and Brixen's landmark cathedral

fortified in the 15th century. In 1525 it was plundered during the German Peasants' Revolt (the Augustinians had fled), and from 1735 all the most important buildings were restored in the baroque style.

You come into the grounds via an entrance dating from the Middle Ages. To your left is an interesting round building, the **Engelsburg** (Angel's Castle). It was originally a chapel dedicated to St Michael and was part of the hospice for pilgrims travelling to Jerusalem — they came through Brixen en route to Venice, from where they embarked. In the 15th century the monastery was fortified with battlements and embrasures as protection against invading Turks; the **Turks' Tower** on the right dates from 1476. Next you come to the dining area and wine cellar on the left, then the first courtyard. In the building above the passageway is the two-storey **library**; a jewel of the rococo, it houses some 65,000

Neustift Monastery

books, manuscripts and maps.

In the first courtyard the **Weltwunderbrunnen** immediately catches the eye. This baroque fountain, which dates from the year 1508, depicts the seven ancient Wonders of the World — and as the eighth Wonder, Neustift Monastery!

Coming into the second courtyard, the **monastery church** is to the right — a building with three naves and a high Gothic choir. Its Romanesque tower is massive. The interior of the church is one of the high points of late baroque, with magnificent ceiling paintings (by Matthäus Günther, 1736) in the form of three gigantic medallions with scenes from the life of St Augustine, and a marble high altar.

The **cloisters** are Gothic. The vault is still covered with some

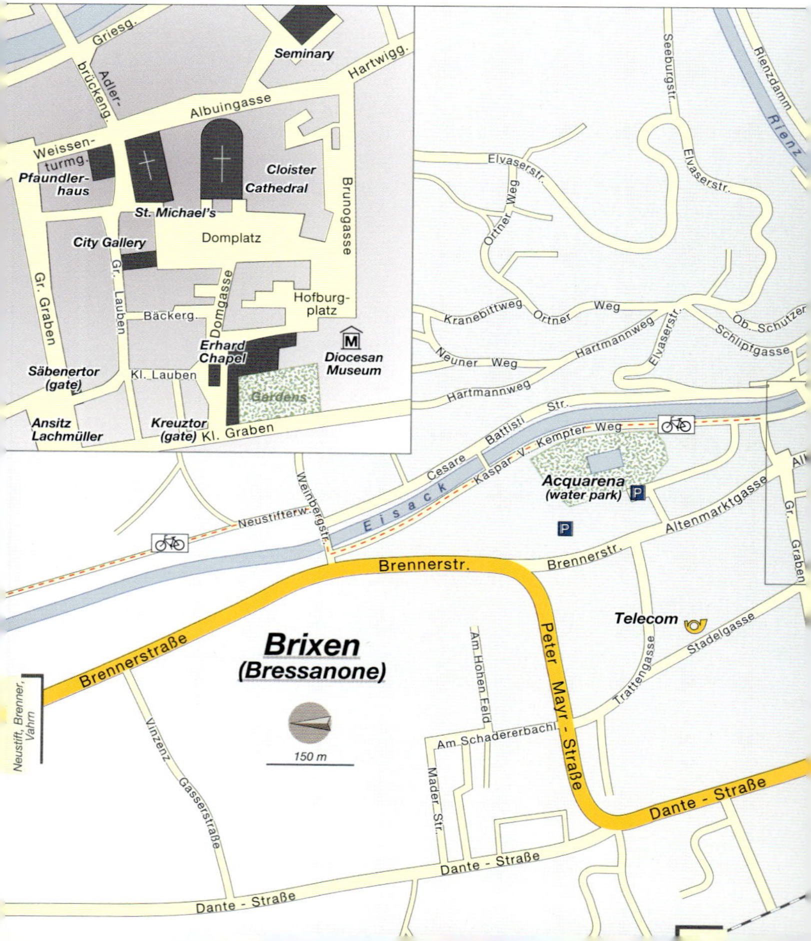

Eisacktal/Valle Isarco

interesting frescoes, although most were ruined by gravestones being inserted at a later date. Finally, don't miss the **historical garden**. *The monastery is usually always open; (paid) car park at the entrance. The courtyards, church and cloisters can be visited daily year round; guided tours Mon-Sat from 10.00-17.00 every hour on the hour (10 €). The garden is open May to mid-Oct. www.kloster-neustift.it.*

Plose

Plose, Brixen's very own mountain, draws walkers in summer and skiers in winter (winter walking is increasingly popular too). Its highest peak, Grosse Gabler at 2561m, rises 2000m/6560ft above the city! It's hardly surprising that its bald summits are already powdered with snow in early autumn and that snow lies around for a long time in early spring.

A road runs via several pretty hamlets and villages to **St Andrä/ S Andrea**, where there is a late Gothic church with a typical high pointed tower. The chapel is an interesting octagonal central building dating from 1696. In this village you'll find the valley station for the **Plose cable car** (Walk 6).

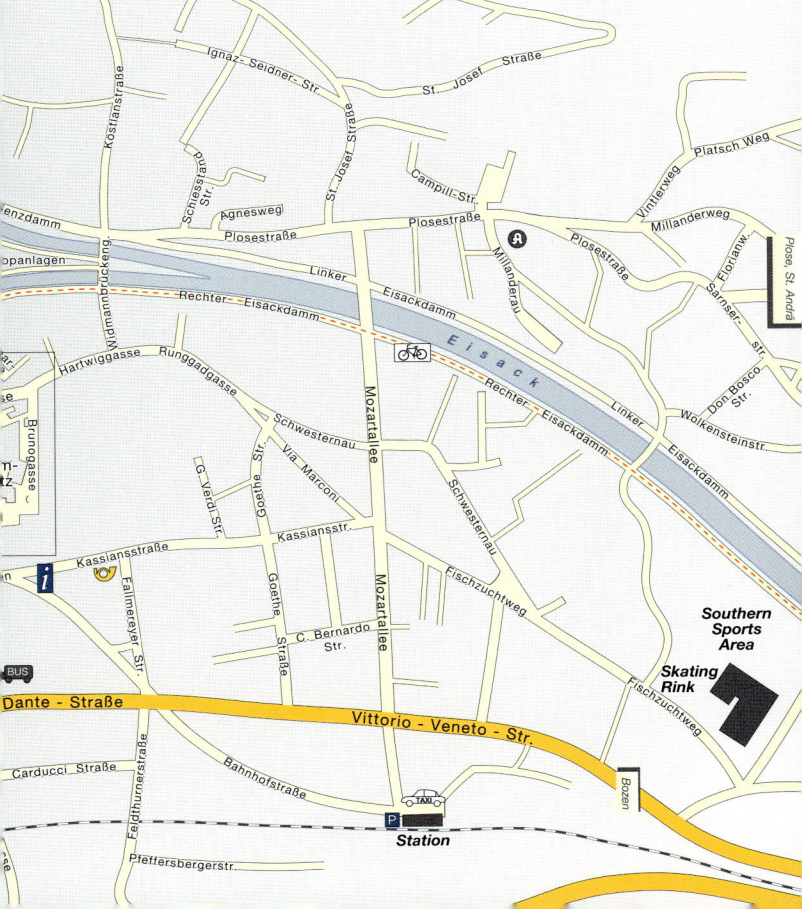

(Operates from end May to the middle of Oct from 09.00-12.00/ 12.45-17.00, in summer 09.00-18.00. The Pfannspitze cable car runs from Jul to end Sep from 09.00-12.15/13.00-17.00. Each costs 16 € one way, up and back 20 €; mountain bikes go free in the Plose cable car only. Plose also has 7 chair lifts serving 43km of pistes; www.plose.org.)

In the hamlet of **Klerant/ Cleran**, a short way downhill from St Andrä, the church of St Nicholas is worth a visit; it has a cycle of frescoes by painters from the Brixen School (around 1475) and a famous naive depiction of an elephant.

Travelling *uphill* from St Andrä, you can get to the top end of the Plose cable car at 2050m by car via Afers and Palmschoss. (There are also **buses** from Brixen which go via the valley cable car station as far as Palmschoss).

Driving via solitary homesteads and the hamlets of **St Jakob** and **St Georg** that make up **Afers/ Éores**, then via **Palmschoss** and the turn-off to the Villnösstal, you come to **Kreuztal** and the top of the cable car station, from where you could start a chair lift, start Walk 6, or take the easy '**Woody Walk**' (ideal for families and strollers.) Alpine meadows stretch up towards the Plose peaks, and in winter chair lifts run almost all the way to the top. There is a superb panorama from here, to the Zillertal Alps in the north, Peitlerkofel/Sass de Putia and the Geisler/Odle peaks of the Dolomites in the east and south, the Sarntal Alps and the Brixen basin in the west.

Lüsner Tal/Valle di Luson

In this narrow, deeply-etched valley there is just one village — Lüsen/Luson. The shady side of the valley, below the northern slopes of Plose, are quite densely wooded, but several big old farmsteads sit on the sunny side.

Here men still make a living from the land; in summer the cattle are driven up to the Lüsner Alm — a broad rolling plateau lying between 1900 and 2200 metres with breathtaking views towards Peitlerkofel and the Dolomites.

Lüsen itself is young. In 1921 a fire destroyed the whole place, including the parish church, which has however been beautifully restored. People come here to walk, to recuperate in peace and quiet, to enjoy the intense greenery and the rustic cooking; they go to bed early. The only 'sight' is the **Pardellermühle**, a mill dating from 1646. The tourist office organises guided tours from May till October, which also include a 'Cultural Walk' through the village.

Klausen/Chiusa

This town lies in a narrow part of the Eisacktal, at the foot of a high isolated rock with several old churches and castles, and crowned by Säben Monastery, the first seat of the bishops of Bozen-Brixen. It wasn't a very amusing place for a bishop — and even less so for the burgers of the little town below, squeezed in between river and rock. But it had the advantage of being easily defended, and remained secure until the 19th century. Moreover everyone — especially every salesman — had to use Klausen's main road to get through the Eisacktal, and had to pay a toll to do so!

Transport: Regional trains stop at the **railway station**; the **bus station** is in the north part of

Klausen's main street: up until just a couple of generations ago, all traffic through the Eisacktal came through this narrow funnel.

town, at the end of the market square (buses to/from Bozen, Brixen, Bruneck, Innichen, and the Villnöss and Grödner valleys). Motorists should note that the old town is a pedestrian precinct.

Sights: Take a walk along the (almost) traffic-free main street. Up until the 1960s all traffic had to funnel through here; today it's a fairly peaceful pedestrian zone. It's best to start out on the north side, by the **Brixner Tor** (gate), with the adjacent late Gothic **Church of the Apostles**. All salesmen had to pass through this gate and, after saying a little prayer in the church, pay their tolls and set out to work.

Follow the main street (called 'Oberstadt' or 'Upper Town' at this point). There's no room here for typical South Tyrolean greenery! Instead you'll see attractively wide houses with coats of arms, bay windows and windows with stone-edged surrounds; today the ground floors are busy with shops and places to eat and drink. Just on the right (at N° 67) is a Renaissance house with beautiful frescoes; N° 59 is the beautiful old Gothic **town hall**; N° 37 (also on the right) is Säbner House, where a wood carver works on the ground floor.

The **parish church of St Andreas** stands a bit below the **Pfarrplatz** (Parish Square). A few late Gothic paintings, statues and galleries still remain from the date of its founding in 1498. From here the main street is called 'Unterstadt' (Lower town), but nothing changes — there are lovely houses left and right. Just before the street ends, the 'Säbner Aufgang' begins on the right, from where you can climb up to the monastery (see below).

On the other side of the Tinne Stream is the somewhat isolated **Cappuchin Monastery** dating from 1701. The Cappuchins only left in 1972; today part of the complex houses the local **museum**. On display is the precious 'Loretoschatz' — a gift from the last Spanish Habsburg empress to her personal chaplain, who came from Klausen. *Museum open from the end of Mar until early Nov, Tue-Sat only 09.30-12.00/15.30-18.00. Entry 4 €, concessions 1.50 €. www.museumklausenchiusa.it.*

The **Säbner Aufgang** is a long climb which begins in the lower town and rises to the **Säben Monastery**. It has been a pilgrims' route for centuries, as can be seen from the Stations of the Cross. After a steep stretch on steps you pass **Branzoll Castle** (not open to the public) with a huge keep. Then you reach the **Liebfrauenkirche**, an octagonal baroque building. In the dome are beautiful frescoes of the Life of Mary. This is the votive church of the inhabitants of

From the Eisacktal you have a good view of Säben Monastery's protected site.

Klausen, who were saved from the Plague by the Mother of God. Via the Benedictine inner monastery one gains access to Säben Monastery's **church** dating from 1687.

Just one more set of steps and you reach the highest point, with the small **Heiligkreuzkirche** (Holy Cross). It rises above many older predecessors, since this prominent and easily-defended site was settled even in prehistoric times. Dating from around 600, it was later rebuilt in late Gothic style as the bishop's palace chapel. The magnificent crucifix on the high altar is by Leonhard von Brixen. *Liebfrauenkirche open from early Jul until All Saints, Tue/Wed/Fri/Sat, 15.00-18.00; Gnaden Chapel, Holy Cross Church and monastery church open daily, 08.00-17.00/18.00. The monastery itself is not open to the public.*

Lajen/Laion
This large villageat the entrance to the Ladin Grödnertal/Val Gardena, base for Walk 14, basks on a sunny terrace at 1100m. The road from Klausen into the valley follows the traces of the old 31km-long railway, built by the Austrian military (in record time) from September 1915 to February 1916, to link Brixen with the upper reaches of the valley.

Tschöfas, **Tanürz** and **St Peter** with its big church (outdoor frescoes!) are isolated villages; St Peter is the last German-speaking settlement below Raschötz, which separates the German and Ladin parts of the valley. This is age-old farming country, with Tyrolean-style twin farmhouses.

Waidbruck/Ponte Gardena
Waidbruck lies at the point where the Eisacktal narrows into a gorge before opening up again at Bozen. It's been a crossroads from Roman times: this is where a road leaves the Eisacktal for the Grödnertal; in Roman times the road over Ritten to Bozen began here.

In the Middle Ages the **Trostburg/Castel Forte** watched over the entrance to the Grödnertal/Val Gardena and still stands there today as if it were ready to spring into defensive action. This castle, where Walther von der Vogelweide (the first great German lyrical poet-knight) grew up in the 12th century, was splendidly rebuilt in the Renaissance — something one can't judge from the outside. Inside, some of the rooms are original, and there is also an exhibition devoted to Oswald von Wolkenstein (14C), the most important lyrical poet between Walther von der Vogelweide and Goethe. *The Trostburg can be reached on foot in 20min from the main square in Waidbruck via the steep old access road, now closed to traffic. Open only on guided tours:*

Easter to end Oct at 11.00, 14.00, 15.00, in Jul/Aug also at 12.00 and 16.00; entry 8 €, concessions 5 €.

Villnösstal/Val di Funes

Few pictures of the Dolomites are as well known as the view shown overleaf — of the **Geisler/Odle** peaks with the little church of St Johann in Ranui in the verdant foreground. And it's just like that: the Villnösstal (Walks 7-13) is one of the few green, quiet and well-farmed valleys in the South Tyrol Dolomites.

Travelling from the Eisacktal you first cross a narrow, deeply-cut and forested gorge, before coming into the wide sunny Villnösstal below St Peter. This attractive farming country once consisted of individual farms and hamlets; today St Peter and St Magdalena, like Teis above the Eisacktal, are more village-like. The peaks of the Geisler group and the equally abrupt **Aferer Geisler/Odles Deores** limit the views. The farmers live from farming, as in the past, but today they also offer farmhouse holidays and let rooms. Taking a holiday here isn't necessarily a doddle: Reinhold Messner, who came from Pitzak in the middle of the valley, learned to climb on **Sass Rigais**, the highest and most eye-catching spike of the Geisler group.

Transport: **Buses** run from Brixen via Klausen railway station as far as St Magdalena and, in summer, four a day go on to the **Zanser Alm** (base for Walks 8-12), which in August is also served by five mini-buses a day from Ranui). Cars pay a toll beyond St Magdalena.

Sights and excursions: In **St Peter** (Walk 7) the parish church of Saints Peter and Paul lies on a sunny terrace above the valley, surrounded by the little village with its inns, post office, bank and shops. More interesting than this much-rebuilt church, however, are two chapels in nearby hamlets.

St Valentin in Pradell has a fine altar triptych dating from the late Middle Ages, with paintings from the life of St Valentine, clearly influenced by Michael Pacher. The fresco of St Christopher on the outside walls is one of the most beautiful in South Tyrol. From here it's a lovely climb up to the little chapel of **St Jakob am Joch**. This also has an altar triptych (from 1517) to admire; like the one in St Valentin's, it comes from the Brixen School. *Both churches are open Jun to end Oct, St Valentin Tue/Thu 16.00-18.00, St Jakob Thu/Sun 16.00-18.00.*

St Magdalena (Walk 13) lies at the point where the Villnösstal narrows again, and the view to the Geisler spires is especially beautiful. The little church of **St Johann** in **Ranui** is an unforgettable spot. It dates from 1744; its slim little tower with the onion dome and painted front, which mimics an entablature, are lovely, but what sets this tower apart is its unusual position: it's at a 45° angle to the nave. The key to the church is in the nearby Ranuihof.

The famous '**Teiser Kugeln**' are stone spheres filled with agate, amethyst or quartz crystals. The parent rock is located by a stream near the village of **Teis/Tiso** in an area of quartz porphyry. Prospecting is forbidden! To see the parent rock, you can take a **guided walk** organised by the Teis Tourist Office. This includes a lovely nature trail and a 'Törggelen' stop (see page 15).

Puez-Geisler Nature Park/ Parco Naturale Puez-Odle

A massive tectonic fault separates the gently sloping meadows of the Villnösstal from the abrupt rock of the Geisler peaks. While the meadows lie above the easily worked red sandstone, the mountain chain is made up of often blindingly white dolomitic rock.

The Aferer Geisler/Odles Deores in the northeast and the Geisler/Odle peaks in the south (the Geisler group), together with the high-lying plateau of the Puez group form part of the Puez-Geisler Nature Park. Thus the park encompasses both German- and Ladin-speaking parts of South Tyrol, as well as parts of the Grödner/Gardena and Gader/Badia valleys.

The park is a truly magnificent **walking area**. One can cross the Puez group from southwest to northeast on a straightforward trail across high alpine terrain, and the Adolf Munkel Weg/Sentiero delle Odle (Walk 10) has always been famous as one of the most beautiful walking trails in the Dolomites. All motorised traffic is forbidden in the park; tents and mountain bikes *are* permitted but, because of the steep trails they're not really an option. So it's much better to take plenty of time to explore on foot, and enjoy the magnificent sight of golden eagles overhead. There are other rare birds in the park, too, like black grouse and capercaillie, but visitors hardly ever see them. The **Naturparkhaus** in St Magdalena is especially informative about geology, as all rock forms can be seen in the nature park. *(Open May-Oct and Jan-Mar, Tue-Sat 09.30-12.30/14.30-18.00, also open Sat/Sun in Jul/Aug); entry free.*

St Johann in Ranui; in the background the Geisler/Odle peaks — where Reinhold Messner learned to climb

You meet up at the **Mineral Museum** *(open Palm Sunday to All Saints, Tue-Fri 10.00-12.00/14.00-16.00, Sat/Sun 14.00-17.00; cl Mon; entry 8 €). Website (www.mineralienmuseum-teis.it) is only in German and Italian, but there are good photos.*

Walk 6: CIRCUIT FROM KREUZTAL/VAL CROCE ON THE PLOSE SUMMIT VIA THE TELEGRAPH

Distance/time: about 10.5km/6.5mi; 4h
Grade: ●! moderate, with an ascent/descent of about 450m/1475ft; beyond the Telegraph you must be sure-footed, with a head for heights. Be aware that the trail is also used by mountain bikers.
Waymarking: red/white; Trail N° 7 to **3**; Trail 6 from **3** to just past **8** and Trail 30 back to the start
Equipment: walking shoes or boots, sun protection
Refreshments: available at the Plose Hut and Ochsenalm
Walking map: Tabacco 030, Brixen-Villnössertal/Bressanone-Val di Funes, 1:25,000
Transport: 🚗 to the large free car park at valley station for the Plose lift in St Andrä (46° 41.868'N, 11° 40.916'E). Or 🚌 321 from Brixen/Bressanone, which stops in the car park (daily, hourly).
Short walk: Telegraph viewing table (●; 6km/3.7mi; 2h30min). Grade as main walk, but there is no exposure. Follow the main walk to the viewing table (**5**), with its superb outlook to surrounding peaks near and far — all of them identified. Return the same way.

The Telegraph is one of several peaks on the Plose massif — the second highest. Ignore the plethora of telecommunications masts and walk on to the viewing table, from where you can see over 100 peaks. The return walk, on the 'Brixen High Route' affords wonderful views into the valley, almost 5000 feet below!

Start out from **St Andrä** by taking the cable car up to **Kreuztal/Val Croce** (**1**). From the top station exit, walk downhill on the wide motor road for a few paces, then turn left uphill on Trail 7 (and 3), signposted to the 'Plosehütte'. When the trail reaches the upper station of a chair lift, you have an especially good view to the Geisler/Odle and Langkofel/Sassolungo groups. Then keep left on the path signposted to the 'Plosehütte' (still Trail 7), climbing the slopes of **Schönjöchl/Giogo Bello**. In winter these slopes are very popular with skiers, as you can see!

Trail 7 runs below a ridge up to your left — to a small **saddle** (**2**), where another trail joins from the left. Go right here, now on the ridge itself and climbing quite steeply to a first **summit** and

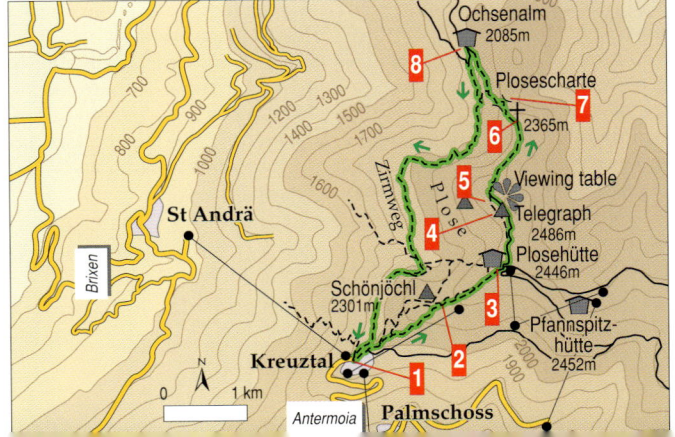

View to the Geisler/Odle peaks from the summit of Plose, with 'alpine roses' in the foreground — a rhododendron species

refuge — the **Plosehütte** with its sunny terrace (**3**; **1h**). Before you tuck in, bear in mind that the hardest part of the walk is ahead of you!

From here continue along the main ridge on Trail 6 (signposting: 'Ochsenalm/Panoramatisch') towards the Telegraph, the second highest summit of the Plose massif. A good track takes you all the way to the **Telegraph** (**4**), with its forest of antennas and old Italian barracks (closed off). A short way further is the circular **viewing table** (**5**; **1h20min**), identifying all the summits which can be seen from here.

From the viewing table Trail 6 is more exposed, at first going steeply downhill along the very narrow ridge, then running more or less level to an ideal resting spot by the **Leonharder Kreuz** (cross; **6**). After a break, follow the zigzags very steeply down 250m/800ft *(dangerous if wet!)* to a gap, the **Plosescharte/Forcella Plose** (**7**), from where you go left through steep meadows to the **Ochsenalm** (**8**; **2h30min**).

From the Ochsenalm follow the motor track downhill and then turn left on the '**Brixen High Route**' (Trail 30), undulating gently along the tree line (most of them stone pines). This route is especially beautiful in the first half of July, when the rhododendrons covering the steep treeless slopes are in bloom. There are tremendous views down into the Eisack/Isarco Valley.

After about 45-50 minutes you pass a trail back down to the Plose Hut, and some 1h30min from the Ochsenalm you'll be back at the upper station at **Kreuztal/Val Croce** (**1**; **4h**).

Walk 7: CIRCUIT FROM ST PETER/SAN PIETRO ON THE BERGBAUERNWEG

Distance/time: about 8.8km/ 5.5mi; 3h15min
Grade: ● easy-moderate woodland and meadow walk with both shady and sunny sections — on roads, forest tracks and meadow paths; ascent/descent 560m/1835ft

Attention: motorbikes!
In the summer the Würzjoch road is beloved of motorbikers, who usually speed up or down. Take care when you're on the road!

Waymarking: from the start to 9 signposted as the 'Bergbauernweg' ('Mountain farmers' track') and from there to 2 as the 'Sunnseitenweg'

Equipment: walking shoes or boots, sun protection
Refreshments: available in St Peter/San Pietro — for instance at the Gasthaus Kabis. En route there are plenty of well-placed benches at viewpoints, ideal for picnicking! After 10, at the Galreidhof, there's a fountain.
Walking map: Tabacco 030, Brixen-Villnössertal/Bressanone-Val di Funes, 1:25,000
Transport: 🚗 to St Peter's car park/bus stop at the entrance to the village (46° 38.488'N, 11° 40.945'E). Or 🚐 340 from Brixen/Bressanone (hourly; last bus back 18.04, on weekdays 20.04).

This idyllic walk runs above pretty St Peter/San Pietro, with lovely views to the Villnösstal/Val di Funes and the Geisler/Odle peaks. It's especially lovely in early summer, before the grass has been cut, when you walk through a waist-high sea of flowers.

The walk starts on the edge of **St Peter** at the bus stop (1): walk northwest uphill into the village. Just past the the council building/tourist office, there's an alley off to the right, signposted up to the **Würzjoch** road (among others). Follow this uphill — in full sight

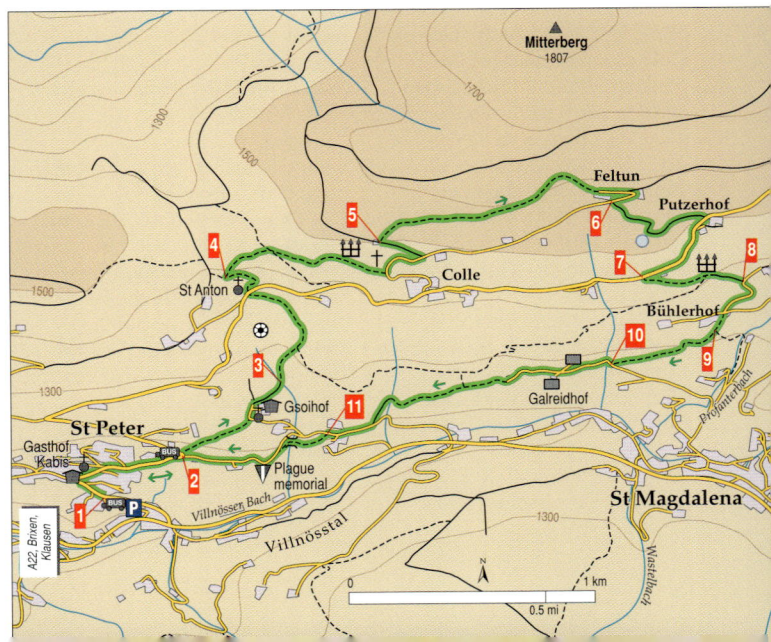

Walking through colourful meadows above St Peter/San Pietro

of the lofty peaks of the Geisler/Odle group on the skyline.

After about 400m the road makes a sharp turn to the west. At the end of this curve there's a bus stop (**2**): here we follow the 'Bergbauernweg' steeply to the right uphill. For about 10 minutes you walk through lush meadows, before coming to a little **chapel** with a bench.

Keep left here. On the right is the **Gsoihof**, dating as far back as 1288. In earlier times its vaulted cellar served in winter as a storage space for the dead, until proper burials were possible in the spring.

Past the Gsoihof, follow the two-wheeled cart track a few meters uphill, then take the meadow path on the right (**3**), signposted 'Bergbauernweg/Vikoler Bild'. At first you're crossing meadows between wooden fences (see above), then you come into mixed woodland.

Out of the woods, the route heads northwest. You walk above a sports ground and soon cross the Würzjoch road. On the far side of the road is the little blindingly white **St Anton/San Antonio chapel** (the 'Vikoler Bild' referred to on the signposting above).

From here it's a steep haul uphill through mixed conifers. Some five minutes from the chapel a path heads off to the right (**4**;

Walk 7: Circuit from St Peter/San Pietro 89

40min). Follow this through the woods, heading east. About 10 minutes later you come to a bench in a clearing. Then there's a bit of downhill walking, shortly passing through a gate. This respite doesn't last long; you're back climbing a meadow path again, with the Geisler peaks ahead. Above you on the left is the wooden **Vikoler Cross** and you come back onto the Würzjoch road.

Follow the road left uphill and take the first left — a farm track signposted 'Bergbauernweg'. In five minutes keep right at a fork (**5**).

At first you walk through more mixed conifers, then after five minutes you emerge from the woods and come to a bench. There's a lovely view from here of St Magdalena with its old church, the Geislers and — in the south — the Raschötz/Rasciesa ridge.

Five minutes later you reach the highest point of the walk. The route describes a curve to the southeast, runs steeply downhill and not long after comes into the old hamlet of **Feltun** with its attractive wooden houses. Walking on asphalt, you now follow a downhill bend and after a few metres/yards turn left on a path through meadows (**6**; **1h40min**).

For the next 10 minutes you're heading straight for the lofty Aferer Geisler/Odles Deores with their highest peak, Tullen (2655m). You pass a drinking tap and eventually come back onto the Würzjoch road, where you meet the **Putzerhof**. Follow the road to the right, into the valley, to the **ruined Gasthof Neujohanis** (**7**). Turn left here. After about 100m through meadows you go through a gate and descend steeply through mixed conifers.

A good 10 minutes from Neujohanis a tarred road comes under foot (**8**). Follow this to the right and five minutes later you come to the **Bühlerhof**. Behind this inn head left downhill through meadows. After some 100m the path splits (**9**; **2h15min**); head right (west) now, always on the 'Sunnseitenweg' which will take you almost all the way back to St Peter. The narrow meadow path runs gently downhill between hazelnut bushes and scattered beech trees.

About 10 minutes from the start of the Sunnseitenweg you come onto a gravel motor track (**10**). Follow this to the right, a little later passing the **Galreidhof** with its drinking water fountain.

Later you go gently downhill with a beautiful view of the Villnösstal through meadowland. Some 15 minutes from the Galreidhof, the path emerges on a tarred road. Follow this to the right; after a good 100m you come to a path heading off to the left (**11**; **2h50min**). Take it: you're back on the Bergbauernweg. Once over a concrete bridge, keep left on the road.

Just a few metres/yards along the asphalt and you pass a well-maintained **plague memorial**, a pillar with a bench nearby — a lovely, final place to take a break. This spot marks the boundary for the inhabitants of St Magdalena who were violently stricken by the plague in 1636. They could go no further than this.

From the plague pillar it's just five minutes back to the curve in the road (**2**) and then another 10 minutes back to the bus stop in **St Peter** (**1**; **3h10min**).

Walk 8: CIRCUIT FROM ZANS VIA THE GAMPENALM

Distance/time: about 6.7km/4.2mi; 2h25min
Grade: ● easy-moderate walking for all the family on wide tracks (cleared in winter); in woods at the start and end; ascent/descent 400m/1300ft
Waymarking: red/white; Trail N° 6, then 6/35 to **7**; Trail N° 33 back to the start
Equipment: walking shoes or boots, sun protection
Refreshments: available at the Zans info hut (**1**; open all year) and at the Gampenalm (**7**; from June to November and from the end of December till mid-March)
Walking map: Tabacco 030, Brixen-Villnössertal/Bressanone-Val di Funes, 1:25,000
Transport: 🚌 from Klausen/Chiusa or Brixen/Bressanone to Zans at the end of the Villnöss Valley/Val di Funes where there is a paid car park at about 5 € for the day (46° 38.170'N, 11° 45.954'E). Or hourly 🚌 340 from Brixen/Bressanone to the terminus, 'Zanserhütte'. Last bus back leaves at 18.43. Outside high season, 🚌 340 only runs to St Peter, from where you have to change to 🚌 339 to 'Zanserhütte' (every two hours; last bus back at 17.37, change at St Peter).

This family-friendly walk at the foot of the mighty Geisler/Odle peaks runs through shady conifer woods and across a high alm full of flowers — to a most attractively sited place to take a break with some refreshments. This walk shares the first section, from Zans to the lovely Gampenalm, with Walk 3.

The walk starts at the **Zans info hut** (**1**), at the large car park. Walk east for a few metres/yards, then follow signposting for the 'Gasthof Sass Rigais' (Trail N° 6). Having passed this inn, take the wide gravel track through the alm meadows. On your right the

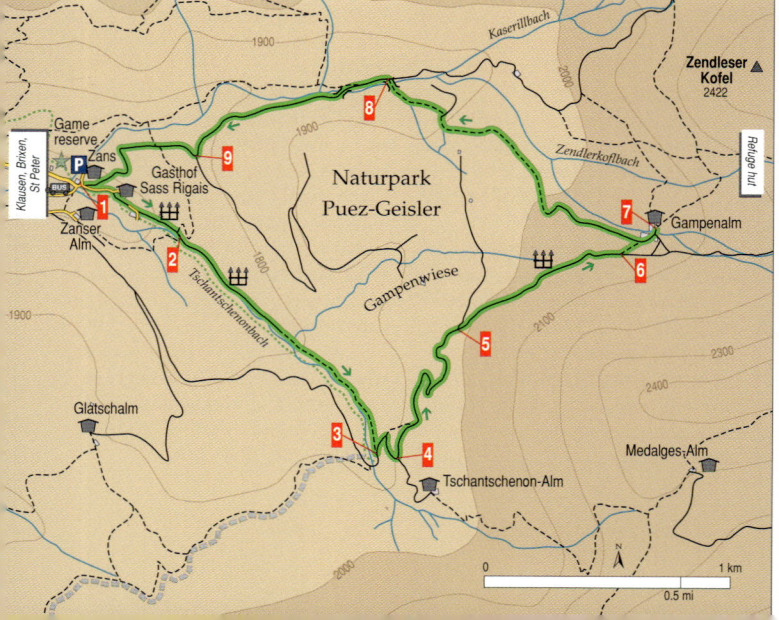

Walk 8: Circuit from Zans via the Gampenalm

mighty towers of the Geisler peaks — Sass Rigais and Furchetta — reach for the sky. About 200m from the inn you go through a cattle gate. On the right there's the splashing sound of the Tschantschenon Stream.

Shortly after going though the cattle gate, you come to a junction (**2**). Keep to Trail 6/35 here, signposted to the 'Gampenalm'. Now you follow this wide gravel track through open woodland. Some 10 minutes after the junction the track narrows and becomes stonier. There's a waymarker here — '35', telling you you're on the right track.

Not far past the waymarker you go through another cattle gate. Then carry on up the steep trail which in many places is stabilised with wooden planks. Following the splashing stream, about 10 minutes later you come to a **lay-by** (**3**) on a wide motorable track. Turn left here. About 100m further on, the track bends to the right (southeast) and quickly forks (**4**; **40min**). Go left for 'Gampenalm' through spruce and pines (the right fork leads to the Tschantschenon and Medalges alms).

On the valley floor the Zanser alms are prominent. Behind them, in the north, the Aferer Geisler/Odles Deores reach skywards — as you continue steadily uphill. Some 10 minutes past the junction a steep section begins, with several hairpins. In another 10 minutes the woods thin out, giving way to alm meadows with scattered larches. Shortly after the meadows begin, the track forks (**5**). A private road goes north downhill to the spread-out Gampen meadows; you head northeast on the wide gravel track. In early summer these rolling meadows embroider a veritable tapestry of blossom.

Now you go through another cattle gate at the edge of the Gampenalm. The long grassy ridge of the Zendleser Kofel rises ahead of you, with the Schlüterhütte/Rifugio Genova in front of it to the south. The buildings on the Gampenalm come into view shortly after. Scattered pines and the odd huge boulder line the track.

About five minutes later you reach an information board with the alm's menu (**6**). Here you leave the main track and take the narrow path through low junipers direct to the **Gampenalm** (**7**). Take a break on their terrace and enjoy a warm apple strudel with vanilla sauce — or maybe just sunbathe in the surrounding meadows.

From here you follow Trail N° 33: it is a bit hidden at the outset, but you'll find it behind the newer stable building on the alm, from

The Zanser Alm

The rock teeth loom ever closer.

where it runs northwest through a cattle gate, gently dropping through widespread flower-filled meadows. On the left you have the Geisler peaks, to the right the Aferer Geisler.

Some five minutes after you've left the alm, the track goes through two cattle gates in a row and then bends. On the right the hillside drops steeply to a stream bed. The track runs in a wide curve through meadows for a while and then comes back to the edge of the slope. Weathered wooden fencing on the left marks the boundary between the path and the Gampen meadows. On the right bushes, junipers and pines grow at the edge of the steep hillside.

Eventually the track heads west and runs through the alm meadows. In the valley floor the washed-out bed of a stream is visible. We reach this stream, the **Kaserill/Caseril**, about 10 minutes later at a wooden boardwalk (**8**; **1h55min**). At the end of the boardwalk the track forks. Head left here on the wide motor track down into the valley. On the left is the Kaserill Stream with plenty of opportunity to take a rest break on its banks and cool your hot feet in the cold water!

After five minutes through mixed conifers you come to a wooden bridge and cross to the other side of the stream. Although the track at first only goes gently downhill, the stream drops into a deep gully.

Some five minutes after the track moves away from the stream, you also go steeply downhill — about 10 minutes later coming to a fork (**9**). Keep right, on the main track here, heading west. You pass another fork and soon come back to the car park (**1**; **2h25min**).

Route variations in the Villnöss Valley/Val di Funes

Most of the walks in this valley start from the info point in Zans. There's a large two-section (paid) car park there, big enough to provide ample space even in high season.

This car park is crossed by many waymarked paths, which all join up at one point or another. So in this book I've tried to use different starting points for the walks — to show the great variety of possibilities in the area.

Walk 9: FROM ZANS TO THE SCHLÜTERHÜTTE/ RIFUGIO GENOVA

Distance/time: about 11.3km/ 7mi; 4h05min
Grade: ● moderate-strenuous, with an ascent/descent of 765m/ 2510ft. On woodland and mountain routes — shady at the outset and the end, but sunny for a long stretch in the middle. There's a steep climb to the Kreuzjoch (**8**) and some skiddy descents.
Waymarking: red/white; Trail N° 6, then 6/35 to **4**, Trail N° 6 as far as **7**, then Trail N° 3/Dolomites High Route to **11**, and finally Trail N° 35
Equipment: walking shoes or boots, sun protection, walking pole(s)
Refreshments: available at the Zans info hut (**1**; open all year), at the Medalges Alm (**8**); the Schlüterhütte (**11**) and the Gampenalm (**12**)
Walking map: Tabacco 030, Brixen-Villnössertal/Bressanone-Val di Funes, 1:25,000
Transport: 🚆 from Klausen/Chiusa or Brixen/Bressanone to Zans at the end of the Villnöss Valley/Val di Funes where there is a paid car park at about 5 € for the day (46° 38.170'N, 11° 45.954'E). Or hourly 🚌 340 from Brixen/Bressanone to the terminus, 'Zanserhütte'. Last bus back leaves at 18.43. Outside high season, 🚌 340 only runs to St Peter, from where you have to change to 🚌 339 to 'Zanserhütte' (every two hours; last bus back at 17.37, change at St Peter).

This panoramic circuit first takes you below the mighty walls of the Geisler/Odle range steeply uphill to the Kreuzjoch/Forcella di San Zenòn. Then you follow the Dolomites High Route against a backdrop of spectacular peaks to the beautifully sited Schlüterhütte/Rifugio Genova. Finally, crossing alm meadows, you come back to your starting point at Zans. The beginning and end of the walk cover the same ground as Walk 8.

The walk starts at the **Zans info hut** (**1**), at the large car park. Follow Trail N° 6 to the **Gasthof Sass Rigais**. Once past this building, take the wide gravel track heading east through alm meadows. On your right there are the lofty peaks of the Geisler/Odle range (Sass Rigais and Furchetta). About 200m beyond the inn you go through a cattle gate and come to a junction (**2**). Keep on Trail N° 6/35 here, heading for 'Gampenalm'. After about 10 minutes the trail narrows and becomes stonier. There's a waymarker here — '35', telling you you're on the right track.

Shortly after you go through another cattle gate, then continue on a steep trail that's stabilised in several places with wooden planks. Following the stream, some 10 minutes later you come to a wide motorable track at a **lay-by** (**3**). Turn left here. Some 100m further on the trail heads southeast and quickly **forks** (**4**; **35min**) once more. Keep right here for 'Tschantschenon/Medalges Alm'.

A wide motor track takes you uphill in two serpentine curves. The mixed conifer wood opens out, offering a view to the mighty rock walls of the eastern Geisler peaks: the Campiller Turm, the Wasserstuhl and the Wasser-kofel/Sas Dalega.

93

Keep right at a fork (**5**) and follow the path signposted to 'Kreuzjoch' (a left here would take you to the Tschantschenon Alm, only 50 or so metres away). Now you are climbing steeply uphill through meadows full of rhododendron and juniper — in early summer a splendour of blooms.

About 10 minutes later the path divides, but it rebraids itself a few metres further on. Take the left-hand path, alongside wooden fencing. With any luck, you'll spot some pink martagon lilies along this stretch. Keep steeply uphill, climbing below giant pines and larch. As you climb higher, the trees give way to views of grassy slopes piercing the rock walls.

After a grassy slope with scattered mountain pines you come to a rubble-filled **gully** (**6**). Soon the trail heads north and goes steeply — and sweatily — uphill for 20 minutes. The Aferer Geisler/Odles Deores rise ahead of you, while in the west you look out to the Villnöss/Funes Valley.

Still climbing, soon other rock teeth are seen in the south — Piz Duleda and the steep scree of the Wasserscharte. Finally you reach the windy **Kreuzjoch** (**7**; **1h35min**) and can take a first break on the bench by the wooden shrine. The view is breathtaking: Piz Duleda and the Puez peaks in the south, the Geislers in the west.

From the Kreuzjoch head north on Trail N° 3 towards 'Schlüterhütte/Rifugio Genova'; you're now on the **Dolomites High Route**. In summer you'll see scores of young people in walking groups on this trail going from hut to hut — all with monster rucksacks.

The **Medalges Alm** (**8**) comes up abruptly after about five minutes — it's set in a hollow, protected from the wind. The trail forks in front of it: keep left, again following 'Schlüterhütte'. Underfoot the surface is quite corregated. In early summer the meadows here are unbelievably splendid. You'll even see edelweiss with some luck.

About 25 minutes past the Medalges Alm you come to a **saddle** (**9**; **2h05min**). In the north the mighty block of the Peitlerkofel/Sass de Putia towers up. Now you're heading down a narrow trail covered with loose stones through another scree. On the right there is a steep drop — *so take care!*

Ten minutes later you come to another saddle. At the end of it a steep path forks west (**10**) down to the Gampenalm, lying below you in meadows. Of course you could shorten the walk here, but the main walk keeps on towards 'Schlüterhütte' (Trail N° 3) and you edge a rocky knoll, Bronsoi.

Past another wooden shrine marking the **Kreuzkofeljoch/ Passo di Poma**, you arrive at the striking **Schlüterhütte/Rifugio Genova** (**11**; **2h30min**). The large wooden refuge dates from 1898 and is very popular. It's set in an broad sunbathing area, protected from the wind, and with a super view of the Geisler peaks — a must for a long break!

From the refuge follow the wide motor track, Trail N° 35, towards 'Gampenalm/Zans'. This is a steep descent on loose gravel, really hard on the knees. The all-encompassing view of the Villnöss Valley is some compensation.

You descend in broad zigzags. About 25 minutes after leaving the refuge you come to the junction for the **Gampenalm** (**12**), which lies just a few metres to the north.

Looking back to the Dolomites High Route

Keep to Trail 35, soon going through a cattle gate with a cattle trough beside it. Then it's down, down, down. The Gampenalm meadows spread out on the right. Closer at hand, the way is edged with attractive pines and spruce and further down you come into a mixed conifer wood.

In about 35 minutes you are back at the 'Tschantschenon Alm' junction (**4**; **3h35min**) From here it's about 30 minutes back to the **Zans info hut** (**1**; **4h05min**).

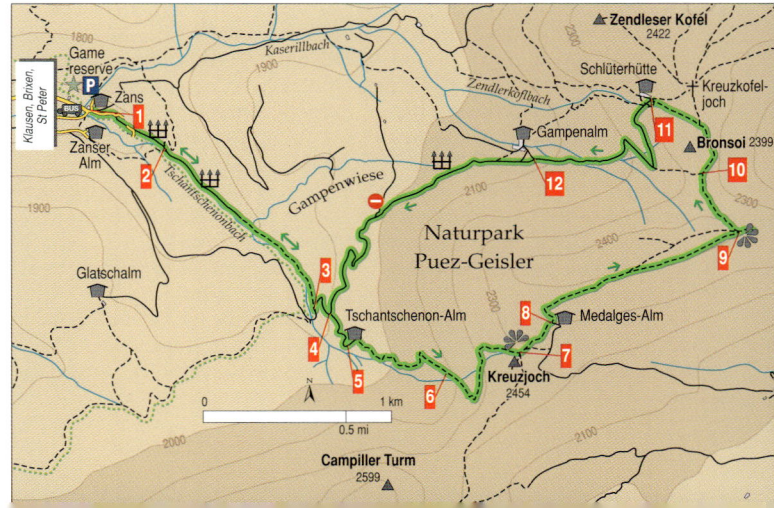

Walk 10: ON THE ADOLF MUNKEL TRAIL (THE SENTIERO DELLE ODLE)

Distance/time: about 13.8km/ 8.6mi; 4h40min
Grade: ● moderate-strenuous, with an ascent of 630m/2065ft and descent of 990m/3245ft. A long, straightforward high-level walk, but on the Adolf Munkel Weg the path is often uneven and full of tree roots. Well-surfaced shady woodland trails to start out; both sun and shade in the middle section, shady at the end, with a short stretch on asphalt.
Waymarking: red/white; Trail N° 36 to **2**, then Trail 35a to **3**; Trail N° 35 (the Adolf Munkel Weg or Sentiero delle Odle) to **10**, Trail 28 to shortly after **13**, and finally Trail N° 33
Equipment: walking shoes or boots, sun protection, walking pole(s)
Refreshments: available at the Zans info hut (**1**; open all year), at the Brogles Hut (**11**) and at the Ranuimüllerhof (just before **14**). There is a long middle section without any possibility for refreshments, so take food and drink! There's a drinking water spring before **4**.
Walking map: Tabacco 030, Brixen-Villnössertal/Bressanone-Val di Funes, 1:25,000
Transport: 🚆 from Klausen/Chiusa or Brixen/Bressanone to Zans at the end of the Villnöss Valley/Val di Funes where there is a paid car park at about 5 € for the day (46° 38.170'N, 11° 45.954'E). Or hourly 🚌 340 from Brixen/Bressanone to the terminus, 'Zanserhütte'. Last bus back leaves at 18.43. Outside high season, 🚌 340 only runs to St Peter, from where you have to change to 🚌 339 to 'Zanserhütte' (every two hours; last bus back at 17.37, change at St Peter). You will end the walk at St Magdalena and take a bus back to Zans.

This long high-altitude walk with outstanding views runs at the base of the Geisler/Odle mountains through extensive meadows to the attractive Brogles Hut. The descent follows the Brogleser Stream to St Magdalena, from where a bus takes you back to Zans. This walk is identical to Walk 11 in the middle section.

The walk starts at the **Zans info hut** (**1**), at the large car park. Head south, cross the Kaserill Stream on a wooden bridge and carry on round the bend above the large car park. At the end of the bend follow Trail N° 36 towards 'Glatschalm/Gschnagenhardtalm', passing the rustic **Zanser Alm** and coming into mixed conifers.

In silence and shade you keep steadily uphill. Some 15 minutes from starting out the trail forks (**2**). Go left towards 'Schlüter-hütte/Rifugio Genova' and 'Gampenalm'. Ten minutes after the fork, the trail heads eastwards. In another five minutes you go through a cattle gate. Now and then the needles of the Geisler/Odle can be seen through the canopy of trees.

Your broad motorable track makes a wide curve uphill to the south. A rustling noise makes itself heard. It's the **Tschantschenon Stream**, and you reach it about 10 minutes from the cattle gate, at a bridge (**3**; **40min**).

Before the bridge, follow the famous Adolf Munkel Weg (Trail N° 35) to the right. It's named for

Walk 10: Adolf Munkel Trail (Sentiero delle Odle)

the first chairman of the Dresden section of the German Alpine Club — the club who built what is today the Schlüterhütte/Rifugio Genova. After a few metres, below on the right, there's a spring in a log trough with crystal-clear ice-cold water. Delicious!

You're walking through a light wood of spruce, pine and larch, where meadows with junipers and rhododendrons come out of hiding between the trees — but the trail is full of roots, so take care lest you twist an ankle!

A good 10 minutes past the bridge you come for the first time to a 'tributary' of the gigantic scree

Climbing to the Adolf Munkel Weg/Sentiero delle Odle

that runs down the flanks of the Geislers. Take a break on a **bench** (**4**) — from where you can size up the dimensions of this colossal scree with its huge imbedded boulders. (Shortly after the bench, there's a narrow path signposted 'Klettergarten' going left into this stone desert.)

Keep on, heading southwest on the Adolf Munkel Weg, ignoring Trail 6 on the right to 'Glatschalm' (**5**) that comes up a short time later. About 30m past Trail 6 you come to the edge of the scree amidst idyllic flat meadows. At the western edge of the scree is a gigantic boulder with a plaque — a tribute to Adolf Munkel.

The trail carries on in a zigzag and comes to another fork to the right for 'Glatschalm' (**6**; **1h15min**). Ignore this turn-off as well and continue on loose gravel through the woods. Spruce, pine, larch, juniper … and always the odd boulder. This is followed by another stretch alongside the scree.

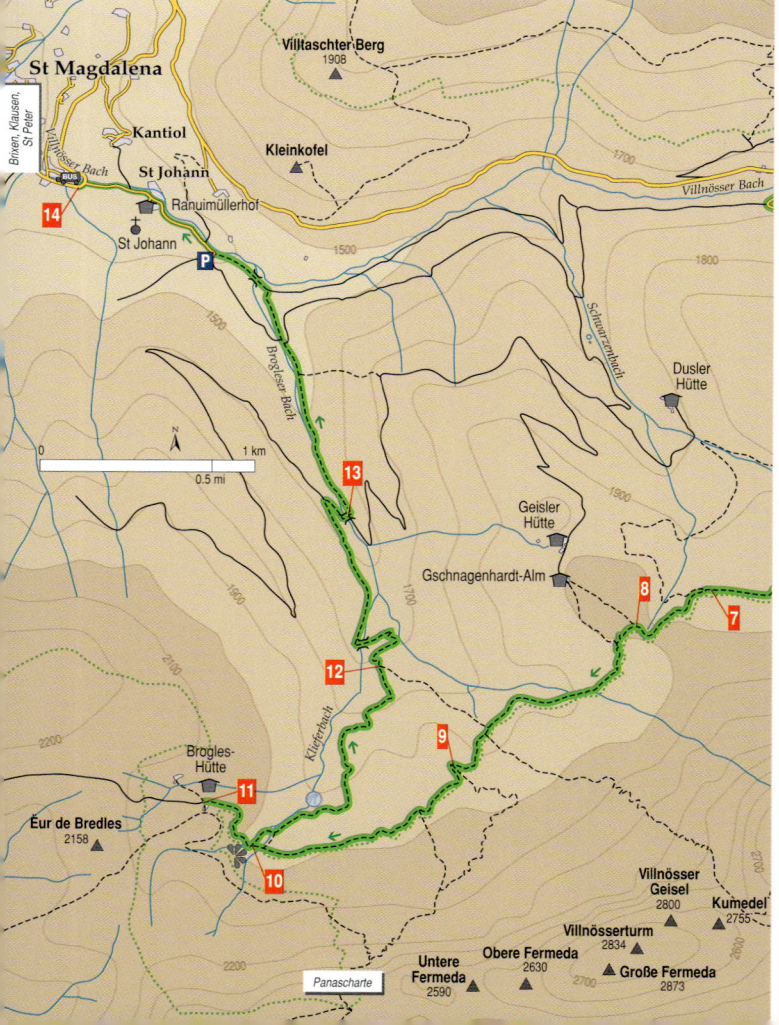

Walk 10: Adolf Munkel Trail (Sentiero delle Odle) 99

Ten minutes later, a trail (**7**) forks right towards 'Dusslerhütte' and 'Geislerhütte'. But keep ahead here again, on the Adolf Munkel Weg, crossing a flat meadow and then climbing a few wooden steps at the end of it. The path is now sandy and full of tree roots; rhododendrons, junipers and hazelnut trees grow at the edges. Shortly after a wooden gate, the trail forks in a hollow (**8**; **1h45min**). Follow the Adolf Munkel Weg to the left downhill here, in the direction of 'Broglesalm' — another sandy trail full of roots. (To the right the way goes steeply northwest uphill to the Gschnagenhardt Alm.) In the south the views open up to the eastern Geisler peaks and Seceda.

Some 10 minutes past the hollow you come to the foot of a massive scree coming down from Sass Rigais. Then you pass a path forking right to 'Villnöss', followed immediately by one heading south to the Mittagsscharte. Again, just keep on the Adolf Munkel Weg, which sometimes makes for very sweaty progress.

Some 10 minutes past the turn-off to the Mittagsscharte your path forks (**9**). (To the southeast a path climbs to the steep Panascharte.) Keep right through mixed conifers for five minutes. Then the woods thin out and you go gently uphill, before crossing a flat meadow.

A few metres past a knoll the trail forks again in a small depression (**10**). To the right it runs alongside the **Kliefer Stream** towards 'Zans' (your ongoing route later in the walk). But since you're likely to be hungry and thirsty by this time, keep left for the moment. Walk steeply uphill through a series of bends for 10 minutes, until you come to the edge of a high alm … and the **Brogles Hut/Rifugio Malga Brogles** (**11**; **3h**) in lush meadows.

Here's where you can take a meal on ancient wooden benches and then sunbathe on the grass. On the north wall of the hut there's a tap where you can fill your water bottles.

Fortified now, walk back for about 10 minutes to the fork at the Klieferbach (**10**) and head northwest on Trail N° 28. You follow the right bank of the stream

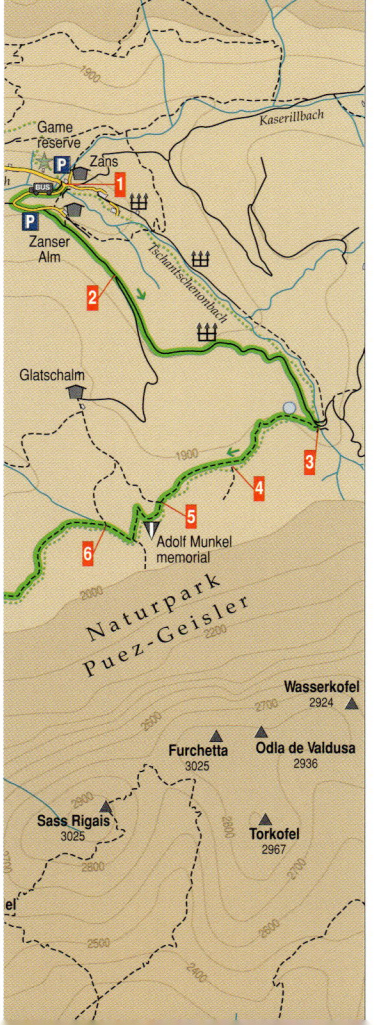

downhill on loose gravel. Some five minutes later the stream leaves you — disappearing into a gorge as a **waterfall**. You continue steeply north downhill through mixed conifers.

A good 20 minutes past the waterfall you reach a crossing (**12**). Take the wide forestry track on the left here, heading downhill through two serpentines. On the way you cross the Kliefer on a wooden bridge and come quickly afterwards to the **Brogleser Stream** (**13**; **4h**). As soon as you cross this stream, keep left and follow the right bank of the stream north through a spruce wood. Ignore two turn-offs to Zans (Trail 34 and later Trail 33.)

After another stream crossing you come to a large car park for walkers. From here follow the tarred road northwest. On the left the lovely little church of **St Johann** rises in the midst of large meadows — the best-known motif of the Villnöss/Funes Valley, reproduced a thousand times in books and on calendars. On the right the **Ranuimüllerhof** offers a last chance for some refreshment.

Not far past the inn your road meets the wide main valley road by the **St Magdalena bus stop** (**14**; **4h40min**). Take the next bus back to the car park/info hut at Zans.

The venerable old Brogles Hut/Rifugio Malga Brogles (before it was rebuilt)

Walk 11: IN REINHOLD MESSNER'S FOOTSTEPS — CIRCUIT FROM ZANS VIA THE GSCHNAGENHARDT ALM

Distance/time: about 9.2km/ 5.7mi; 3h05min
Grade: ● easy-moderate walk for all the family, with an ascent/ descent of 435m/1425ft. Mostly shady paths through woods and in the mountains, but on the Adolf Munkel Weg the path is often uneven and full of tree roots.
Waymarking: red/white; Trail N° 35 to **9** and from **4** to **9** the Adolf Munkel Weg; then Trail N° 36
Equipment: walking shoes or boots, sun protection, walking pole(s)
Refreshments: available at the Zans info hut (**1**; open all year), at the family-friendly Geisleralm before **11** (open from the end of May till the beginning of November and again from the end of December to the end of March; closed Mondays in winter and Tuesdays/Wednesdays in summer). But in the opinion of the author the Gschnagenhardt Alm (**10**) and Dusler Hütte (**12**) are far more beautiful.
Walking map: Tabacco 030, Brixen-Villnössertal/Bressanone-Val di Funes, 1:25,000
Transport: 🚍 from Klausen/Chiusa or Brixen/Bressanone to Zans at the end of the Villnöss Valley/Val di Funes where there is a paid car park at about 5 € for the day (46° 38.170'N, 11° 45.954'E). Or hourly 🚍 340 from Brixen/Bressanone to the terminus, 'Zanserhütte'. Last bus back leaves at 18.43. Outside high season, 🚍 340 only runs to St Peter, from where you have to change to 🚍 339 to 'Zanserhütte' (every two hours; last bus back at 17.37, change at St Peter).

This pleasant circuit beside the Geisler/Odle peaks follows trails to the beautifully sited Gschnagenhardt Alm (Reinhold Messner's 'nursery'; see the panel overleaf) and — further along — to the quiet Dusler Hut. In the middle section the walk follows the same trail as Walk 10, the Adolf Munkel Weg — incredibly beautiful, but full of tree roots to trip you up!

The walk starts at the **Zans info hut** (**1**), at the large car park. Head south and cross the **Villnöss Stream** on a wooden bridge. Just on the far side of the bridge take the wooden steps on the left-hand side of the track and climb under pines. After the steps turn left at the T-junction; about five minutes after starting out you're passing the **Zanser Alm** (**2**). From here follow Trail N° 35, signposted to 'Glatschalm' and 'Gschnagenhardt Alm'.

A boardwalk takes you over a swampy meadow. At the end of it, go gently downhill and shortly after cross a wooden bridge, heading north. Cross the **Tschantschenon Stream** on another bridge and come to a fork (**3**). Turn right here on Trail N° 6/35 towards the 'Gampenalm'.

Continue on a wide gravel track, heading southeast through a loose grouping of trees. Some 10 minutes from the fork the trail narrows and is stonier. A marker at this point (N° 35) tells you that you're on the right trail.

About five minutes later you go through a cattle gate. Continue on the steep trail (stabilised with wooden logs in several places). Following the splashing stream, you come to a lay-by at a wide

101

Reinhold Messner's nursery — the Gschnagenhardt Alm

Reinhold Messner — for many South Tyrol's most famous son — comes from the Villnöss/Funes Valley. Although his homeland is pretty laid back about that, you'll still see reminders of him at the Gschnagenhardt Alm, where he spent summers as a youth.

Next to the calling cards of bearded 'extreme' climbers is a panoramic map of the Geisler range on which they've marked all of Messner's first ascents. So they make it subtly clear that the climber who has mastered every peak on earth over 8000 metres (26,000 feet) had his early training here on this alm and … so rumour has it … still comes and goes.

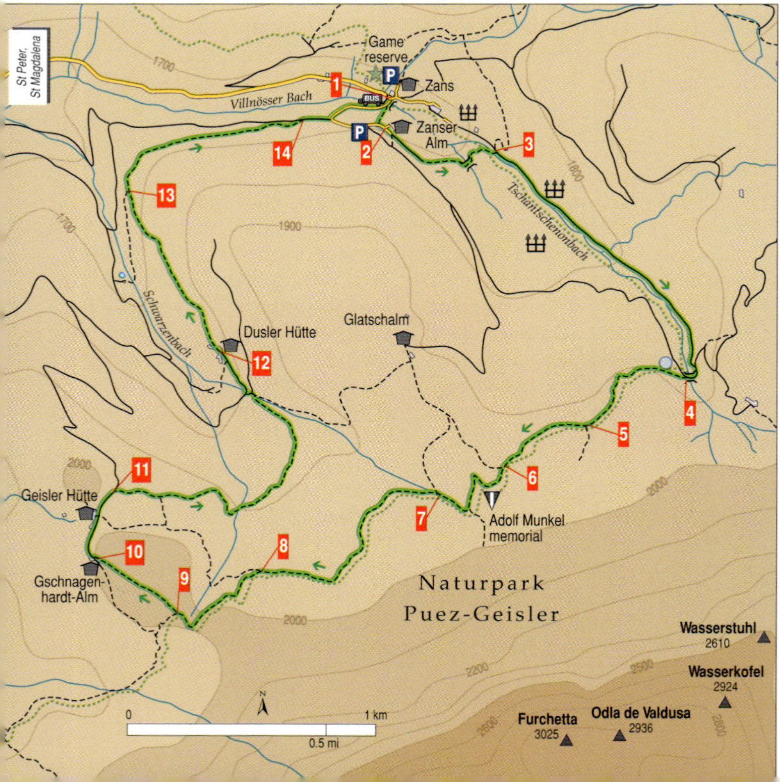

Taking a break at the idyllic Gschnagenhardt Alm/Malga Casagno

motorable track about 10 minutes later. Go right here, after a few metres crossing the stream on a **bridge** (**4**; **40min**). Once over the bridge, keep left.

The **Adolf Munkel Weg** (Trail N° 35) begins here. A few metres along, there's a spring on the right, in a log trough a bit below the trail. The water is crystal-clear and ice-cold — delicious! You're walking through a light wood of spruce, pine and larch, where meadows with junipers and rhododendrons come out of hiding between the trees. The trail is full of roots, so take care lest you twist an ankle!

A good 10 minutes past the bridge you come for the first time to a 'tributary' of the gigantic scree that runs down the flanks of the Geislers. Take a break on a **bench** (**5**) — from where you can size up the dimensions of this colossal scree with its huge imbedded boulders. (Shortly after the bench, there's a narrow path signposted 'Klettergarten' going left into this stone desert.)

Keep on, heading southwest on the Adolf Munkel Weg. There are giant boulders on both sides of the trail, overgrown with trees and shrubs as if in a magical wood.

About 10 minutes from the bench ignore Trail 6 on the right to 'Glatschalm' (**6**). A short way further on you come to the edge of the scree amidst idyllic flat meadows. At the western edge of the scree is a gigantic boulder with a plaque — a tribute to Adolf Munkel.

The trail carries on in a zigzag and comes to another fork to the right for 'Glatschalm' (**7**; **1h15min**). Ignore this turn-off as well and continue on loose gravel through the woods. Spruce, pine, larch, juniper … and always the odd boulder. This is followed by another stretch alongside the scree.

Ten minutes later, Trail 36a (**8**) forks right towards 'Duslerhütte' and 'Geislerhütte'. Keep ahead here again, on the Adolf Munkel Weg, crossing a flat meadow and then climbing a few wooden steps at the end of it.

The path is now sandy and full of tree roots; rhododendrons, junipers and hazelnut trees grow at the edges. Shortly after a wooden gate, the trail forks in a hollow (**9**; **1h40min**). Keep right here, steeply uphill towards 'Gschnagenhardt Alm'. In the south the view opens out to the eastern Geisler peaks and to Seceda. We're climbing log-stabilised steps between mighty pines.

Five minutes past the hollow you come to the edge of the extensive Gschnagenhardt meadows falling gently to the north and shortly after onto the gravel road to the eponymous **Gschnagenhardt Alm/Malga Casagno** (**10**; *see* 'Reinhold Messner's nursery' on page 102).

Sunny tables and benches invite you to rest awhile with a raspberry spritzer, or some Austrian-style pancakes *(Kaiserschmarrn)* or pancake soup *(Frittatensuppe)*. The endless, gently rolling meadows are a dazzling sea of flowers in early summer before the grass is cut … luring you to take a noontime nap. To the north you look out to the Aferer Geisler/Odles Deores and — when the weather is clear — all the way to the main Alpine ridge.

When you are ready to continue the walk, head north downhill and in just a few metres you'll be at the **Geisleralm** with its large play area — an alternative place to take a break if you're in a family group with young children. Carry on along the wide motor track through pine wood. After just about 100m, at the fork (**11**), go right on narrow Trail 36 … another trail full of roots to trip you up. In 30 minutes you'll be down at the **Dusler Hut** (**12**; **2h25min**).

Rustic wooden benches invite you to pause again here, with a spectacular view south to the rock walls of the Geislers. The Dusler Hut operates as a cattle ranch in summer and is also open in winter for snow walkers.

At the northern end of the alm you pass through a cattle gate and now walk gently through the meadows. The trail widens out and runs into woods. It heads steadily downhill over more tree roots and stones — take care here. There are often wooden logs stabilising the trail.

About 15 minutes past the alm, at a fork (**13**), keep right for 'Zans'. The way levels out through mixed conifers. Below you, on the left, you hear the rush of the Villnöss Stream. Soon you reach a wide motorable track (**14**), which takes you back via the big car park to the **Zans info point** (**15**; **3h05min**).

Walk 12: FROM ZANS TO THE WÖRNDLELOCH ALM

Distance/time: about 6.5km/4mi; 2h20min (1h20min out, 1h back)
Grade: ● easy-moderate, with an ascent/descent of 470m/1540ft. Straightforward; on wide forestry tracks and paths; a few steep bits. No shade on the heights.
Waymarking: red/white; Trails 32/35 at the start, then Trail 33 to the first stream crossing; Trail 32 to **5**, then Trails 31/31a; all well signposted
Equipment: walking shoes/boots, sun protection, walking pole(s)
Refreshments: available at the Zans info hut (**1**; open all year), spring just before **3**, at the Kaserill Alm **4** and simple snacks at the Wörndleloch Alm **6**

Walking map: Tabacco 030, Brixen-Villnössertal/Bressanone-Val di Funes, 1:25,000
Transport: 🚌 from Klausen/Chiusa or Brixen/Bressanone to Zans at the end of the Villnöss Valley/Val di Funes where there is a paid car park at about 5 € for the day (46° 38.170'N, 11° 45.954'E). Or hourly 🚌 340 from Brixen/Bressanone to the terminus, 'Zanserhütte'. Last bus back leaves at 18.43. Outside high season, 🚌 340 only runs to St Peter, from where you have to change to 🚌 339 to 'Zanserhütte' (every two hours; last bus back at 17.37, change at St Peter).

This walk, off the beaten track, takes you into the wild, lonely valley called Wörndleloch at the foot of the Aferer Geisler/Odles Deores. Here, at the eponymous Wörndleloch Alm/Malga Busa, are the grazing slopes for the rare Grey Geisler breed of cattle. They are prized for their high quality beef, available in several valley restaurants.

The walk starts at the **Zans info hut** (**1**). Following 'Wörndleloch' signposting, climb Trails 32/35 in an easterly direction; the going, through a mixed conifer wood, is quite steep. Some 10 minutes from the start you cross the Zans Nature Trail and keep ahead, east uphill, on the wide forestry track.

Around five minutes after the crossing, keep left at a fork (**2**) signposted to 'Wörndleloch'. Soon the **Kaserill/Caseril Stream** is rustling along on your left. The climb ends; continue along on the level and shortly find yourself at the same height as the mountain stream beside you. Its mighty gravel bed makes you wonder just what a weight of water must come down into the valley when the snow melts.

The quaint Kaserill Alm

In five minutes you cross the stream on a wooden bridge and then ignore a left turning signposted to Tullen (the highest peak in the Aferer Geisler/Odles Deores). On the right, a few metres further on, you see a spring where you can slake your thirst.

Shortly after the spring you pass a right turn (**3**; **35min**) to the Gampenalm; keep ahead here. Just a short way further on you cross the stream again and follow it steeply uphill. On your left is the southern flank of the **Aferer Geisler**, reaching for the sky; in the east is the rugged top of the Zendleser Kofel/Col di Poma with its high summit cross.

After the stream has left you, you come to the quaint **Kaserill Alm** (**4**). If you've got an appetite for a favourite cheese, you can find it here: whether fresh, hard or soft — take your pick and enjoy a hearty snack!

Your forestry track goes further for about 10 minutes and then forks. Keep left on Trail N° 32. Five minutes later, after a serious pull uphill, you come to another fork (**5**). Go left for 'Wörndleloch', quickly going through a gate. Now you're in the kingdom of the Grey Geisler breed of cattle (see panel opposite).

Looking back there is a mighty panorama: from the Geisler peaks in the south over the Villnöss/Funes Valley and the Sarntal Alps/Alpi Sarentine in the distance to the fissured Aferer Geisler — what a sight!

Keep uphill, heading northeast. Passing two unmanned alm huts and some huge larch trees, you penetrate deeper into the ever-narrowing Wörndleloch Valley, bordered by the Zendleser Kofel and the Aferer Geisler. The rolling alm hillsides are full of marmot burrows.

Some 15 minutes from the fork you go through another cattle gate. Right afterwards you cross a stream bed (dry in summer) on a wooden bridge. Ahead you can see your goal, and five minutes later you reach the **Wörndleloch Alm** (**6**; **1h20min**).

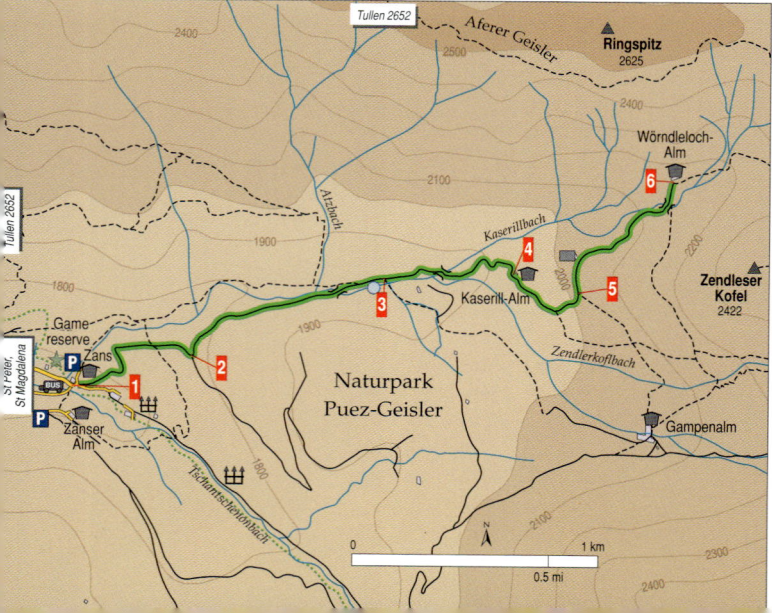

Walk 12: From Zans to the Wörndleloch Alm

The damp coolness of morning saturates the air around the Geisler/Odle peaks.

It's a family-run business. In the summer the four children help out. Walkers can have a drink and a snack and at the same time learn more about the Grey Geislers, which graze the steep slopes here from June to October.

All this — and the view to the mighty teeth and ridges of the Geislers with their seemingly endless scree slopes — a landscape with primeval force, which one can admire again and again.

After this break, return the same way to the **Zans info hut** (**1**; **2h20min**).

Sheep and cattle — traditional and modern success in the Villnöss/Funes Valley

The Villnösser Brillenschaf (literally 'spectacle-wearing sheep', named for the black rings round their eyes) have attained national celebrity. But they have a less well-known big brother, the Grey Geisler breed. Both illustrate the many successful efforts to preserve local livestock breeds and promote them to tourists.

The Brillenschaf, hundreds of years old and once the dominant breed, was almost extinct by the 1970s, but has increased to about 600 today. It provides tender meat and its delightful, friendly face is used more and more on advertising. In summer these sheep graze the extremely steep slopes of the Flitzer Scharte, so walkers seldom see them. You can, however, book an excursion to their grazing area with the tourist office — combined with a lunch in the Pitzock restaurant in St Peter (www.pitzock.com).

Unlike the sheep, in summer Grey Geislers graze the extensive meadows around the Wörndleloch Alm. An association founded under the direction of Günther Pernthaler, who owns the alm, determined that only animals of this specific breed can graze in this valley. They want to raise purebred cattle of the highest quality. For farmers in this area the switch from milk to meat is something of a risk. So it is to be hoped that the cattle follow in the footsteps of the sheep and that local gastronomy will support the cattle as they do the sheep — with advertising and perhaps special tasting weeks.

Walk 13: AROUND THE AFERER GEISLER/ODLES DEORES

Distance/time: about 17.3km/10.7mi; 6h
Grade: ● moderate-strenuous, with an ascent of 650m/2130ft and descent of 1100/3600ft. Straightforward, but long and tiring, with a few steep bits. No shade on the heights.
Waymarking: red/white; Trail 33 from the start to **4**; Trail 35, then AV2 to **8**; Trail 4 and Günther Messner Steig to **11**, then Trail 11 and shortly on Trails 11A and 32 to finish
Equipment: walking boots, sun protection, walking pole(s)
Refreshments: available at the Zans info hut (**1**; open all year), and at the Gampenalm (**3**; from June to November and from the end of December till mid-March), Schlüter Hut (**4**; from mid-Jun to mid-Oct)
Walking map: Tabacco 030, Brixen-Villnössertal/Bressanone-Val di Funes, 1:25,000

Transport: 🚌 to St Magdalena; park near the bus stop (46° 38.481'N, 11° 42.919'E). Then take hourly 🚐 340 to its terminus, 'Zanserhütte', at the end of the Villnöss Valley/Val di Funes. Or take the same bus from Brixen/Bressanone. The walk ends back at St Magdalena.

● **Alternative, shorter walk:** For a really great family walk, follow the main walk to the Schlüterhütte with its magnificent, far-reaching views (**4**; about 2h). Have lunch at the hut: specialities include various polenta dishes, and the desserts are especially tasty, too — carrot and buckwheat tart, apple strudel with vanilla sauce, and — rare for mountain huts — yoghurt with fresh fruit. Afterwards, relax with a drink while the kids explore the wide meadows. Return the same way (3h30min-4h in all; about 8km/5mi; ascent/descent 600m/1970ft).

The Aferer Geisler/Odles Deores are the somewhat smaller counterpoint to the Geisler/Odle peaks. They hem the Villnöss/Funes Valley to the northeast. Seen from the Peitlerscharte/Forcella di Putia, they merge with steeply rising Peitlerkofel/Sass de Putia in the distance, with the next mountain range to the north being Plose (Walk 6). This walk takes in the northern part of the Günther Messner Steig, to make a circuit around the Aferer Geisler (the southern part of this trail, which crosses the peaks, is climbers' country). The trail was named in memory of Reinhold Messner's brother, who died in a mountaineering accident when climbing with his brother in the Himalayas.

The **walk begins** at the **Zanser Alm bus stop** (**1**): follow the motorable track signposted to the Gampenalm and Schlüterhütte (Trail 33). When you reach an alm

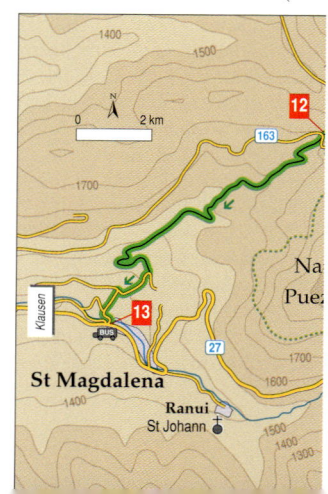

Walk 13: Around the Aferer Geisler/Odles Deores 109

after 1.5 km, cross the usually dry **Kaserill Stream** (**2**) to the right (well waymarked). On the far side, a good path (still Trail 33) sees you climbing steeply, sometimes on log-stabilised steps. When the trail levels out a bit, there is a fine view to the Geisler peaks.

Soon you're at the **Gampenalm** (**3**; **1h15min**). Pass the alm and go right, uphill, on a steep path (still Trail 33), keeping the motorable track to the Schlüterhütte over to your right.

It's a fairly tiring zigzag ascent to the **Schlüterhütte/Rifugio Genova** (**4**) and then up to the somewhat higher **Kreuzkofeljoch/ Passo Poma** (**5**; **2h**), from where there is a superb view to Kreuzkofel in the Fanes group on the far side of the Gadertal/Val Badia. Pilgrims on foot use this pass when coming from the

Walkers at the Kreuzkofeljoch/Passo Poma

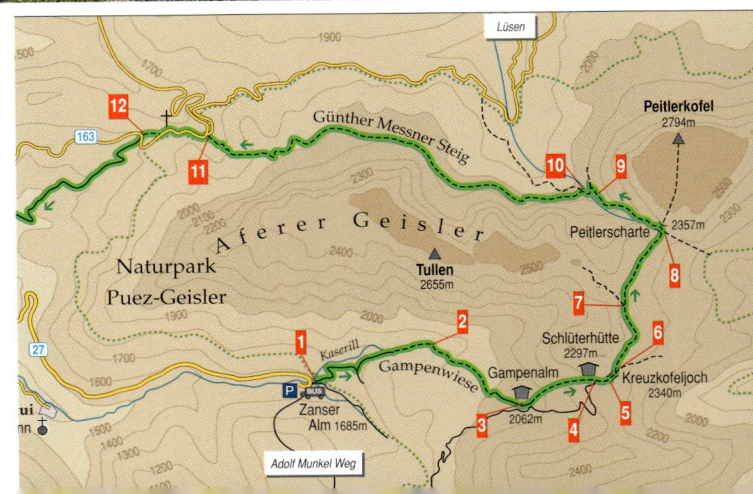

View west from the Peitlerscharte/ Forcella di Putia

Hochabtei/Alta Badia and Gader/ Badia valleys on their three-day Corpus Christi procession to Klausen/Chiusa and the Säben Monastery.

From the Kreuzkofeljoch head left on almost-level Trail AV2 (the 'Alta Via' or Dolomites High Route 2) towards 'Peitlerkofel/Sass de Putia', which rises loftily ahead. At the first fork (**6**) go left, at the second (**7**) keep right (left is the southern part of the Günther Messner Steig across the peaks of the Aferer Geisler, only suitable for climbers). The normally crowded **Peitlerscharte/Forcella di Putia** (**8**; **2h45min**) is where all those heading for Peitlerkofel stop to rest — as can be seen, sadly, both on the ground and in the nearby vegetation.

Now head left downhill on a gravelly zigzag path (Trail No 4 and AV2, also the Günther Messner Steig). At a fork (**9**) after about 20 minutes, keep left. Cross a stream (usually there's some water) and, at the next fork (**10**), go left again (even though most people will be going *right* here, to their parking places on the road from Lüsen. The mountain with the rounded top is Plose.

You're quite alone here. Larches and Arolla pines, Alpine meadows and easily-crossed screes make up the next hour and a half on the northern part of the Günther Messner Steig (the last 15 minutes of which is a *very steep descent*). A massive scree descending from the Aferer Geisler is to your left.

On reaching the road (**11**; **4h15min**), head left and, after 10 minutes, by a crucifix, go right on a waymarked woodland trail (Trail 11; ignore a path to the right a few paces beforehand). You cross the asphalt road again in five minutes and now follow a forestry road closed to vehicles (**12**; Trail 11, later forking left on Trail 11A then, further downhill, right on Trail 32, into a little valley. The road rises slightly and finally descends again.

You leave the woods near a bench (**5h30min**) and see the church of St Magdalena against the backdrop of the Geisler/Odle peaks. Pass a first farmstead and, 100m further on, join Walk 7 for just 200m — to the next farm. Continue along the road here, to the valley floor in **St Magdalena** and the **bus stop** (**13**; **6h**).

Walk 14: THE POSTAL TRAIL FROM LAJEN/LAION TO ST ULRICH/ORTISEI

Distance/time: about 11.6km/ 7.2mi; 3h40min
Grade: ● moderate, with an ascent of 445m/1460ft and descent of 310m/1015ft. A rather long high-altitude walk on meadow paths, forestry tracks and bits of road with moderate traffic; in sun and shade; no great problems
Waymarking: signposted as 'P' or 'Poststeig' throughout, usually with the name of the next village
Equipment: walking shoes or boots, sun protection

Refreshments: plenty of opportunities in Lajen/Laion, St Peter (Gasthof Überbacher) and St Ulrich/Ortisei; a spring at 9
Walking map: Tabacco 05, Val Gardena-Alpe di Siusi/Gröden-Seiseralm, 1:25,000
Transport: 🚗 several parking places in Lajen/Laion — for instance at the sports ground by 1 (46° 36.639'N, 11° 34.028'E). Or hourly 🚌 351 between St Peter and St Ulrich; last bus back at 19.34

This long high-altitude walk follows in the footsteps of the postmen of yore. It runs on the south side of the Gröden/Gardena Valley, through meadows and woodlands, with spectacular views of the Dolomites. It's especially beautiful in October, when the trees shimmer gold and dark red.

The walk begins in **Lajen/Laion** at the little chapel **Maria Einsiedel** (1) — opposite Ploner's butcher shop, at the corner of Walther von der Vogelweide and Kesselweg. Follow the main road east towards 'Tschöfas/St Peter'.

About five minutes from the start, turn left on Tschöferer Weg (2). You pass the **Pension Baumann** and continue for about 15 minutes through lush meadows between walls, hedges and hazelnut bushes. To the south you're looking out to Schlern/Sciliar, in the east to Platt- and Langkofel/Sassopiatto and -lungo, backed by the Sella group.

Once in the hamlet of Tschöfas, turn left at the crossroads (3) and immediately after turn right, following the 'Poststeig' fingerpost waymarker. Soon the road peters out into a track. Continue east downhill, then before long, gently uphill again. In front of you are Langkofel and Sella and, although they're getting closer, they're still some way off.

Some 15 minutes from the start of the track, it forks. Keep right for 'Poststeig' (4; **40min**), following a narrow meadow path past hedges

Starting out on the Postal Trail

and bushes. In a few minutes you cross another track and go downhill into the woods.

Then there's a steep five-minutes uphill section, before you follow fencing downhill to the road to St Peter (**5**). Walk along the road for a scant 100m, then turn right into the woods at the 'Poststeig' fingerpost.

Now you follow a wide track and cross a splashing stream. Eventually you find tar underfoot as you cross steep meadows and come to the large, recently renovated **Oberfelsonnerhof**. Walk between the buildings and uphill, until you come back up to the **road to St Peter** (**6**).

Follow the road to the right till you come into the village and reach — behind the huge parish church dating from 1716 — the marketplace with its fountain and the **Gasthof Überbacher** with its beautiful panorama terrace — a nice place for a break. There are public toilets by the Raiffeisen Bank (signposted).

Leave St Peter on the main valley road (watch out — there's no pavement!). A good five minute past the end of the village, in a sharp curve, you come to a lane forking off to the left (**7**; **1h30min**). Follow the signposting 'Pedrutscher Hof' uphill here, forking left again after just a few metres in a mixed wood.

The woods open up soon and offer an attractive view to the western flanks of Balest above St Ulrich, covered with scree. The trail kinks southwards — again in the woods — and runs uphill in wide curves. Still in the woods, follow a path signposted 'Poststeig' to the right (**8**). Walking through meadows, you approach the **Pedrutscherhof**. Soon the trail runs through thick conifers woods, where stones and boulders are covered with moss.

Right: view to Langkofel/Sassolungo from the Postal Trail

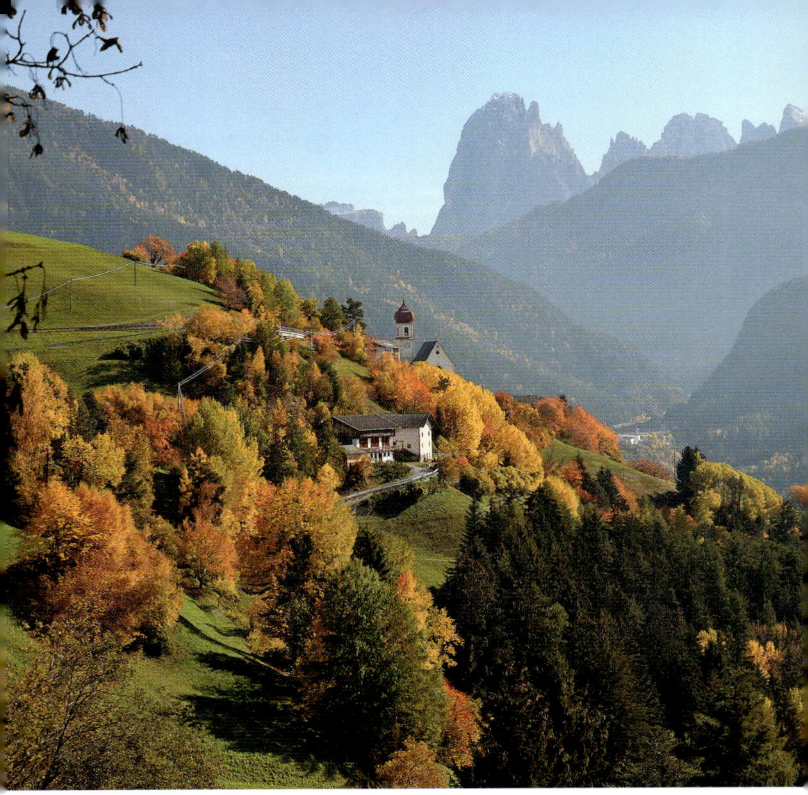

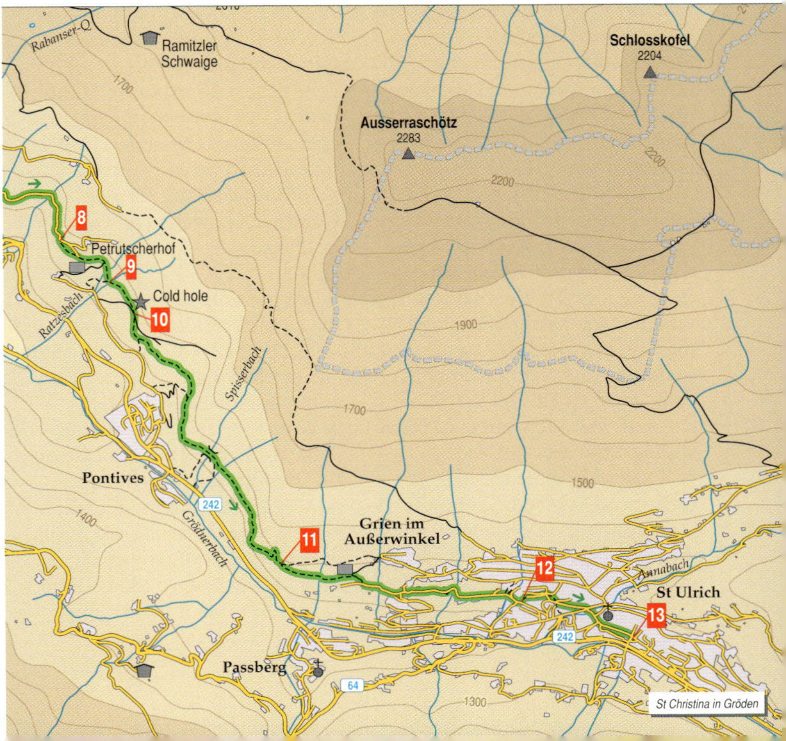
Rabanser-Q.
Ramitzler Schwaige
1700
Schlosskofel
2204
Ausserraschötz
2283
2200
2200
8
Petrutscherhof
9
Cold hole
10
Ratzesbach
1900
Spisserbach
1700
Pontives
242
1500
1400
Grödnerbach
11
Grien im Außerwinkel
12
Annabach
St Ulrich
13
242
Passberg
64
1300
St Christina in Gröden

Shortly after crossing a stream, the trail forks (**9**). Head left and cross another stream shortly afterwards — it starts just above the trail and offers a chance for a cooling drink!

Now you proceed in gently ups and downs through a shady conifer wood, heading south. Moss-covered stones and rock make the atmosphere quite magical … a fairies' wood. The trail is soft, full of roots, and criss-crossed by rivulets.

About 20 minutes from the spring at the stream, you come to a huge rockfall with massive porphyry blocks above the trail. An icy breath emanates from this protected microclimate — the so-called '**Cold Holes**' (**Kalten Löcher**), where numerous cold air currents come as a surprise in the usually warm and dry alpine summer climate.

Not far past the rockfall the trail forks (**10**; **1h25min**); go right here towards 'Pontives'). After a further 100m ignore the turning down right to Pontives and keep up on the Poststeig. Below is the main valley road, with the Pontives industrial area.

Climbing gently, just under 10 minutes from the Pontives fork you cross the **Spisserbach** and keep left just past this stream crossing for 'St Ulrich'. A few minutes later you're climbing through the foothills of a gigantic **rockfall**. Above you, seemingly endless scree fields reach up to the sky, with just a few birch and larch amongst the rock debris.

Once out of the rockfall you walk through woods again. On the right a weathered wooden fence protects you from the steep drop down to the road. Shortly, you're climbing another steep stretch on log-supported steps. Then, reaching a rocky plateau, a bench gives you a change to take a break.

Shortly after the bench, at a fork (**11**; **2h55min**) follow the Poststeig to the right. From here you descend gently through open pines, until you reach the edge of the wood five minutes later. The scattered houses of St Ulrich lie before you here. At the end of the valley is the mighty Sella.

Go downhill at a wall, then pass below an old double farmstead from where tar comes underfoot all the way into St Ulrich. Then you walk along Streda Nevel between houses and some old inns to the centre of town.

Some 20 minutes after coming onto tar, you cross a stream and a few metres further on the Post Trail turns left into Fr Tavella Street (**12**), only accessible to pedestrians and cyclists.

After a good 100m you cross Tavella Street and straight away follow the walkway to the right, below the road. Another 100m further on, between houses, you come to Streda Station. Head left on this road, passing the old **locomotive of the former Grödner/Gardena railway**. You're heading for St Ulrich's parish church.

At the roundabout in front of the church, head right (signposted to 'Sacun/St Jakob') for the centre and stroll along the pedestrian zone. After walking gently downhill for about 10 minutes you come to **St Ulrich's bus station** (**13**; **3h40min**). There are numerous cafés and restaurants nearby, where you can take well-deserved refreshment before catching your bus back to Lajen.

6 SEISER ALM AREA/ALPE DI SIUSI

Seis • Völs • Kastelruth • Seiser Alm

Walks: 15-23; *walking tips:*
Laranz Woods (page 116); Tisens and Tagusens (page 119)
Access: cable car from Seis/Siusi; up to 26 buses a day between Bozen/Bolzano, Völs/Fiè, Seis and Kastelruth/Castelrotto; up to 7 a day between Völs and Gröden/Val Gardena via Seis and Kastelruth. Free shuttle bus with six lines between the Panider saddle, Kastelruth, the valley station, Seis and Völs. In high season buses run every quarter- or half-hour from 08.00-19.00; single journey 2.50 €. On the alm itself there's the alm bus between Compatsch (the mountain station for the Seis cable car) and Saltria, 2.50 €. An 'express' bus runs from Seis to Saltria (19 € return).

Which card?
You can buy a '3 in 7' Combicard for 45 €, allowing 3 trips in a 7-day period to the Seiser Alm by cable car or the 'express' bus, plus the use of all shuttle buses, from the Alm bus to the Night-liner. There are also Combicards for 7/14 days (58/88 €). There are 'Nordic passes' in winter with similar prices. And, of course — a 'gold' Combicard ... For information see www.seiseralm.it.

Websites www.seis.it
www.voels.it
www.kastelruth.com
www.seiseralm.it
www.bolzano-bozen.it
Opening hours: see individual attractions

Völs/Fiè, Seis/Siusi and Kastelruth/Castelrotto lie on a plateau high above the Eisacktal/Valle Isarco. Rising 1000m above them are the broad meadows and pastures of the Seiser Alm/Alpe di Siusi, one of the most extensive pasturelands in the Alps. Even higher — another 600m up — is the high limestone plateau of Schlern/Sciliar. It is not often that one sees such a breathtakingly beautiful landscape, so don't be surprised if you're not alone. During the autumn harvest festival in Kastelruth, you can't get a room in the area for love nor money; it's a weekend to avoid. Instead, why not visit in early spring, with mild days and so many wild flowers in bloom. Or in summer, when sports possibilities are endless and there's a chance to swim in an ice-cold lake. Or late autumn, when the larches stand out bright yellow in front of the limestone flanks of Schlern.

Seis/Siusi

Even for a province with as many spectacular backdrops as South Tyrol, few villages are as blessed as Seis. It lies in a green basin below the wild, bare Santner peaks, an offshoot of the adjacent Schlern. Once a small farmers' hamlet, it is now a first-class holiday centre. There are good hotels and *pensions*, the cuisine is excellent, and **walking possibilities** are first class.

Seis has an old tradition as a summer resort: people have been coming to the Ratzes baths since 1715, and in the 19th century the Norwegian playwright Henrik

Ibsen bought himself a house here. In the forest above the village are the remains of **Hauenstein Castle**, where Oswald von Wolkenstein (see Walk 17 on page 116) lived.

Transport: There is a large **car park** by the **bus station**, at the corner of Schlern and Valier.

Sights: There's little of note in Seis itself, even the baroque parish church is nothing special. But the church of **St Valentin** (see Walk 15) above the town, definitely *is* worth a visit. From here you'll have the best possible view of Schlern (take binoculars too!). The little church with its slender tower and golden onion dome has lovely frescoes inside and out, dating from the end of the 14th century. *Only open for guided visits Jul/Aug on Thu 14.00-15.00.*

The ruins of the Salegg and Hauenstein castles

Salegg Castle was first mentioned in a document in 1148 and probably belonged to the Lords of Kastelruth/Castelrotto in the Middle Ages. Only remnants of the wall remain now, and the same is true of Hauenstein Castle. The latter was built by the von Hauenstein family and only later fell to the Wolkensteins, who enlarged it and made it more livable. One of their family members was the poet Oswald von Wolkenstein (commemorated by a marble plaque). After the Peasants' Revolt in 1525, the castle was abandoned and fell into disrepair. According to a legend, an underground passage connects the two castles. Both castles are visited during Walk 17.

● **Walking tip**: **Laranz Woods** (see Tabacco 1:25,000 map N° 05). There's a little walk in the Laranz Woods west of Seis, which would be nothing special except for the giant mushrooms of all varieties scattered around. None are poisonous; they are all painted sculptures — done by Robert Winkler, a talented wood carver who has come to an arrangement with the park authorities to display them there. His work is also on display en route from Hauenstein Castle to Salegg Castle (Walk 17).

Völs/Fiè

The setting of this old village on one of the hills overlooking the plateau is most attractive, and the church square is particularly harmonious.

Transport: There are two **car parks**, both on the main village road — one near Boznerstrasse, the second on the other side of the village, near the start of the trail to Hauenstein Castle.

Sights and excursions: Inside the old parish Church of the Ascension (**Maria Himmelfahrt**), with its slender clock tower and eye-catching onion dome, is a Romanesque 13th-century crucifix and an altar triptych (1489) by the master craftsman Narziss of Bozen. The vicarage near the **cemetery chapel of St Michael** houses the small but interesting **parish museum**. This has a most attractive collection, especially of late Gothic sculptures taken from various chapels in the parish for safe-keeping. *Parish museum open only in summer for guided tours, Tue/Fri at 11.00.*

Right: the Seiser Alm/Alpe di Siusi in early summer, full of flowers, with Schlern/Sciliar and the Santner peaks in the background

View from Kastelruth's Calvary Hill (Kastelruther Kofel or Kalvarienberg) down onto Tisens

Schloss Prösels/Castello Presule: The forerunner of the little castle you see today was originally given by the Kaiser to the Bishop of Brixen in 1027. Centuries later, Leonhard von Völs, governor under Kaiser Maximilian, had it rebuilt in modern Renaissance style, turning it into a prestigious castle complex which spread its fame.

Some rooms are magnificent — like the large sitting room with fireplace and wooden beamed ceiling, the riders' room with Renaissance panelling and wonderful wood carvings on the balustrade of the large staircase. The walls were painted with frescoes, and in the castle chapel Hans Leonhard Schaufelein — a master from the Dürer School, showed what modern art was north of the Alps. The contrast between the late Gothic building technique and the Renaissance paintings, frescoes and wood-carvings are often especially striking — as in the loggia of the inner courtyard, where portraits in the Renaissance style are displayed between the late Gothic arches. *Castle open from May-Oct daily (ex Sat). Can only be visited on a guided tour: in Jul/Aug at 10.00, 11.00, 13.00, 1400, 15.00, 16.00; Jun/Sep at 11.00, 14.00, 15.00, 16.00; other times at 11.00, 14.00, 15.00. Entry 10 €, concessions 6 €.*

South Tyrol has few good swimming lakes, so the little lake in Völs (**Völser Weiher** in German — or Völs *pond*; **Lagetto di Fié** in Italian) has become popular for swimming. You can reach the lake by car on roads from Völs or start Walk 16 there. Read more about the little lake on page 125.

Kastelruth/Castelrotto

Kastelruth is an extremely pleasant place for a holiday — green and beautifully sited, with the Seiser Alm and Schlern in the background and with a mostly intact historical old centre at the foot of its castle hill (which today lacks a castle). It has top-class infrastructure: excellent hotels and a wide variety of pastimes for both summer and winter. Kastelruth is often full up, so book early.

Transport: There is a large **car park** near the village centre by the **bus station**.

Sights and excursions: The old part of Kastelruth has some houses with outside frescoes, like Felseck House, the Gasthof zum Wolf and the Mendelhaus (shown on page 18). But the village landmark is the massive detached **clock tower** of the baroque parish church of Saints Peter and Paul (1756-58) with its onion dome. The church itself, which is also very large, is more recent (19C).

A steep lane rises from the village centre (by the solid Gasthof Turmwirt on the right). You can either follow this lane or take the track to the right, just where the lane starts. Either way you will reach the **Kalvarienberg** (Calvary Hill, also called the **Kastelruther Kofel**). The well-waymarked circuit takes about 30 minutes. There was once a castle atop this hill, but it was destroyed in 1202. The rump of the keep was converted into two baroque Calvary chapels; next to them is another chapel dating from the 17th century.

● **Walking tip: Tisens and Tagusens** (see Tabacco 1:25,000 map N° 05). By following way-marked Route 1 from Kastelruth you can walk to the nearby village of **Tisens** in half an hour. Start from Klausplatz in the centre: follow Plattenstrasse, then turn right after 150m on Sabine Jäger, a very lightly-trafficked road that goes all the way to Tisens. Like so many other churches in South Tyrol, **St Nicholas** at Tisens has a huge St Christopher on the outside wall.

From Tisens you could carry on to **Tagusens**. To walk there (allow 1h), follow waymarked Route 2, which forks right where the motor road makes a left-hand curve in the valley, about 750m *before* Tisens. The trail crosses the wooded Moosbüchl and takes about 50 minutes from the turn-off. Tagusens is a solitary outpost set above the exit from the Grödnertal (the village opposite is Lajen, where Walk 14 begins). Below the hamlet is the chapel of **St Magdalena**. Its tower dates from the 14th century, the nave (later rebuilt in baroque style) from about 1500. The baroque altar, with a painting by Franz Xaver Unterberger is especially lovely.

Don't miss the school museum in Tagusens, which cleverly depicts what classrooms were like about 50 years ago (the building was used as a school up until 1993). *Museum open from Easter to All Saints, Mon/Wed/Fri from 10.00-16.00; no entry fee, donations welcome.*

Seiser Alm/Alpe di Siusi

The Seiser Alm is well known as one of the most beautiful holiday destinations in all Europe, and with good reason. Hardly any other mountain area can offer so much throughout the seasons and yet remain so little changed by tourism. Dominated by Schlern/Sciliar and the Rosszähne/ Denti di Terrarossa — and with Langkofel/Sassolungo in the east, the Seiser Alm is pure heaven for those who want an active holiday.

Transport: It is strictly forbidden to drive on the Alm, and the road from Seis/Kastelruth to **Compatsch** (where all the infrastructure is concentrated) is closed in summer from 09.00-17.00; you can only reach the alm via the cable car from Seis. (The only exception is that overnight guests can obtain special licences from their hotels or the tourist board, but even they must use the roads before 10.00 and after 17.00.) The **cable car** runs from Seis daily from 08.00-19.00 (in case of rest break or maintenance stoppage there is a shuttle bus); one way 13 €, up and back 19 €, families 28.50/41 €; www.seiser almbahn.it.

The rolling high plateau of the Seiser Alm, lying between 1700-1800m and 2100-2300m, is bedded with soft stone, which collects surface water. So there are many little ponds and wet places with interesting vegetation and, between them, large areas of meadows and pastures which have been grazed by cattle from time immemorial. Before machines and chemical fertilisers became common, the meadows were managed by hand and brought in moderate but high-quality returns. To judge how good the hay was, you only have to taste the local milk, butter and cheese. The locals have known for centuries how good the oil from this hay was for treating arthritis and bone diseases; the '**hay baths**' now offered to tourists date back to a traditional treatment for the local people.

If you cross the plateau with its alms and sprinklings of huts where dry hay is stored for the winter (and then taken by sledge into the valley), you come into the mountainous region — as spectacular as the Alm itself.

From the plateau one can climb mighty **Schlern** which rises so majestically over Völs and Seis (Walks 20, 22); the same is true for the well-named **Rosszähne** (Ross 'teeth'). Schlern is a fantastic

---

Hay baths — a Völs speciality

For many people a summer holiday in Völs will be their first opportunity to take a 'hay bath' — as generations of local farmers did to keep themselves fit and fresh. The Hotel Heubad is a reminder of the time, in the early 20th century, when a doctor, Josef Clara, first sent tourists here for the hay. And they loved it.

So what is a 'hay bath'? The 'bath scrubber' buries the guests in a hay-pit and fills it with hay up to their necks, then covers them with towels and leaves them to their fate: they sweat. After 10 to 25 minutes (depending on age, gender and general state of health), if their pulse has risen substantially, the guest has sweated enough and then moves on to a rest room to recuperate, wrapped in warm blankets.

As with the sauna, this is the time for the client to take a lot of liquid on board — not alcoholic, of course — but who's to say if the guest's hand reaches for the wine bottle rather than the water? After that one must eat heartily, and South Tyrolean cooking fits the bill perfectly.

The effect of the hay bath is detoxification through sweating and a good feeling in one's body; the joints especially are lubricated, and arthritic pains are lessened or even disappear entirely. When the pains come back, just take another hay bath...

---

mountain for its panoramas and much loved by climbers — especially the Santner and Euringer crags that rise up from the plateau. These were named for the first climbers to tackle them,

Johann Santner and Gustav Euringer. The Rosszähne (Walks 21, 22) also attract rock climbers: from the Tierser Alpl Hut the Maximilianweg traverses the ridge towards Schlern. In *via ferrata* terms, it is not a difficult route.

Bozen/Bolzano

Bozen, the capital of South Tyrol, lies outside the area of this guide. But many visitors to the Dolomites travel via Bolzano or take a day trip to the town, which is situated in a sunny south-facing basin, surrounded by vineyards in the north. Of the 100,000 inhabitants, about 75% are Italian-speaking; English speakers are more used to the name Bolzano. But the old town still exudes a Middle Ages/baroque German character.

Transport: All trains running between Munich and Verona, Milan, Rome and Venice stop at Bolzano's **railway station**. It is also the **hub of the SAD bus company**, which has a very large network covering the whole of South Tyrol. There is a **covered car park** south of the rail station.

Sights: The meeting place of the town is **Waltherplatz**, with cafés, shops and a large memorial dedicated to Walther von der Vogelweide (see 'Waidbruck', page 82). It's a good place to begin a **stroll around the old town**.

The square is dominated by the parish cathedral church, the Gothic **Dompfarrkirche**; its 62 m-high tower is finely-carved late Gothic. Once inside, don't miss the Gothic chancel and baroque high altar. There is also a museum. *Church open daily 11.00-17.00; museum Tue-Sat 10.00-12.30, entry 3 €.*

The **Dominikanerkloster** is a Dominican monastery and late Gothic hall church with three naves; the choir has beautiful baroque ornamentation. There are frescoes from the Giotto School in the Johanneskapelle and more frescoes dating from around 1490 by Friedrich Pacher in the cloister (which is only accessible from the adjacent conservatory of music). *Church open Mon-Sat from 08.00-18.00, Sun from 12.00-18.00; cloisters open Apr-Oct, Sat only, from 10.00-12.00.*

From here it's just a short way along Goethestrasse to the photogenic **Obstplatz**. This busy fruit and vegetable market has been serving the town for centuries. The **Lauben** is here too: the main shopping street, with old-established shops and modern boutiques under the arcades of impressive town houses.

From the Obstmarkt walk along Franziskanergasse to the **Franziskanerkirche** — late Gothic inside and out, with a Nativity by Hans Klocker (1500) on the reredos. Then step into the Italian part of Bozen on the west side of the river, where you come to the **Piazza della Vittoria** (Siegesplatz), a square and war memorial dedicated to Bolzano's Italian Fascists — a source of contention since South Tyrol has autonomy.

In the **Gries district** one finds the large **Muri Benedictine Abbey**. Only the lovely late Gothic monastery church is open to the public. In the late Gothic **Gries parish church** there is a magnificent carved altar by Michael Pacher dating from 1475, depicting the coronation of Mary. *The anteroom of the monastery church is open daily from 09.00-19.00, and you can get a good view of the church; Gries parish church is open from Apr to Oct, Mon-Fri, 10.00-12.00, 14.30-16.00.*

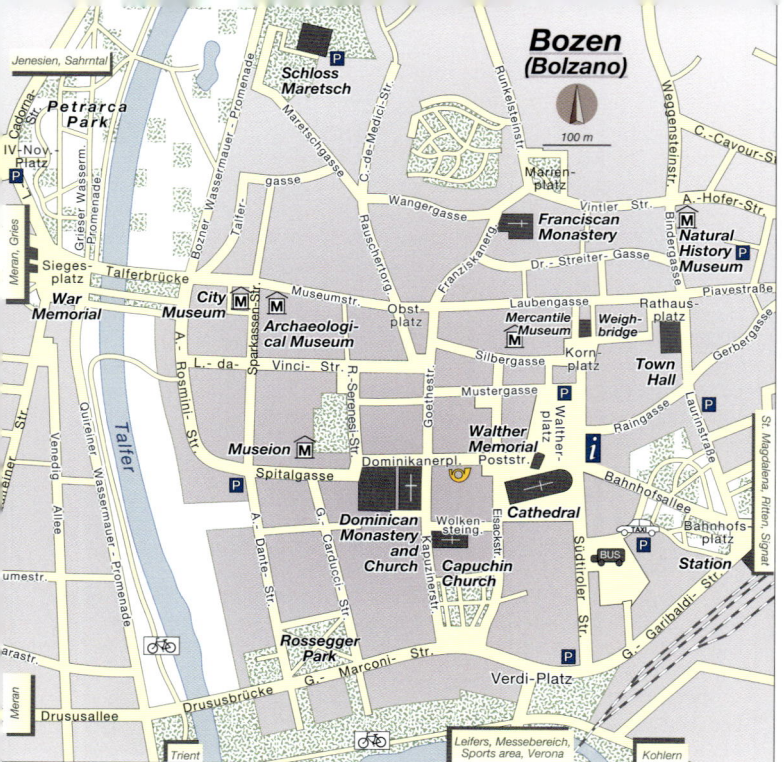

On the **north side of town** is **Runkelstein Castle**, an easy stroll (there's also a free shuttle from Waltherplatz). Dating from the Middle Ages, it has some very unusual frescoes depicting country life — for example men and women playing ball, lance-throwing competitions and round dancing under the trees. *Daily (except Mon) 10.00-18.00 (entrance fee 8 €).*

Chief among the town's museums is the **Archaeological Museum**, also called the 'Ötzi-Museum' in honour of its most famous exhibit. Ötzi, the 'man in the ice', is displayed on the first floor, in a darkened room behind armoured glass in a cold-storage chamber at -6°C. There's information about his discovery by hikers in 1991; radiocarbon dating revealed the body to be more than 5000 years old. *Open Tue-Sun 10.00-18.00; daily in Jul/Aug/Dec; entry 9 €; families 18 €.*

The three-story **Stadtmuseum** (City Museum) exhibits the art, culture and customs of Bolzano and South Tyrol. *Open Tue-Sun 10.00-18.00; entry free.*

The **Naturmuseum Südtirol** is a modern museum focussing on the natural history of South Tyrol, with eye-catching dioramic displays. *Open Tue-Sun from 10.00-18.00; entrance fee 7 €; concessions 5 €; families 14 €.*

The **Museion** is a museum for modern art, with continually changing displays. *Open daily (ex Mon) from 10.00-18.00 (Thu until 22.00); entry 7 €; concessions 3.50 €.*

The **Merkantilmuseum** is an impressive baroque town house, once the commercial court. *Open daily (ex. Sun) 10.00-12.30; entry 4 €; concessions 2 €.*

Walk 15: FROM KASTELRUTH/CASTELROTTO TO SEIS/SIUSI VIA ST VALENTIN

Distance/time: about 3km/1.9mi; 1h
Grade: ● easy, with an ascent of 100m/325ft and descent of 180m/50ft; good surfaces underfoot
Waymarking: red/white; Trail N° 6 from the start to **3**, then Trail 7 to the end
Equipment: walking shoes, sun protection
Refreshments: plenty of opportunities in Kastelruth and in Seis
Walking map: Tabacco 05, Val Gardena-Alpe di Siusi/Gröden-Seiseralm, 1:25,000
Transport: 🚗 park in Kastelruth, opposite the lane where the walk starts at **1** (46° 34.022'N, 11° 33.603'E). Then take one of 🚌 several buses a day from Seis back to Kastelruth. Or park in Seis (car park behind the bus station at 46° 32.690'N, 11° 33.782'E). Take a bus to Kastelruth to start, then walk back to your car in Seis.

For almost the whole of this short, easy walk you have Schlern and the wild spikes of adjacent Santner in front of you. Near the end of the walk you can visit the church of St Valentine. It's only open for guided tours on Thursdays in July and August between 14.00 and 15.00, but the outside frescoes can be enjoyed all year round.

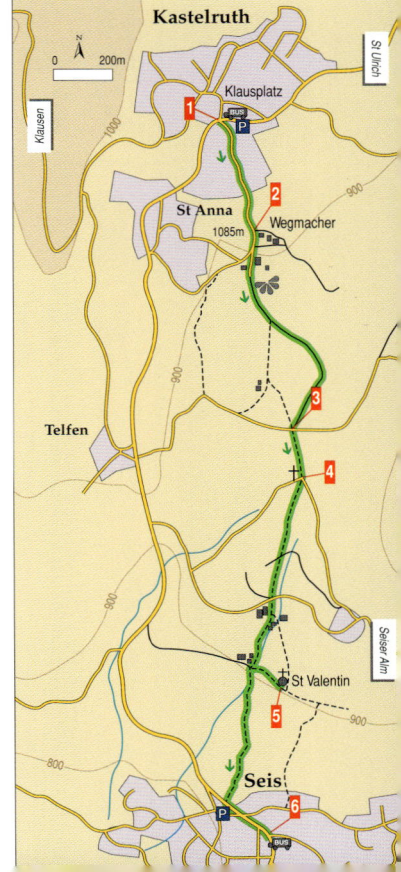

Begin in **Kastelruth**: after looking around **Klausplatz**, return to the main trunk road, cross over and walk south up the lane (Marinzenweg) signposted to various hotels (**1**). You soon see Trail 6 waymarking as you climb gently away from the village.

Just over 400m uphill, at a Y-fork, go right on a lane marked as a cul-de-sac (**2**). Under 100m further up, at the next tarred Y-fork, go left. Now at its highest point — and with fantastic views to Schlern and the Santner peaks ahead —, the lane becomes a cinder track; from here just continue in the same direction, following the good Route 6 waymarking.

Crossing a lane with a plethora of signposts (**3**), you join Route 7 and keep ahead to a three-way fork... which you may not even notice at first. Two hard surface tracks make a Y-fork here, and there is a shrine on the right. Take the grassy path (**4**) in between the tracks, gently descending (there is a sign for Trail 7 here, but it's not obvious at first). This path runs straight across meadows, crosses the Seiser Alm road and comes to a group of houses. On the left, 150m further on and a little off the route, is the church of **St Valentin** (■); you'll have seen its tower and golden onion dome on the approach.

After visiting the church, keep straight downhill to nearby **Seis**. Meeting the main road, follow it to the left for just over 150m, to the **bus station/car park** (■; **1h**).

Early summer at the church of St Valentin, with the snow-touched Santner peaks of Schlern/Sciliar in the background

Walk 16: CIRCUIT FROM VÖLS/FIÈ LAKE TO THE TUFFALM AND THE HOFER ALPL

Distance/time: about 7.4km/ 4.3mi; 2h35min
Grade: ● easy-moderate, with an ascent/descent of 480m/1580ft; fairly steep ascent; shady; good surfaces underfoot, but watch out for tree roots!
Waymarking: red/white; Trail 1 from the start to **5**, Trail 1A to **7**, Trail 3 to **8**, Trails 8a/8 to shortly after **9**, then Trail 2 back to the start at Völser Weiher
Equipment: stout walking shoes, swimming things
Refreshments: plenty of opportunities: at the start by Völser Weiher in the Gasthof Waldsee at **1**, at the Tuffalm (**4**; Apr-Nov and during the Christmas holidays) and at the Hofer Alpl (**7**; Apr-Nov and during the Christmas holidays, end Dec-early Mar only Fri-Sun).
Walking map: Tabacco 029, Schlern-Sciliar/Rosengarten-Catinaccio-Latemar, 1:25,000
Transport: 🚗 park at the large car park for the Völser Weiher/Lagetto di Fiè, signposted, 2km above Völs/Fiè (46° 31.269'N, 11° 31.193'E). Or take 🚌170 from Bolzano or 🚌 176 from Seis to Völs (alight at the roundabout). From there it's about half an hour on Trail N° 1 to Völser Weiher. Last 🚌 back to Seis: 170 at 19.52; 176 at 17.43.

This family-friendly circular hike leads along good forestry tracks past the small lakes called Völser Weiher and Huberweiher to the picturesque Tuffalm and then the idyllic Hofer Alpl, with plenty of opportunity to enjoy alm cuisine and end the day with a swim.

The walk begins at the entrance to the car park at the **Infopoint** (**1**). Follow signposting for Trail N° 1 ('Völser Weiher') past the tennis courts, then past the Gasthof Waldsee and the reed-filled banks of **Völser Weiher/Lagetto di Fiè** (see the panel on page 127). Beyond a barrier, the Huberweiher opens up on the left (but this lake is not suitable for bathing!).

About 10 minutes after starting out, at a fork in the path (**2**), follow Trail N° 1 towards 'Tuffalm', heading right through shady mixed conifers. This is a steady ascent, where pieces of path uneven from gnarled roots alternate with cobbled sections and — where the route is particularly steep — you're climbing log-stabilised steps. In the south, you continually catch glimpses of the northern walls of Hammerwand/Croda del Maglio and the spikes of Tschafatsch/Monte Giavaccio between the treetops.

About 20 minutes after the fork, you go through a cattle gate. This marks the end of the forest, and the walk continues uphill over wide alpine pastures to a fork (**3**). On the left, just five minutes away to the left, you come to the **Tuffalm** (**4**, **40min**) on a meadow hilltop. This hut was once chosen as the most beautiful alm in South Tyrol! Whether or not you're hungry, this detour rewards the hiker with a great view of the valley basin around Bozen/Bolzano and the Ritten/Renon. And a midday nap on the extensive grass surrounds is always possible…

Walk back to the fork at **3** and go left on a wide gravel path into the forest. About 15 minutes past the Tuffalm, the path finally turns southwest and crosses the bubbling **Völser Bach/Rio di Fiè**, which rises high above you in the walls of the Jungschlern/Piccolo Sciliar. A good 10 minutes after crossing the stream, at a junction (**5**), take the lower path, Trail No 1A towards 'Hofer Alpl'. This trail is full of roots; it leads downhill through the forest until, about 15 minutes later, you come to a wide motor track (**6**). Go left here and, after a few metres, turn right with Trail 1A towards 'Hofer Alpl'.

The forest opens up and you arrive at **Hofer Alpl** (**7**; **1h25min**) with its panoramic terrace and petting zoo with goats and rabbits — just the place for children. But the cheese dumplings, together with the view over the Bolzano basin and the Ritten — guarantee that the parents also get their money's worth.

From the Hofer Alpl take steep, skiddy Trail N° 3 steeply downhill, first through alpine meadows, then through conifers. The Hammerwand rock face, Völs and Prösels/Presule Castle come into view now and again. About 20 minutes from the Hofer Alpl, the path forks in the middle of a larch grove (**8**). Keep right on Trail 8a, for 'Tuffalm' and 'Völser Weiher' until a wide motor track (Trail N° 8) comes in from above and leads you steadily downhill.

Almost 5 minutes after that fork, a **reservoir** with some benches comes up on the left. The path forks on its north bank (**9**; **2h**). Stay on Trail N° 8 and cross the Völser Bach again on a bridge about 10 minutes later (a few metres above the bridge a path leads to a shallow paddling and bathing area). From here take Trail

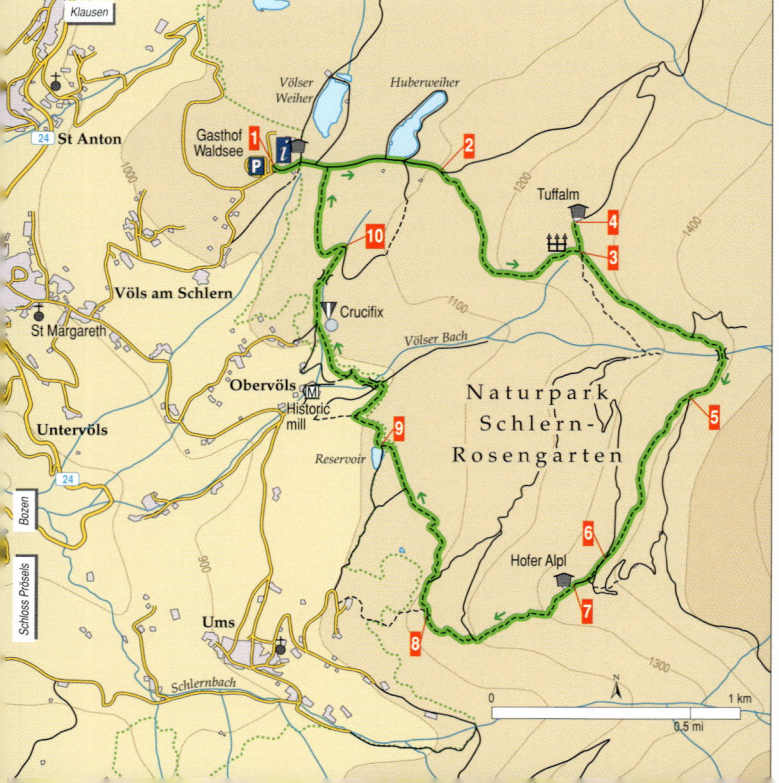

Völser Weiher/Lagetto di Fiè
South Tyrol doesn't have many bathing lakes, so Völs, with its pond, is rather special. It was originally created as a carp fishing lake for the lords of Schloss Prösels/Castello Presule, since fish was needed for the many annual fasting days. The shore is boggy in places, and sometimes the pond dries up, but there is a small bathing complex and a little Gasthaus nearby serving regional dishes. There are also rowing boats for hire. It is definitely worth jumping into the cool water after the hike!

Top: Völser Weiher/Lagetto di Fiè in winter; above: the Hofer Alpl

N° 2, going slightly uphill towards 'Völser Weiher'.

Pass a walled spring and an old **crucifix** and then continue uphill through mixed conifers. A trickling stream ripples to the right, and you soon cross it on a wooden walkway. About 10 minutes past the crucifix, your path joins a wide motor track (**10**). Follow the signpost for Trail N° 2 to 'Völser Weiher', a little later rejoining your outgoing route. Retrace steps for a good five minutes, back to the starting point (**1**; **2h35min**).

Walk 17: ON THE OSWALD VON WOLKENSTEIN TRAIL

Distance/time: about 3.9km/ 2.4mi; 1h35min
Grade: ● easy-moderate, with a fairly steep ascent/descent of 240m/800ft on forest and mountain paths. Plenty of shade
Waymarking: red/white; Trail N° 2 from the start to **3**, Trail 3 to **7**, then Trail 8 back to the start
Equipment: sturdy shoes
Refreshments: available at the Hotel Salegg and in Seis

Walking map: Tabacco 029, Schlern-Sciliar/Rosengarten-Catinaccio-Latemar, 1:25,000
Transport: 🚗 park at the large car park for the Seiser Alm/Alpe di Siusi cable car (46° 32.435'N, 11° 33.829'E). Or take 🚐 170 bus from Brixen/Bressanone or Bolzano to Seis bus station and from there 🚐 176 to the valley station of the cable car — or walk there in 10 minutes. Last 🚐 176 at 18.07; last 🚐 170 to Brixen 17.49, to Bolzano 19.46.

This shady circuit leads through the dense forests of conifers below mighty Schlern/Sciliar, past the legendary Salegg and Hauenstein castle ruins. It's a walk for all the family, with numerous information boards and play areas along the way ensuring child-friendly entertainment. Still — especially in fog and bad weather — the castle ruins (see panel on page 116) appear almost mysteriously gloomy.

The walk begins at the **entrance to the car park** for the Seiser Alm cable car (**1**). Follow the road a few metres uphill to a left bend.

Then take the lane to the right (**2**), towards 'Hotel Salegg, Oswald von Wolkenstein Weg'. You find yourselves in a shady

Walk 17: Oswald von Wolkenstein Trail

conifer wood, with scattered boulders.

After a few minutes, the road forks. Take the upper road and reach the **Hotel Salegg** in five minutes. The **Oswald von Wolkenstein Circuit Trail** (3) begins just in front of the hotel, and you follow it uphill from here. It leads across a clearing with a beautiful view of Seis and then climbs through shady forest via some steep hairpin bends — at times on a log-stabilised path.

Almost 20 minutes from the hotel you come to junction (4; **35min**). (To the left you can reach the sparse remains of **Salegg Castle** after about 50m via a wooden boardwalk (see 'The ruins ...' on page 116). They consist of just a tower fragment and some remains of the wall. The view of Seis and Schlern is impressive, though, and a comfortable bench invites you to rest.)

Back on the slightly ascending main path you pass information boards, rest areas and play stations for children, which introduce them to the mysterious world of the Middle Ages.

About 15 minutes past the turn-off to the Salegg ruins, a path branches off to the right (5): it ends after about 100m under an overhanging rock wall with seats. Here, a notebook with stories and songs from the Middle Ages invites the walker to read and sing.

Back on the main path, after five minutes you come to some stairs (6; **55min**). Climb up here, through a crevice, to finally reach the ruins of **Hauenstein Castle** via a steep stone staircase. Here, too, we enjoy the view of Seis and Schlern.

Again back on the main path, continue through the forest. Soon afterwards, you come to a fork by a well (*the water is not potable!*). Follow Trail N° 3 from here, heading east towards 'Seis'. A few metres further on, on the right, there is a mighty wooden **knight's throne** in the forest; next to it are tables and benches — everything is set up for a medieval banquet!

Not far past the throne you go through a barrier, and immediately afterwards head left at a fork (7) on Trail 3. This motorable track makes for a gravelly descent. After a few metres, Trail 3 heads left, back to Hotel Salegg, but you keep straight ahead on Trail N° 8.

A good 10 minutes past this fork you reach the upper end of the car park for the valley station of the Seiser Alm cable car and in about five minutes you're back at the starting point (1).

Left: the ruins of Hauenstein Castle, dating from the 12th century and later the home of the Wolkensteins, one of whose members was the poet Oswald von Wolkenstein.

Medieval atmosphere: a foggy day in the forest; below: Oswald von Wolkenstein

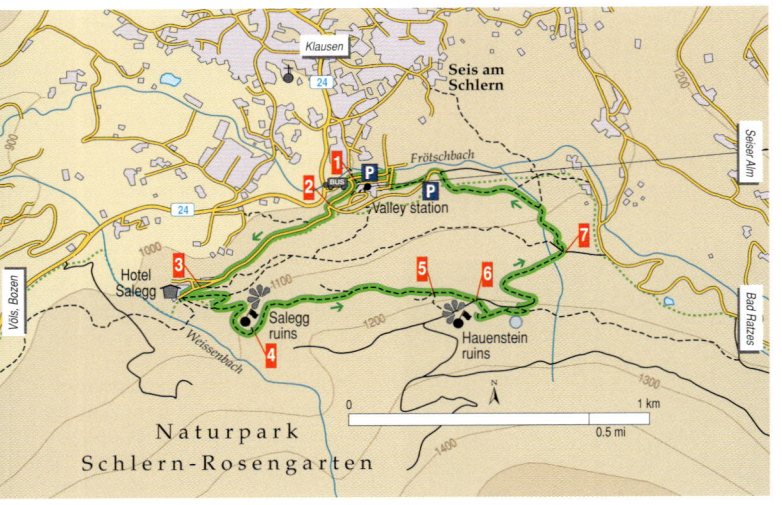

Oswald von Wolkenstein Ride

This horse riding competition in honour of the poet Oswald von Wolkenstein takes place at Prösels Castle and in the three villages of Seis/Siusi, Völs/Fiè and Kastelruth/Castelrotto at the end of May and early June. As in Middle Ages tournaments, equestrian teams meet each other. At this folk festival there are also bands, groups dressed in medieval costume, jesters and artists.

Walk 18: CIRCUIT FROM COMPATSCH TO THE PUFLATSCH/BULLACCIA SUMMIT

Distance/time: about 9.1km/ 5.6mi; 2h55min

Grade: ● easy-moderate, with an ascent/descent of 435m/1425ft on wide tracks and mountain paths. Hardly any shade

Waymarking: marked throughout 'PU' for '**P**uflatsch-**U**mrundung' ('Puflatsch circuit'); after **13** also marked red/white Trail N° 14

Equipment: hiking boots and walking poles for the descent, sun protection

Refreshments: available in Compatsch (**1**), in the Puflatsch Hut after **3** and at the Arnika Hut (**7**). But there are many pleasant resting spots en route, so perhaps take a picnic with you.

Walking map: Tabacco 05, Val Gardena-Alpe di Siusi/Gröden-Seiseralm, 1:25,000

Transport: 🚗 There is a large car park for hikers in Compatsch

Remember: You are only allowed to take your car to the Seiser Alm before 09.00 and after 17.00.

(46° 32.394'N, 11° 37.050'E; € 19/day). Alternatively, you can park in Seis at the valley station (46° 32.435'N, 11° 33.829'E) and take the cable car (end of May to beginning of November, ascent and descent € 19, families € 41) to Compatsch. Or take 🚌 170 from Brixen/Bressanone or Bolzano to Seis bus station and from there 🚌 10 (Seiser-Alm-Express) to Compatsch (free of charge with the guest card, otherwise € 19). Alternatively, take 🚌 176 or a 10-minute walk to the valley station of the cable car. The cable car or one of the free shuttle buses (in high season every quarter to half hour) will take you up to Compatsch. On the Seiser Alm itself, 🚌 11 (€ 2.50) runs between Saltria and Compatsch. Last 🚌 11 back to Saltria at 18.40, last 🚌 10 to Seis (bus station) 19.10, last 🚌 176 from the valley station to the bus station 18.07 and from there last 🚌 170 to Brixen 17.49 or to Bolzano 19.46.

This leisurely family hike leads through broad alpine meadows to the mystical 'Witches' Benches' and over a heather-like plateau. There are several refreshment stops in rustic huts and panoramic views of the Eisack/Isarco Valley, the main Alpine ridge and the entire Seiser Alm/Alpe di Siusi plateau with a host of Dolomites peaks in the background.

The walk starts at the **ticket kiosk** (**1**) of the large Compatsch car park: head in the direction of the centre for a few metres, then take a road off left signposted to 'Puflatsch/Bullaccia'. Rising slightly, you pass the mountain station of the cable car and follow the road westward. On your left is the post-modern building of the Alpina Dolomites Hotel. The rock faces of Schlern/Sciliar and the Santner peaks are straight ahead.

At the end of the hotel complex, the road turns northeast (signpost: 'Puflatsch/Arnikahütte'). Continue through alm meadows to a fork (**2**; **15min**). On the right is your return path after completing the circuit. For now, follow the lane (Trail 14) straight ahead towards the 'Arnikahütte', heading steeply uphill through a small pine wood. About 10 minutes later the woods open out to alpine meadows again. Keep

132 Dolomites, Book 1: North and West

straight ahead again at a Y-fork (**3**) with the signpost 'PU (Puflatsch-Umrundung)'. Shortly afterwards, ignore the left fork to the Puflatsch Hut (Trail 12b).

The ascent runs gently through meadows past several alpine huts. Ignore a left turn and continue on an earthy mountain path until you meet a wide motor track (**4**) on a hilltop. Follow this a few metres downhill into a hollow and then back up again.

About 10 minutes after the hollow, at a fork (**5**; **45min**), go right on a narrow earthen path and through a small stand of rhododendrons. There are two alpine huts on the left. At the end of the rhododendrons you cross a small wooden bridge.

This is followed by a short stretch through pines, then meadow again — until, about 10 minutes from the fork you reach a bench with views to Kastelruth/

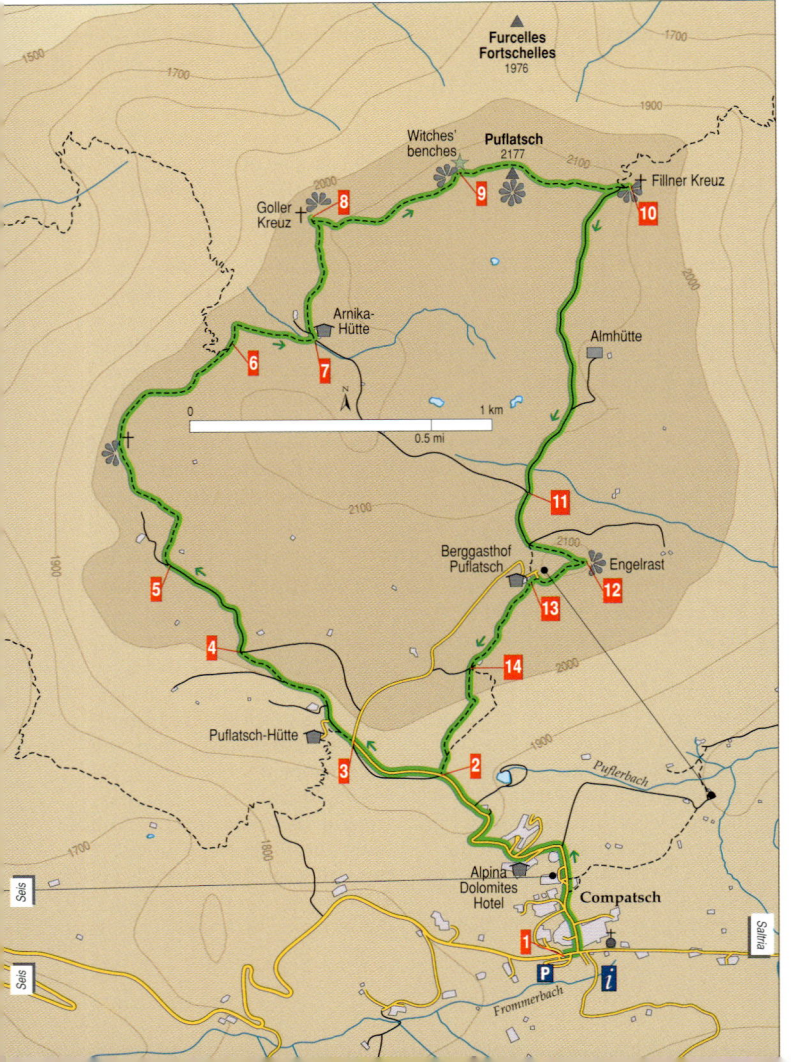

Walk 18: From Compatsch to the Puflatsch/Bullaccia summit

Castelrotto and the main Alpine ridge in the west.

Passing another bench and a wooden cross, the path now leads along the western edge of the Puflatsch/Bullaccia plateau. As you walk, there are beautiful intermittent views through the pines and bushes to the valley 1000m/3300ft below.

At the next fork (**6**) there is a steep path left downhill to Kastelruth which you ignore. A little later you come to a large wooden cross. The path then leads through a small wooden gate and straight to the **Arnika Hut** (**7**). Two trails meet in front of the terrace here: you can either take a rest at the cozy hut or hike north through junipers in the direction of the 'Hexenbänke'. (The other trail leads east: it's a short-cut back to the mountain station of the Puflatsch cable car, which you'll pass later.)

It is increasingly rocky underfoot as you carry on uphill. About 10 minutes past the hut, you reach the edge of the slope at a cross, the **Goller Kreuz** (**8**). As you follow the path along the edge, you view widens to take in the Rosszähne/Denti di Terrarossa and Schlern/Sciliar in the south.

About 10 minutes past the cross, the stony path brings you to the '**Witches' Benches**' (**9**) — a staircase-like, weathered formation of porphyry columns. With a little imagination, they can be interpreted as benches with a backrest. The shape and fantastic all-round view probably gave rise to stories linking them with tribunal sites or sun cults — but there is no reliable evidence for this. Perhaps nearer to the point are legends about the Schlern witches gathering here to avoid severe storms over the Seiser Alm — especially if you've experienced one of these rapidly approaching thunderstorms with menacing black clouds yourself ...

If you follow the path a few metres further, you will reach the **highest point of Puflatsch/ Bullaccia**. There are no crosses or markings, just a bench, but if you look around, you realise: it doesn't get any higher! You are rewarded with a 360-degree panorama that is second to none (from west to east): the main Alpine ridge, the Grödner/Gardena Valley, the Geisler/Odle peaks, the Sella group, Langkofel/Sassolungo, Plattkofel/Sassopiatto, the Rosszähne, Schlern — truly unbelievable! It is also easy to see how barren the northern part of Puflatsch is: the scattered rocks, junipers and rhododendrons — the whole thing reminiscent of the Peak District or Scottish Highlands.

The path continues east along the northern edge of the escarpment, where well-placed benches invite you to take a breather. Following wooden fencing, you arrive at the **Fillner Kreuz** (**10**) a good 10 minutes after the Witches' Benches. This cross also makes a fine lookout point.

Here the route turns south towards 'Puflatsch-Bergstation'; the path is wide and runs through junipers. Soon after the cross you cross a boggy valley; there is an alpine hut on your left. Some 20 minutes past the cross, at a fork (**11**), keep straight ahead (where a right turn would lead to the Arnika Hut). You can already see the Puflatsch mountain inn ahead.

From here on, the heathland is replaced by alpine meadows. At the next fork, below the inn, take Trail N° 14 signed to '*punto*

Heading back to Compatsch from the Fillner Cross, with Langkofel/Sassolungo and Plattkofel/Sassopiatto in the background

panoramico'. In just under five minutes this leads to the **Engelrast viewpoint** ('Angel's Rest'; 12). A South Tyrolean artist created this viewing platform from which **53** three-thousand-metre peaks can be admired — their names engraved on a viewing table.

From the viewing table head southwest towards the mountain station of the cable car. Cross its route and immediately afterwards you'll be standing in front of the panorama terrace of the **Berggasthof Puflatsch**, one of the cheapest places to stop for refreshments in the Seiser Alm area.

Take the path (13; **2h20min**) branching off to Compatsch in front of the terrace. It leads first over soft meadow ground and then on gravel for about 10 minutes. After crossing a track (14), the downhill path is very steep and a bit washed-out.

The Compatsch hotel complexes can already be seen below. After a few steep hairpin bends, your path soon meets the tarred road (2) to Compatsch. From here retrace your steps along your outgoing path back to the car park in Compatsch in under 15 minutes (1; **1h55min**).

Walk 19: FROM COMPATSCH ACROSS THE SEISER ALM/ ALPE DI SIUSI PLATEAU

Distance/time: about 12.2km/ 7.6mi; 3h35min
Grade: ● easy-moderate, but quite long, with an ascent/descent of 390m/1280ft on wide tracks and paths
Waymarking: red/white throughout; Hans and Paula Steger Weg to **3**; Trail N° 2 to **6**, 13a to **7**; 13 to **8**, Trails 6/5a/5b to **11**, and finally Trail 10
Equipment: hiking boots and walking poles
Refreshments: available in Compatsch (**1**), at the Hotel Panorama (**4**), at the Laurin Hut and Spitzbühl Hut (**11**). There's a spring at **12**.
Walking map: Tabacco 05, Val Gardena-Alpe di Siusi/Gröden-Seiseralm, 1:25,000
Transport: 🚗 There is a large car park for hikers in Compatsch

Remember: You are only allowed to take your car to the Seiser Alm before 09.00 and after 17.00.

(46° 32.394'N, 11° 37.050'E; € 19/day). Alternatively, you can park in Seis at the valley station (46° 32.435'N, 11° 33.829'E) and take the cable car (end May-early Nov, ascent and descent € 19, families € 41) to Compatsch. Or take 🚌170 bus from Brixen/Bressanone or Bolzano to Seis bus station and from there 🚌10 (Seiser-Alm-Express) to Compatsch (free of charge with the guest card, otherwise € 19). Alternatively, take 🚌176 or a 10-minute walk to the valley station of the cable car. The cable car or one of the free shuttle buses (in high season every quarter to half hour) will take you up to Compatsch. On the Seiser Alm itself, 🚌11 (€ 2.50) runs between Saltria and Compatsch. Last 🚌11 back to Saltria at 18.40, last 🚌10 to Seis (bus station) 19.10, last 🚌176 from the valley station to the bus station 18.07 and from there last 🚌170 to Brixen 17.49 or to Bolzano 19.46.

This circuit from Compatsch on the classic 'Hans and Paula Steger Trail' leads across lush wet meadows (sometimes on boardwalks) and through shady forests — first towards Saltria and then with panoramic views over extensive Alpine pastures.

The walk starts at the **ticket kiosk** (**1**) of the large Compatsch car park: head east on the road (closed to car traffic during the day) towards Saltria. Either just in front or behind Compatsch's ultra-modern church, follow Trail N° 30 (signposted after the church). You come onto a wide paved hiking path that leads you across meadows, the Hans and Paula Steger Trail (see panel overleaf).

A scant 10 minutes from starting out, the path becomes narrower. Soon afterwards wooden boardwalks lead you over a small mountain stream. Then, slightly uphill, you reach the road (**2**) to Saltria a little later. Cross it and follow the sign to the Hotel Steger-Dellai (formerly owned by Hans and Paula Steger) uphill through mixed conifer woods.

Past the hotel and its small pond, at a junction, keep to the Hans and Paula Steger Trail (where to the right leads to the Gostner Schwaige). Meadows and forest alternate. Approximately 15 minutes past that fork, the trail

Boardwalks cross the wet meadows.

forks (**3**; **35min**). Leave the Hans and Paula Steger Trail here and follow signposted Trail 6 right towards the 'Panorama' mountain station.

First you pass some pines and spruce, then the trees give way to the endless Alpine pastures that characterise the Seiser Alm. The Rosszähne/Denti di Terrarossa, Maximiliansteig/Via Ferrata Maximilian, Schlern/Sciliar and the Santner peaks frame the scenery.

You climb this wide hiking trail gently uphill for quite a long time, then you cross the route of a ski lift and shortly afterwards reach a crossroads. Take the tarred road straight ahead — to the striking **Hotel Panorama**.

At the western end of the hotel grounds, a path (**4**; **1h05min**) branches off to the south (Trail N°

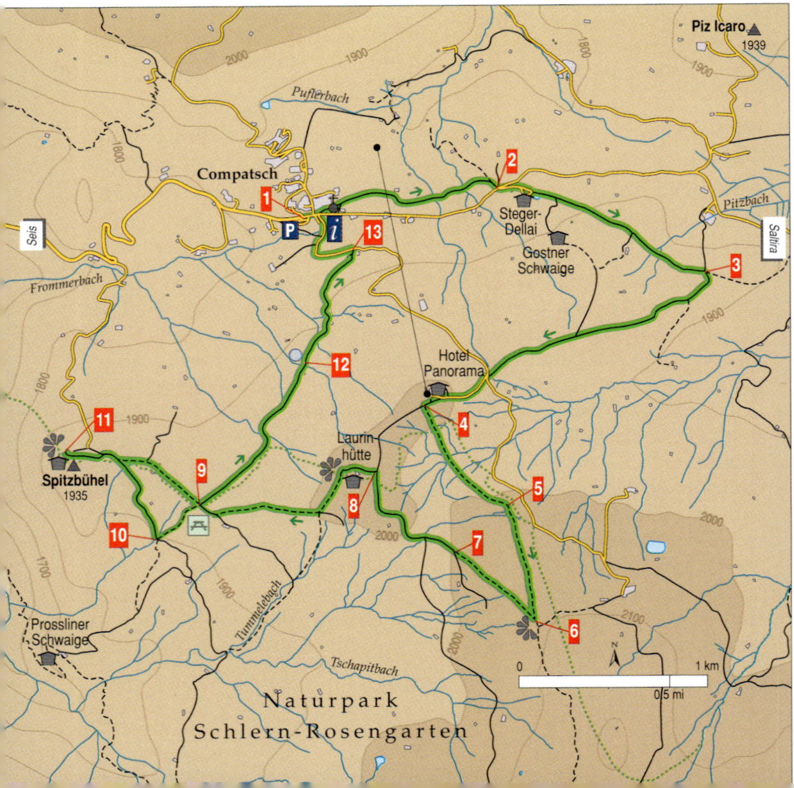

The Hans and Paula Steger Weg

The Hans and Paula Steger Trail runs from Compatsch to Saltria and is the classic walk on the Seiser Alm/Alpe di Siusi plateau. It's accessible to everyone, with information boards about the natural history, flora and fauna of the Alm. The trail is dedicated to the Bavarian-South Tyrolean mountaineering couple Hans and Paula Steger. She was a swimmer, high diver, skier and extreme climber. He was a mountaineer, ski instructor and later became the coach of the Italian national Alpine team. In 1949 they bought the Dellai Refuge (today the Hotel Steger-Dellai), renovated and managed it. Together they set up a foundation to promote and preserve the Seiser Alm/Alpe di Siusi Nature Reserve. Hans Steger died in 1989, Paula Steger in 2001.

2, signposted to the 'Tierser Alpl Hütte'). Take this path — running partly on wooden boardwalks over the wide, somewhat boggy plateau and through a depression.

About 15 minutes after the depression, continue to the right in the direction of 'Tierser Alpl' at a signpost (**5**). This takes you uphill, sometimes on more boardwalks. After you've climbed some steps paved with planks, you come to a junction (**6**; **1h40min**) about 20 minutes past the last signpost. This junction, surrounded by several boulders, is the highest point of the hike.

Turn sharp right and continue in a northwesterly direction on Trail N° 13a now, following 'Spitzbühlhütte'. You descend, with soft meadow underfoot, for about 15 minutes, heading for wide alpine meadows speckled with many small huts. The

View south across the Seiser Alm/Alpe di Siusi

Puflatsch/Bullaccia plateau rises to the north. Then your path joins a stony motor track (**7**), which leads you northwest to a lift station and some huts. Shortly afterwards you reach another motor track in a depression. Follow the signs to the Spitzbühl Hut and the Hotel Panorama. In the distance, the Geisler/Odle peaks tower up in front of you.

About 10 minutes after the signpost you come to a junction (**8**) and follow signs to the **Laurin Hut** with its flagpole and large terrace with a fine view to Schlern/Sciliar. This is a good place to take a break.

Immediately past the hut, the path leads south through a swampy meadow. Cross this on boardwalks and, shortly afterwards, at a fork, go right downhill on a wide track. Soon after that fork, keep right at a large boulder but, no more than 100m further on, turn left at a bench (**9**). Head downhill, again with soft meadow underfoot.

After the bench, the path merges with a concreted motor track (**10**; **2h35min**). Follow this track to the right uphill through the meadows towards 'Spitzbühlhütte'. You finally come to a road. Go left here, and after a few metres go left again on a gravel path. This goes past the mountain station of the chair lift and downhill to the **Spitzbühl Hut** (**11**). From the nearby edge, there is a spectacular view down to Seis and Kastelruth. With its good thermal conditions, this is a popular meeting place for 'pilots', who launch their model aircraft and metre-wide drones here in summer.

After taking some refreshment, walk back to the road in about five minutes and follow the sign to 'Compatsch' (first Trail N° 5, then Trail 5a). Passing several alpine huts, a good five minutes later you reach the bench (**9**) you passed on your outgoing route. Go left now, on Trail N° 10.

After a short boggy section you pass a **spring** (**12**) with deliciously cool drinking water. On the left you can already see the Compatsch hotels. After a short ascent, the meadows end and you follow a wide motor track between elders downhill to the road (**13**) to Compatsch. Follow the road to the left in a wide arc and about 10 minutes later you'll be back at the ticket kiosk in Compatsch (**1**; **3h35min**).

Walk 20: FROM COMPATSCH TO SCHLERN/SCILIAR

Distance/time: about 9.5km/ 5.9mi; 4h10min
Grade: ● ❗ very strenuous; steep scree-covered 'Tourist Path'. Ascent 1045m/3430ft, descent 440m/1445ft. You must be sure-footed, with a head for heights. Little shade; very hot in summer
Waymarking: red/white; Trail N° 10 as far as **9**, Trail 1 and the 'Touristensteig' to **12**; Trail 4 for the detour to Petz (**13**)
Equipment: hiking boots, walking poles, sun protection
Refreshments: available in Compatsch (**1**), at the Prossliner Schwaige (dairy hut; **6**) and at the Schlernhaus (**12**), spring at **3**
Walking map: Tabacco 05, Val Gardena-Alpe di Siusi/Gröden-Seiseralm, 1:25,000
Transport: 🚗 There is a large car park for hikers in Compatsch (46° 32.394'N, 11° 37.050'E; € 19/day).

Remember: You are only allowed to take your car to the Seiser Alm before 09.00 and after 17.00.

Alternatively, you can park in Seis at the valley station (46° 32.435'N, 11° 33.829'E) and take the cable car (end May-early Nov, ascent and descent € 19, families € 41) to Compatsch. Or take 🚌170 bus from Brixen/Bressanone or Bolzano to Seis bus station and from there 🚌10 (Seiser-Alm-Express) to Compatsch (free of charge with the guest card, otherwise € 19). Alternatively, take 🚌176 or a 10-minute walk to the valley station of the cable car. The cable car or one of the free shuttle buses (in high season every quarter to half hour) will take you up to Compatsch. On the Seiser Alm itself, 🚌11 (€ 2.50) runs between Saltria and Compatsch. Last 🚌11 back to Saltria at 18.40, last 🚌10 to Seis (bus station) 19.10, last 🚌176 from the valley station to the bus station 18.07 and from there last 🚌170 to Brixen 17.49 or to Bolzano 19.46.

This hike from Compatsch to Schlern/Sciliar is probably the most spectacular on the Seiser Alm/Alpe di Siusi. I prefer to extend it over two days: on day one you hike from Compatsch across the plateau on the steep Touristensteig to the Schlernhaus/Rifugio Bolzano and on to Petz/Pez, the highest point on Schlern. On day two, Walk 00 takes you from the Schlernhaus via the Tierser Alpl Hut/Rifugio Alpe di Tires and Plattkofel Hut/Rifugio Sasso Piatto to the Saltria cable car. But if you're really fit and have only one day in the area, Walk 22 covers much of the same ground as a day hike.

The walk starts at the **ticket kiosk** (**1**) of the large Compatsch car park: head east on the road (closed to car traffic during the day) towards Saltria. After about 100m turn right at the tourist office on a street bristling with signposts. For the moment, follow the sign for 'Laurinhütte'.

You head uphill on this wide tarred road past pines, spruce and pastureland. After a wide bend to the left, fork right on Trail N° 10 (**2**) in the direction of 'Saltner Hütte'. As you rise up a wide gravel path, the landscape widens out and carpets of flowers are spread before you. Rosszähne/ Denti di Terrarossa and Schlern border the meadows on the

139

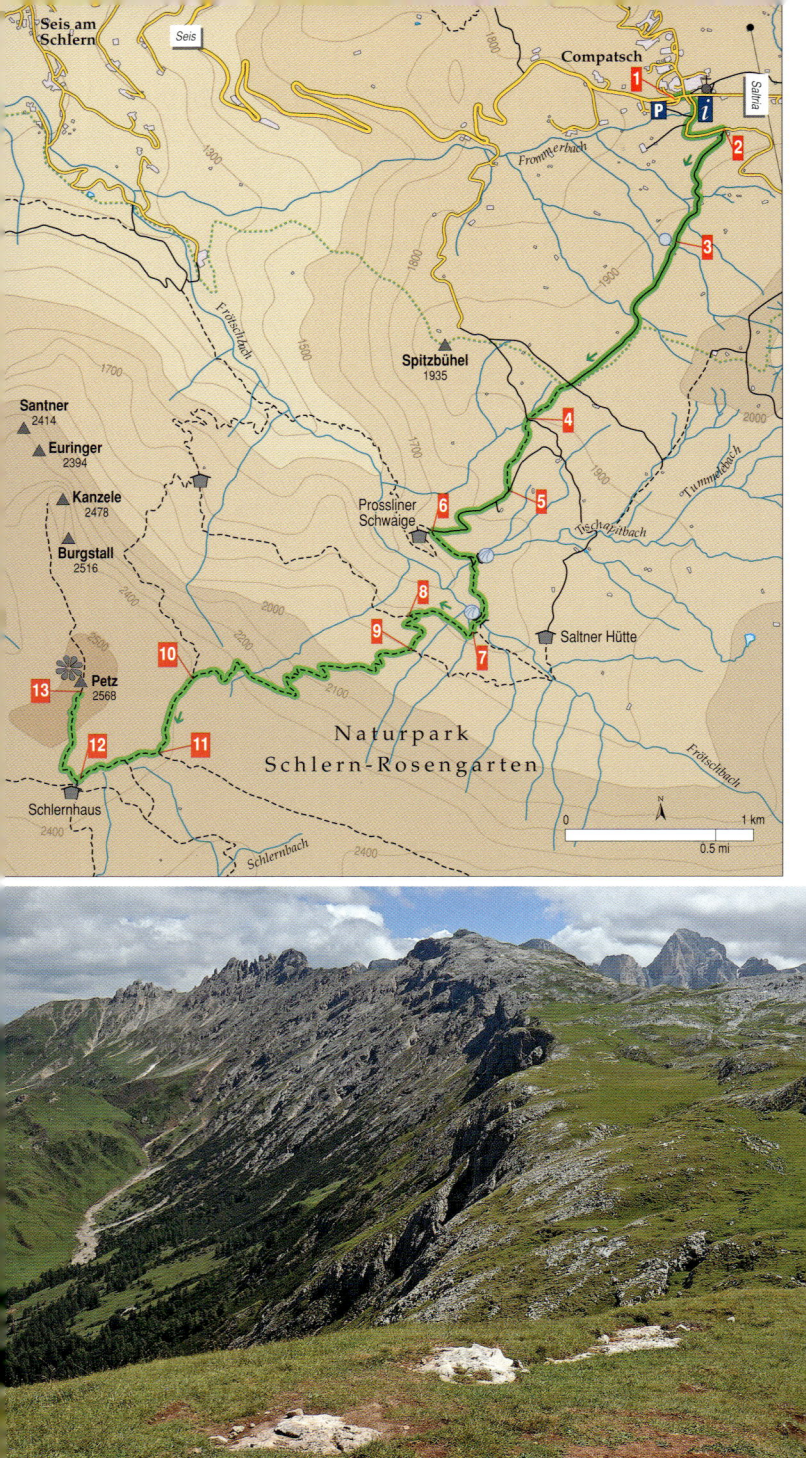

Walk 20: From Compatsch to Schlern/Sciliar 141

horizon. About 15 minutes after turning right, you come to a **spring** (**3**; **30min**) near several alm buildings. Its fresh water offers a welcome cooling off!

Continue through the meadows with a view to Schlern and the Santner peaks. You'll spot cotton grass growing in boggy places. About 15 minutes after the spring, keep straight ahead at the next junction on Trail 10 towards the Saltner Hut, heading downhill on a meadow path. In the southeast a wide valley with alpine meadows and cows opens up to view — with the Saltner Hut in the middle.

You cross the motor track (**4**; **55min**) leading to the Saltner Hut and keep following Trail 10 further south, towards 'Prossliner Schwaige', always heading towards Schlern. About 10 minutes later, on a ridge, you come to another motor track (**5**). Follow this track to the right, in the direction of 'Schlernhaus' and 'Prossliner Schwaige'. The dairy **Prossliner Schwaige** (**6**; **1h20min**) is picturesquely located, with Schlern towering above; it's an idyllic place to stop for a break. But if you're drawn to the summit, you'll continue on narrow trail N° 10 towards 'Schlernhaus'.

Go through a cattle gate and immediately afterwards cross a wooden bridge over the **Tschapitbach**, a stream which flows into the Frötschbach. Huge blocks of limestone lie in the stream bed.

On the right, below you, hidden behind pines, the Frötschbach rushes down into the valley in a gorge. Going downhill, you're in the bottom of the gorge about 10 minutes after crossing the Tschapitbach. You cross the rushing Frötschbach on a rustic wooden bridge with a view of a small waterfall.

After almost five minutes of gentle ascent, having crossed another bridge, you come to a boardwalk (**7**). Follow this to the right, steeply uphill, in the direction of the 'Schlernhaus'. First it goes through an open stand of pines and then through shady spruce trees. At its end the path forks at a bench (**8**). Keep left here. The path takes you uphill in two steep hairpin bends through mixed conifers, and soon you come to an alpine meadow.

About 10 minutes after the bench you reach a junction (**9**; **2h**) at another bench with a wide view of the Seiser Alm, Puflatsch/Bullaccia and the Geisler/Odle peaks in the northeast. This is where you join the **Touristensteig** ('Tourist Trail'; N° 1), a mountain path covered with loose scree,

Heading east on the Schlern/Sciliar high plateau

which stretches southwest up the steep flank of Schlern and **requires your utmost concentration**.

You now climb through endless mountain pines where stone steps and wooden planks constantly stabilise the loose rubble. This ascent, on a well-used path, is exhausting and sweaty.

After a just under an hour, the rocky sections alternate with pine woods and grassy slopes. The views are becoming more and more spectacular: to the southeast you see the elongated Schlern plateau as far as Roterdspitz/Cima di Terrarossa — the highest of the Schlern peaks — and behind it the mighty walls of Rosengarten/Catinaccio. During the last stage of this climb, steps and a handrail help you, and finally you have reached the edge of the plateau.

Trail N° 1B branches off to the right (**10**; **3h15min**) to the Gamssteig. You keep to the 'Tourist Trail' which leads you further south, below Petz. After about 10 minutes of gentle ascent on a well-paved path, keep right at a fork (**11**), following 'Schlernhaus'. Once past a scree field that stretches down from the summit of Petz, you come to the stone-built **Schlernhaus/Rifugio Bolzano** (**12**; **3h35min**) — but actually the Schlern *houses*. There are four buildings in all, the oldest dating

Walk 20: From Compatsch to Schlern/Sciliar

from between 1883 and 1885. In the main building there is wonderful wood paneling in the dining room. Do stop and enjoy the grandiose panorama!

The Touristensteig ends at the Schlernhaus, but Trail N° 4 now leads you uphill on rock-strewn grass slopes. After a few metres you're climbing steeply on loose scree. Edelweiss is not uncommon on both sides of the path here.

As you struggle up this wide scree slope up the mountainside, individual trails are increasingly lost. Finally, about 20 minutes past the Schlernhaus, you reach the rocky **summit plateau of Petz/Pez** at a large metal cross (13). What a panorama! To list all the peaks on view would need a separate book. In the north is the main Alpine ridge, in the east numerous 3000m peaks, in the southeast the Rosengarten. Even Bolzano can be seen deep down in the haze of the Eisack/Isarco Valley.

It takes about 15 minutes to get back to the 126-bed **Schlernhaus** (12; **4h10min**) on the same skiddy path (*take care descending!*), where an overnight stay is recommended, before setting out on Walk 21 the next day. But really fit walkers could retrace steps to Compatsch in about three hours.

Cross on the Petz summit

Walk 21: FROM THE SCHLERNHAUS/RIFUGIO BOLZANO TO THE SALTRIA CHAIR LIFT

Distance/time: about 13.6km/ 8.4mi; 4h50min
Grade: ●❗ strenuous and long; steep ascents (585m/1920ft overall) and descents (945m/ 3100ft overall) on mostly stony paths. You must be sure-footed, with a head for heights. Little shade; very hot in summer
Waymarking: red/white; Trail N° 4 as far as **11**, Trail 9 to **13**, then Trail 7A
Equipment: hiking boots, walking poles, sun protection

Refreshments: available at the Plattkofel Hut (**11**) and Tierser Alpl Hut (**6**); *possibly* at Berghaus Zallinger (**13**) and the Williams Hut (**14**); springs just past **8** and at **10**
Walking map: Tabacco 05, Val Gardena-Alpe di Siusi/Gröden-Seiseralm, 1:25,000
Transport: Walk 20 takes you to the Schlernhaus, where this walk begins. You return on the Florian chair lift to Saltria (€ 2.50) and from there take alm 🚐 11 (€ 2.50) to Compatsch (last bus at 18.55).

Day two of the spectacular Seiser Alm/Alpe di Siusi hike, described below, follows on from Walk 20. You begin by heading east across the lonely plateau. You walk below the rugged Rosszähne/Denti di Terrarossa to the Tierser Alpl Hut/Rifugio di Tires, then carry on — in a landscape full of

Walk 21: From the Schlernhaus to the Saltria chair lift

flowers — to the Plattkofel Hut/Rifugio Sasso Piatto. The mighty rock faces of Rosengarten/Catinaccio and later Plattkofel/Sasso Piatto are always in view.

Start the walk early in the morning at the **Schlernhaus** (**1**); head for 'Tierser Alpl/Plattkofelhütte'). In 10 minutes you reach a fork (**2**) where, turning right on Trail N° 4, takes you to the Tierser Alpl Hut. The entire Schlern/Sciliar plateau, up to Roterdspitz/Cima di Terrarossa spreads out in front of you. Large alpine pastures are interspersed with rocks, scree, mossy areas and little puddles. The wind carries the chime of cowbells across the wide plain.

You then carry on slightly downhill for about 15 minutes to a large cairn (**3**; **25min**). It's a good trail marker in winter and on foggy, rainy days. In the south are the alpine buildings of the Aicher stables. In the southwest, the white building of St Kassian Church stands out: an early mass is held in this church on Schlernkirchtag in mid-August (the rest of the day is then dedicated to having fun with friends and lots of beer drinking ...).

The path initially climbs gently but steadily and is marked with some more cairns. The meadows dwindle increasingly — replaced by rubble and rocks; the path is soon covered with loose stones. About 25 minutes past the large cairn, the plateau narrows at another depression called **Plörg**. From here your trail goes steeply uphill through rocks and scree. The view back to Petz and the Seiser Alm — which can be seen in its entirety now — is fantastic.

About 15 minutes past the Plörg depression, keep right at fork (**4**; **1h05min**) towards 'Tierser Alpl'. (Going left — east — here leads to Roterdspitz/Cima di Terrarossa and the Maximiliansteig/Via Ferrata — so it's climbers' territory only!) Shortly afterwards you go through a cattle gate on the ridge which stretches up to the Roterdspitz. A great view of the rock faces of Rosengarten awaits you.

For about five minutes you go south downhill on steep hairpin bends. At the so-called **donkey ridge**, the path turns east and now leads below the ridge and its rocky eruptions towards the Tierser Alpl

Heading for the Tierser Alpl Hut/Rifugio di Tires below steep rock walls

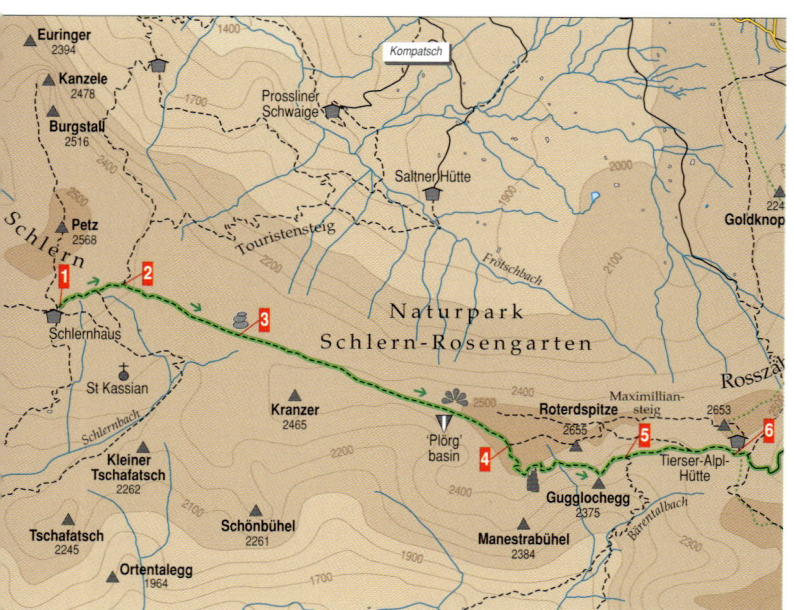

Hut. On your right, the slope breaks off steeply into the Bärenloch, the ascent from the Tschamintal/Valle di Ciamin.

About 15 minutes after the end of the switchbacks, you reach a hilltop, **Gugglochegg**. From here you can clearly see the way to the Tierser Alpl Hut. Head gently downhill for about five minutes, to reach a fork in the path in a depression (**5**). Climb up to the left on a wide path out of the hollow. (A steep path goes south into the Bärenloch.) To your right is a small valley with a stream and sheep.

After about 20 minutes of leisurely climbing, you're in front of the **Tierser Alpl Hut** (**6**; **1h55min**; photo on page 151), below the prominent peaks of the Rosszähne. Its sun terrace invites you to take a well-earned rest. And my tip here is their wonderful *Kaiserschmarrn* — a golden-yellow poem made of flour, eggs, powdered sugar, butter and dried wild flowers on top!

From the hut it's but a few steps to a saddle, the Tierser Alpl Joch. Here the trail forks, and you turn right on Trail N° 4 towards 'Plattkofelhütte'.

A wide motor track initially leads you in a deep curve to the east, then steeply downhill to the southeast *(take care, loose scree!)*. In front of you Plattkofel/Sasso Piatto, Sella, Marmolada and the wide green Duron Valley. After about 20 minutes of knee-punishing descent, the skiddy trail gives way to solid ground. Go down gently now for about 10 minutes, past a mossy depression, to a large cattle gate (**7**).

Continue on Trail 4 on darker, alluvial soil to the **Mahlknecht-joch/Passo Duron** (**8**), where

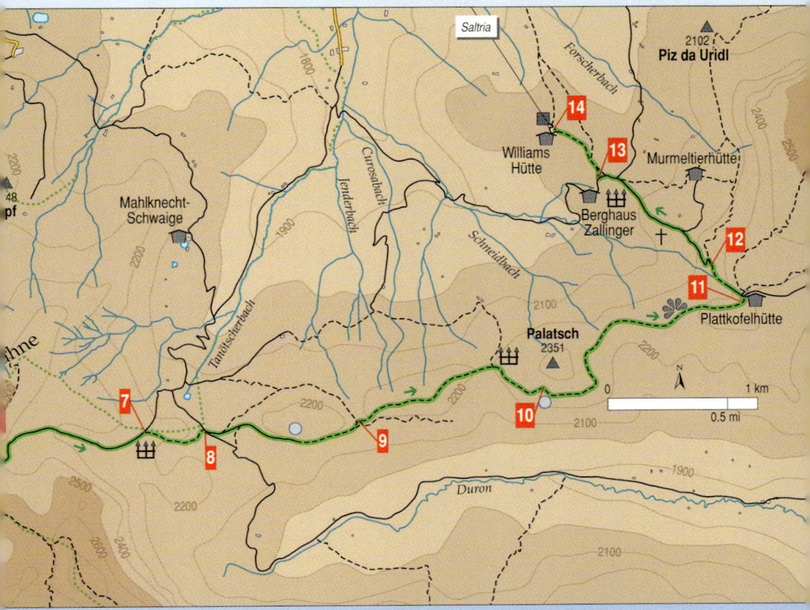

Walk 21: From the Schlernhaus to the Saltria chair lift

you continue east. Soon afterwards you find a **spring** at the left of the path, where you can fill your water bottles. Opposite is a shepherds' shelter.

About 10 minutes after the source you reach the meadow ridge at a junction on a saddle (**9**; **3h**). Climbing left up grassy slopes, you always have Plattkofel and the Sella group in view. After about 15 minutes you go through a cattle gate. About 10 minutes later you pass another **spring** (**10**), this time at the right of the path. Shortly afterwards, there's another cattle gate.

A little later the path turns north and leads in a wide curve above some alpine huts to another saddle on the meadow ridge. To the north you have a beautiful view of the Zallinger Mountain Hut, the Williams Hut with the mountain station of the Florian chair lift and the eastern part of the Seiser Alm. Mighty Plattkofel is also close by.

Sunset on the Rosengarten group/Catinaccio

Hiking more or less along the ridge top, you reach the **Plattkofel Hut/Rifugio Sasso Piatto** (**11**; **4h05min**). Maybe you're ready for some soup with bacon dumplings, polenta and an elderberry spritzer on its terrace! The hut is also the starting point and staging post for the circuit of Langkofel and Plattkofel — that's its *raison d'être*. Due to its exposed location on the Fassajoch, it is usually windier and cooler here than elsewhere.

Thus fortified, hike on: take the very steep motor track northwest towards the Berghaus Zallinger. This track is covered with a lot of loose rubble and can be very slippery. It goes along a steep grassy slope.

About 10 minutes past the Plattkofel Hut, at a junction (**12**; this is where you would access the Sella Pass or the Langkofel/Plattkofel circuit), stay on the wide motor track to a large crucifix. From there you go steeply downhill through mixed conifer forest for 20 minutes. The path forks at a cattle gate. Keep left on a wide motor track towards 'Berghaus Zallinger'. After 100m the track forks again (**13**; to the left is the Berghaus Zallinger, only a few meters below), but you turn right here and climb for about 10 minutes on a gravel track through an open mixed conifer wood to the Williams Hut (**14**; **4h50min**). Here's where the hike ends — on its sun terrace. The Florian chair lift takes you to Saltria in a few minutes, and from there you take the bus back to Compatsch.

Top left: heading for Plattkofel/Sassopiatto and the Plattkofel Hut/Rifugio Sassopiatto (bottom left)

Walk 22: FROM THE SEISER ALM/ALPE DI SIUSI TO SCHLERN/SCILIAR AND THE TIERSER ALPL HUT

Distance/time: about 19.3km/ 12mi; 7h
Grade: ●❗ strenuous and long; alm tracks and paths; steep scree-covered 'Tourist Path'. Ascent/descent about 800m/2625ft. You must be sure-footed, with a head for heights. Little shade; very hot in summer
Waymarking: red/white; Trail N° 10 as far as **3**, Trail 5 and then the 'Touristensteig' to **6**, Trail 1 (still the 'Touristensteig') to **7**, Trail 4 to **9**, then Trail 2 to **12**, and finally Trail 6 to the end
Equipment: hiking boots, walking poles, sun protection
Refreshments: available in Compatsch (**1**), at the Saltner Hut (**4**), the Schlernhaus (**6**; a detour off the route), and at the Tierser Alpl Hut/Rifugio di Tires (**8**)
Walking map: Tabacco 05, Val Gardena-Alpe di Siusi/Gröden-Seiseralm, 1:25,000

Remember: You are only allowed to take your car to the Seiser Alm before 09.00 and after 17.00.

Transport: 🚗 There is a large car park for hikers in Compatsch (46° 32.394'N, 11° 37.050'E; € 19/day). Alternatively, you can park in Seis at the valley station (46° 32.435'N, 11° 33.829'E) and take the cable car (end May-early Nov, ascent and descent € 19, families € 41) to Compatsch. Or take 🚌170 bus from Brixen/Bressanone or Bolzano to Seis bus station and from there 🚌10 (Seiser-Alm-Express) to Compatsch (free of charge with the guest card, otherwise € 19). Alternatively, take 🚌176 or a 10-minute walk to the valley station of the cable car. The cable car or one of the free shuttle buses (in high season every quarter to half hour) will take you up to Compatsch. On the Seiser Alm itself, 🚌11 (€ 2.50) runs between Saltria and Compatsch. Last 🚌11 back to Saltria at 18.40, last 🚌10 to Seis (bus station) 19.10, last 🚌176 from the valley station to the bus station 18.07 and from there last 🚌170 to Brixen 17.49 or to Bolzano 19.46.

For those who haven't the two days needed for Walks 20 and 21, here's a hike that covers many of the high points in just one day. From the start to waypoint 3 and from waypoint 6 to 7, this walk is identical to Walk 20, but it deviates to the Saltner Hut for some fresh alm milk and from there picks up the 'Touristensteig' at its start. Then from waypoint 7 to number 9 the route mirrors Walk 21, but leaves it at the Tierser Alpl Hut/Rifugio di Tires to head back down to Compatsch. See pages 140-148 for some photos of the views on offer and more detailed descriptions of the route.

The walk starts at the **ticket kiosk** (**1**) of the large Compatsch car park: head east past the bus stop, and then take the first right turn, heading south on the road bristling with walkers' signposts. Just past the first left bend, turn right on Trail 10 (**2**). You rise gently over alm meadows, walk under the lift to the Laurin Hut, and rise to a ridge (1957m). From here walk 100m downhill, to a motor track leading to the Saltner Hut (**3**).

At this point you deviate from Walk 20, which *crosses* this track. Follow the track (Trail 5) left, to the pleasant **Saltner Hut** (**4**; **1h45min**), a dairy farm with rustic food and fresh alm milk, just at the start of the climb to Schlern. Cross the stream and go right on the '**Touristensteig**' (**5**), a path covered with loose scree, which stretches southwest up the steep flank of Schlern and **requires your utmost concentration**. You ascend rapidly in deep zigzags, huffing and puffing up through mountain pines. Walk 20 comes in from the right (**6**) on Trail N° 1.

When you come to the meadows of the **Schlern/Sciliar plateau**, you can stride out across almost level ground to a fork (**7**; **3h15min**). The **Schlernhaus**

Right: the Tieser Alpl Hut/Rifugio di Tires, at the foot of the Rosszähne; below: the Schlernhaus buildings, with Rosengarten/Catinaccio in the distance

(actually there are four buildings; see the photo below) are to the right and are worth a visit, but the main walk goes left here.

You are now following Trail 4 over the Schlern plateau, with a beautiful view to Rosengarten/

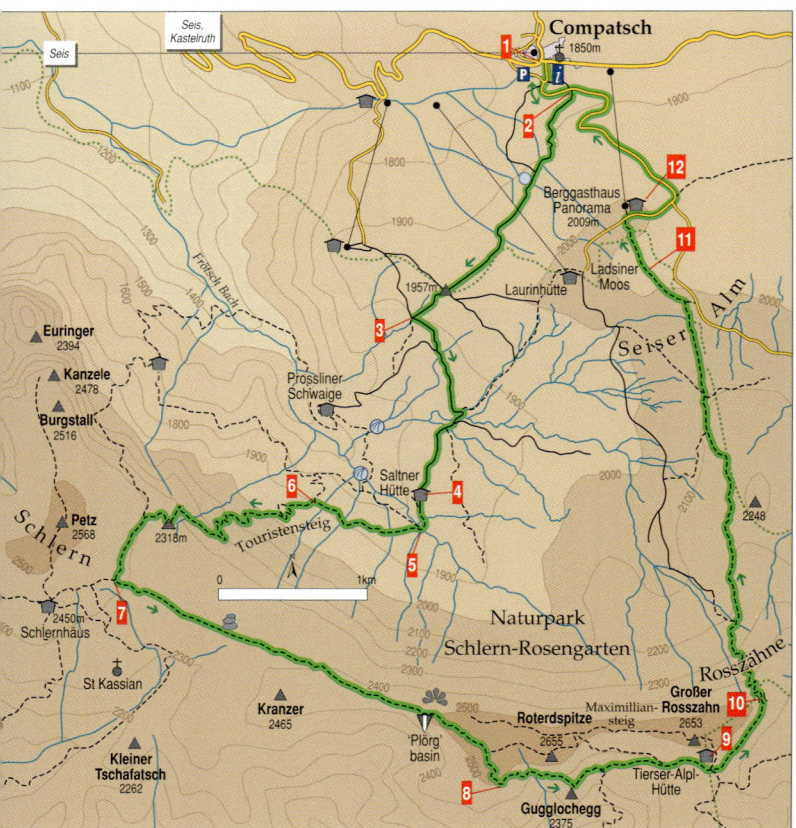

Catinaccio. Beyond a saddle there is another ascent — to the **end of the plateau under the Rosszähne/Denti di Terrarossa** (8; **4h**), where the trail heads right, into a wild gorge. For the next half hour you must be sure-footed and have a head for heights; the path is good, but narrow and, if you slip, it's a long way down …

Beyond a traverse at the foot of the **Rosszähne** and the path forking through the Bärenloch to Tiers/Tires you climb again, to the **Tierser Alpl Hut** (9; **4h45Min**), which has been in view for quite some time. It sits on a saddle between the Rosszähne and Rosengarten.

After taking a break, carry on to the left on Trail 2 to the **Rosszahnscharte/Forcella Denti di Terrarossa** (10). Again you need to be sure-footed on the steep descent over loose rubble in a corrie above the Seiser Alm. Then the route heads right and is less steep. Keep left at a fork, crossing meadows and a damp little valley (the **Ladinser Moos**; 11). When you reach the **Panorama Hotel** (12; **6h**), you can either take the chair lift, or walk down the road to **Compatsch** in an hour (**7h**).

Walk 23: CIRCUIT FROM COMPATSCH VIA THE TIERSER ALPL HUT/RIFUGIO DI TIRES

Distance/time: about 16.9km/ 10.5mi; 5h45min
Grade: ●❢ strenuous and long; steep climb on the Rosszähne and steep descent from the Tierser Alpl Hut. Ascent/descent 780m/2560ft overall. Skiddy mountain paths on the Rosszähne. You must be sure-footed, with a head for heights. Little shade; very hot in summer
Waymarking: red/white; Trail N° 10 as far as **3**, Trail 5b to **4**, Trail 13a to **6**, Trail 2 to **9**, Trail 4 to **10**, Trail 8 to **12**, and finally Trail 7
Equipment: hiking boots, walking poles, sun protection
Refreshments: available in Compatsch (**1**), at the Laurin Hut, the Tierser Alpl Hut/Rifugio di Tires (**9**), the Mahlknecht-schwaige/Rifugio Molignon (**13**) and the Almrosen Hut (**14**). Take plenty of water! There's a spring between (**2**) and (**3**).
Walking map: Tabacco 05, Val Gardena-Alpe di Siusi/Gröden-Seiseralm, 1:25,000

Remember: You are only allowed to take your car to the Seiser Alm before 09.00 and after 17.00.

Transport: 🚗 There is a large car park for hikers in Compatsch (46° 32.394'N, 11° 37.050'E; € 19/day). Alternatively, you can park in Seis at the valley station (46° 32.435'N, 11° 33.829'E) and take the cable car (end of May to beginning of November, ascent and descent € 19, families € 41) to Compatsch. Or take 🚌170 from Brixen/Bressanone or Bolzano to Seis bus station and from there 🚌10 (Seiser-Alm-Express) to Compatsch (free of charge with the guest card, otherwise € 19). Alternatively, take 🚌176 or a 10-minute walk to the valley station of the cable car. The cable car or one of the free shuttle buses (in high season every quarter to half hour) will take you up to Compatsch. On the Seiser Alm itself, 🚌11 (€ 2.50) runs between Saltria and Compatsch. Last 🚌11 back to Saltria at 18.40, last 🚌10 to Seis (bus station) 19.10, last 🚌176 from the valley station to the bus station 18.07 and from there last 🚌170 to Brixen 17.49 or to Bolzano 19.46. Panorama chair lift from the Panorama Hotel down to Compatsch (mid-May to mid-Oct, one way € 7, return € 10).

This long and varied circuit leads us first over the high plateaus of the Seiser Alm/Alpe di Siusi. You climb the steep rubbly corrie of the Rosszahnscharte/Forcella Denti di Terarossa to reach the Tierser Alpl Hut/Rifugio di Tires. This is followed by a long descent on the northern walls of the Rosengarten/Catinaccio massif via the Mahlknecht Hut/Rifugio Molignon (where you should see lots of marmots) and back across the Seiser Alm.

The walk starts at the **ticket kiosk** (**1**) of the large Compatsch car park: head east on the road (closed to car traffic during the day) towards Saltria. After about 100m turn right at the tourist office on a street bristling with signposts. For the moment, follow the sign for 'Laurinhütte', heading uphill between pines, spruce and alpine pastures.

Shortly after the road makes a wide curve to the east, fork right on a wide gravel track (**2**)

154 Dolomites, Book 1: North and West

signposted to the 'Saltner Hütte' (Trail N° 10). The track rises between elderberries and scattered pines. Soon the landscape expands, and the vegetation makes way for extensive meadows. In early summer, carpets of flowers are spread out here, while the Rosszähne/Denti di Terrarossa and Schlern/Sciliar border the horizon.

About five minutes after the start of the alpine meadows, you climb over a cattle gate in a small depression. A little later you come across a refreshing **spring** near several alpine buildings. Continue through the meadows with a view to Schlern and the Santner peaks. You'll notice cotton grass growing in boggy places. The chirping of birds, and the clanging of cowbells fill the air. Otherwise all is silence.

About 15 minutes past the spring, at a fork (**3**; **35min**), turn left on Trail 5b, signed to the 'Tierser Alpl Hütte'). Almost

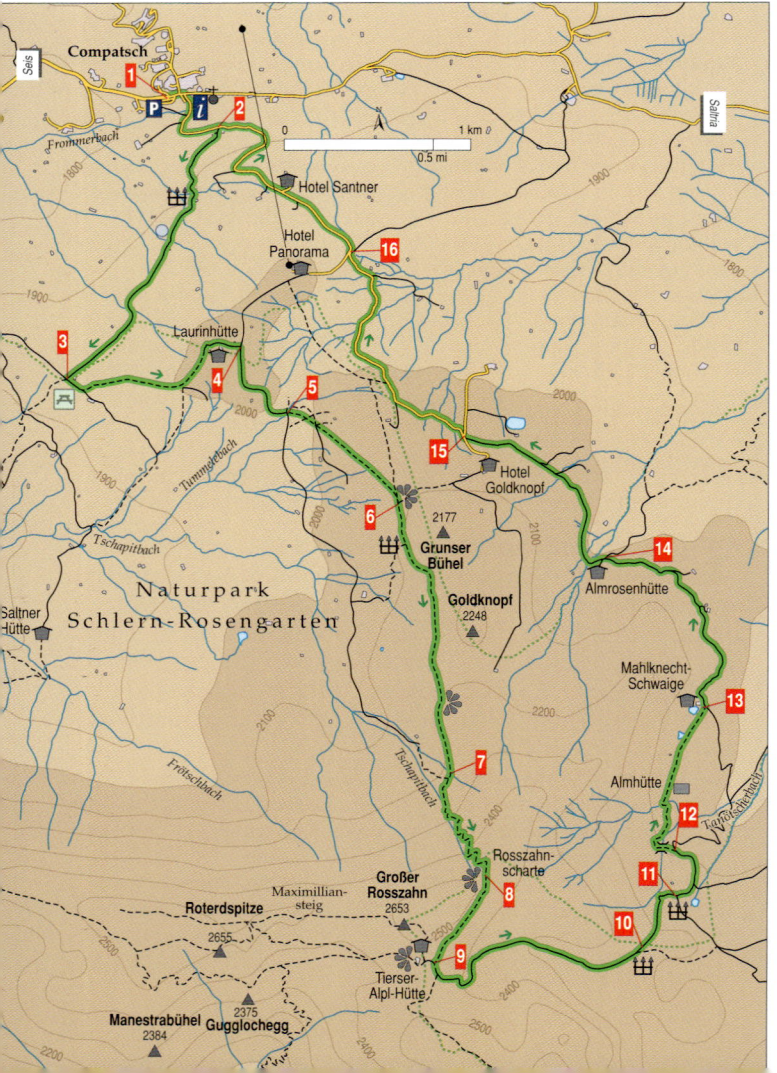

Panoramic views at the Rosszahnscharte/Forcella Denti di Terrarossa

100m further on, path 5b branches off again to the left at a boulder. Follow it slightly uphill, hiking towards the mountain station of a ski lift and the Laurin Hut next to it. You cross swampy ground on a wooden footbridge. On the right you can already see the Rosszähne with its gap *(Scharte)*.

About 15 minutes after the fork, you come to the Laurin Hut with its flagpole and can take a break on its sun terrace. From here you follow a wide motor track below the ski lift. Immediately afterwards, you come to a fork (**4**). Go right here on Trail N° 13 towards 'Tierser Alpl/Saltner Schwaige'.

After about 10 minutes, at the next fork (**5**; **1h15min**), keep to path 13a in the direction of 'Tierser Alpl/Goldknopf'. Some 150m further on, the trail forks three ways: take the middle prong (Trail 13a). This meadow path leads you over marshy ground straight to the green crest of the **Grunser Bühel/Col del Spiedl**.

After about 15 minutes you meet Trail N° 2, which leads up from the mountain station next to the Hotel Panorama. Keep right and, a few metres further on, you reach a **bench** (**6**) with a great view of the Seiser Alm, Schlern and Puflatsch/Bullaccia. Continue walking towards the Rosszähne (a left goes to the Hotel Goldknopf). Your path rises steadily.

Shortly after the bench, at a cattle gate, ignore a fork to the right (to the Saltner Hut) and stay on Trail 2. Eventually you cross a stream on a wooden footbridge and climb through increasingly stony terrain. About 20 minutes from the cattle gate, when you're on a hilltop, there is an interesting view of the Seiser Alm below you.

From the hilltop you carry on through black, eroded terrain. Soon you have to cross a rocky stream bed *carefully* on damp stones (**7**; **2h**). Then the path is paved with coarse stones as it approaches the scree above.

The actual entry into the scree cirque begins about 10 minutes after the stream bed. You have to climb steeply uphill for 35 minutes in sweaty hairpins. Even in summer the path crosses old snow fields. Keep stopping — not only to catch your breath, but to enjoy the grandiose panorama of the Seiser Alm, Schlern and Compatsch in the north!

156　Dolomites, Book 1: North and West

When you finally reach the Rosszahnscharte (8), a carved wooden bench invites you to take a break. In front of you, in the south, the huge rock face of the Grasleitenspitze/Cime del Principe and the lonely Duron Valley in the southeast. Behind you the view stretches from the Seiser Alm to the main Alpine ridge. What a panorama!

After a long break (there are plenty of quiet places between the rocks), continue southwest through scree fields towards 'Tierser Alpl'. Some 15 minutes beyond the pass, on a knoll, you come to a fork in the trail (9; 3h)

Below lovely flowers ... but above there's still snow!

Walk 23: Circuit from Compatsch via the Tierser Alpl Hut 157

below steep rock faces. (To the right, a few metres away, is the **Tierser Alpl Hut/Rifugio di Tires** at the foot of the Maximilian *via ferrata*. The hut was completely renovated and expanded in 2015.)

But you head left down a wide motor track towards 'Mahlknechtschwaige'. This gravel track describes wide curves as it runs downhill: it is *skiddy, so take care!* About 20 minutes after forking left, the track becomes more earthen and black. A boggy valley opens up on our right, where contented cows graze in summer.

About 10 minutes after the end of the scree-covered track you're standing at a large cattle gate (**10**) with a fence. Your ongoing route descends steeply north just alongside the border of the Schlern Nature Park — a real pain in the knees! (A path branches off to the east to the Mahlknechtjoch.)

About 10 minutes past the cattle gate, you pass an old transformer building on the left; behind it there's a small church, hidden in the forest. You go through a cattle gate and immediately afterwards keep left at a fork (**11**). A few metres further on, ignore a right turn to Berghaus Zallinger. Almost five minutes later, turn left (**12**; **3h45min**) towards the 'Mahlknechtschwaige'.

Past a wooden gate you come to a kind of ravine: several metres high, densely overgrown slopes on both sides of the trail lead you to the bottom of a small gorge. You cross a rushing mountain stream on a wooden plank bridge and continue downhill beside railings.

After a small cattle gate, you move away from the gorge, wade through a small side stream and master one last ascent, rising to a small alpine hut. The slopes to your left are dotted with marmot burrows. Their piercing whistling can be heard almost any time of day. If you take your time, you will be able to watch them romp around between the rocks.

A good 10 minutes after the gate you reach **Mahlknechtschwaige/Rifugio Molignon** (**13**). Geese waddle about by a small lake. Cows graze in the neighbouring pasture. An idyllic place to fortify yourself with bacon dumpling soup or apple strudel!

From the hut follow wide Trail N° 7 towards 'Almrosenhütte' and 'Compatsch'. At first you rise, then, a little later, it's gently up and down through alpine meadows, with pines, boulders and rhododendron. Then the path leads steeply downhill to the **Almrosen Hut** (**14**; **4h25min**). It owes its name to the huge carpets of dark red rhododendron.

Your way towards 'Compatsch' now leads north over a small mountain stream. Then it rises steeply for about 10 minutes. Afterwards you wander through the gentle, wide meadows of the Seiser Alm. About 20 minutes past the hut, at a fork (**15**), keep ahead down the road (still Trail 7, signed to 'Compatsch').

Some 20 minutes past the junction, the road rises between alpine huts. At the top, at a junction (**16**; **5h15min**) keep to the tarred road to Compatsch. (Or turn left to the Hotel Panorama and eponymous chair lift if you've had enough!). Shortly after the junction, you pass the huge Hotel Santner. Keep descending in wide curves, looping below the chair lift, for the next 20 minutes, until you come back to **Compatsch** and the starting point (**1**; **5h45min**).

7 THE ROSENGARTEN/CATINACCIO AREA

Tiers and the Tierser Tal • Steinegg • Eggental • Welschnofen • Rosengarten • Karersee • Latemar • Deutschnofen

Walks: 24-30; *walking tips:* Weisslahnbad (page 159), the 'Elizabeth Promenade' (page 162), Lake Karer/Carezza circuit (page 165)

Websites
www.eggental.com
www.tiers.it
Opening hours: see individual attractions

The rose garden … why would anyone give this rugged, untamed mountain range such a romantic name? There's a secret behind it: when seen from the Tierser Tal/Val di Tires, Eggental/Val d'Ega or Regglberg, the mountain walls glow red after sunset — as if by magic.

Before it was transformed into a massif, the mountain was a rose garden, and King Laurin was its master. It doesn't matter if you find this hard to believe, because the legend is so pretty anyway (see page 163). And you won't escape the legend — it's everywhere around you when you're in Tiers/Tires, Welschnofen/Nova Levante, Deutschnofen/Nova Ponente and at Lake Karer/Carezza. There are Laurin inns, Laurin lifts, Rose Garden hotels and endless Laurin souvenirs.

The proper name of this tourist region is Rosengarten-Latemar, taking in not only Rosengarten/Catinaccio but the adjacent, equally rugged (but less legendary) Latemar range. The area is also home to South Tyrol's most important place of pilgrimage — the church of Maria Weissenstein/Santuario di Pietralba, near the friendly holiday village of Deutschnofen on Regglberg, a mountain characterised by meadows, wooded hills and sprinklings of solitary farms and hamlets.

Tiers and the Tierser Tal/ Tires and Val di Tires

One can hardly imagine a wilder ravine than the far reaches of the Tiers Valley. Up until the 1970s, when a small road was built, there was no motor access from the Eisack/Isarco Valley to Tiers, the only real village in the valley.

The long isolation of Tiers is still noticeable today, at least in the village itself. With the new road came tourism — a whole range of hotels, guest houses, holiday homes and private rooms for rent. The skiing and **walking areas** of Rosengarten, Lake Karer and the Latemar are all nearby, affording good business opportunities. But what attracts visitors above all is the magnificent natural setting, with the massive walls of the Dolomites in the background and the age-old farming traditions — including harvesting the hay by hand in the mountain meadows and cheese-making on the alms.

Transport: Transport is easy here; the road is good, and there are frequent **buses** to and from Bozen: up to 10 times daily on weekdays and five a day on Sundays. Two or three buses a day go all the way to the Karer Pass. There is also a free **walkers' bus**

The Rosengarten/Catinaccio area

from the beginning of May till about June 20, when the school holidays start and the summer timetables for the local SAD bus company provide good scheduling for walkers.

Sights and excursions: Tiers/Tires is made up of three sections: the village itself with the parish church, the hamlet of St Zyprian/San Cipriano, and the spa area at Weisslahnbad. The **parish church** of St George has a Romanesque tower; the late baroque porch (1766) was built onto the late Gothic choir.

The road from Tiers to Lake Karer runs below the walls of the Rosengarten. It is one of the most beautiful high-altitude roads in the whole Alps. There are several places to **park and walk**.

● **Walking tip: Weisslahnbad**
Signposted Trail 4 leaves from the upper/northern part of Tiers to the isolated **plague chapel of St Sebastian** in a clearing in the woods. This was built in 1635, the year of the Plague, after 124 people had died — almost the entire population.

From the chapel walk the motor track (Trail 4, then 4a) to **Weisslahnbad**, where people have long sought relief from rheumatic pain. The hot water is slightly acidic, with low-level radioactivity. The baths, in the hotels, are now regulated by the local government.

From Weisslahnbad walk down to **St Zyprian/San Cipriano** and, from the chapel at the junction, follow Oberstrasse back to Tiers, with a fine view over the Tierser Tal and to the Rosengarten group (allow 2h-2h30min out and back, ascent/descent 420m; see Tabacco map 1:25,000 N° 05).

> **Tschamin/Ciamin Valley and Schlern Nature Park**
> If you walk from Weisslahnbad up into the **Tschamintal/Valle di Ciamin** which divides Schlern/Sciliar and Rosengarten (Walk 25), you will come face to face with wild primeval nature. Just how wild can be judged by the fact that a neighbouring valley is called Bärenfalle (Bears' Trap) and that the climb to Schlern is called the Bärenloch (Bears' Hole). This valley is part of the **Schlern Nature Park**. Not far beyond Weisslahnbad you pass the Park Information House and a restored sawmill (see panel on page 173). There is a **car park** (driving beyond this point is forbidden) and an inn. **Naturparkhaus open Jun-Oct, Tue-Sat 09.30-12.30/14-17.30; Sun in Jul/Aug.**

West of Tiers, in the narrow valley between Tiers and Blumau, is the hamlet of **Breien/Brie**. There's nothing to see except for a little church on the sunny slopes 200m above the hamlet, dedicated to **St Catharine of Alexandria**. The Gothic wall paintings on the southern outside wall depict her martyrdom. To get there, walk 40 minutes along the track from the bus stop, keeping left at a fork. The upper frescoes may be shaded by the overhanging roof; noon is the best time for photography.

Steinegg/Collepietra

Steinegg, part of Karneid, lies on a sunny terrace at the lower end of the Tierser Tal. It can be reached from Blumau or from the Eggental below Birchabruck/San Florian d'Ega. This road only dates back a few decades; before, there were only trails and a bad haulage track.

Since the road was built the village grows a little every year: visitors who appreciate the freshness in summer and the beauty of autumn have spread the word — how beautiful it is up here when the sun shines, while the Etsch and Eisack valleys are lost in mist.

The local **museum** below the church is interesting, and at the edge of the village there are some earthen pyramids composed of a most attractive moraine rock. *Museum open from Palm Sunday to 31 Oct for guided tours only. Information at www.museum steinegg.com.*

Eggental/Valle d'Ega

Welschnofen/Nova Levante is the largest village in the Eggental. The valley itself begins as a narrow gorge at the eastern edge of Bolzano and splits into two at Birchabruck — the Eggental and Welschnofen branches. Both the new and old roads over the Karer Pass into the Fassa Valley run via Welschnofen; today these are the most travelled stretches on the Great Dolomite Road.

But you don't have to be a fan of high-mountain roads (and none is greater than the Dolomite Road) to come here, since the landscape alone is reason enough — Rosengarten and Latemar, widespread woodlands, and many **walking trails** with well-placed huts. And then there's Lake Karer/Carezza as a focal point, its waters reflecting the image of Latemar.

Welschnofen/Nova Levante

The village can be reached via the Great Dolomite Road from the Eisack/Isarco Valley; take the Bolzano Nord exit from the motorway. Coming from the east take the Fassatal road via Vigo and the Karer Pass.

You can drive through the old part of Welschnofen in the wink of an eye — from the Mondschein Inn to the church only takes five minutes. The modern part of the village, with its hotels, pensions and the like is bigger, but you can easily miss it out. To get to the ski area you follow the road to Lake Karer or down to Birchabruck/San Floriano and then up to

Alm below the Rosengarten

On the Great Dolomite Road

The first part of what is today the famous Great Dolomite Road between the Eisack/Isarco Valley at Bolzano and Cortina d'Ampezzo was the road through the Eggental to Welschnofen. The wild gorge of the Karneid Stream between the Eisacktal and Birchabruck below Welschnofen was an insurmountable obstacle for road-builders up until the middle of the 19th century. The gorge walls are only a few metres apart at their narrowest points, and when the water was high the gorge was impassable.

But some clever engineers found the solution: they built the road as a succession of suspension bridges below the rock overhangs and so far above the stream that even high water did not reach them; the rock itself was breached with tunnels.

By 1860 Welschnofen was finally accessible on the Eggental through road. Up until then Welschnofen had been part of Kardaun; by 1870 the villagers were proud to announce their own municipality.

At this point a Viennese, Dr Theodor Christomannos (see photo caption on page 193) came along with his idea of a Dolomite Road to run all across the Austrian Dolomites from Bolzano to Cortina. A huge hotel for tourists near lovely Lake Karer above Welschnofen (the Grand Hotel Carezza, see 'Walking tip' overleaf) soon attracted many tourists to the area, and the local businessmen smugly thought that the road would stop there. But in the same year (1896) the Karer Pass was breached, and by 1909 the road had been extended to its current length of 110km.

From the Karer Pass the road runs through the Fassa Valley (Vigo, Pozza and Canazei in the province of Trento) to the Pordoi Pass, then down to Arabba in Buchenstein (Belluno Province) and from there over the Falzàrego Pass to Cortina d'Ampezzo. Whether you travel the Great Dolomite Road by car, motorcycle or even bicycle, today you'll be on a very well engineered asphalt road. It's not steep at any point (the maximum gradient is 12%), but it's full of curves (caravans can't use it east of the Fassa Valley).

Obereggen/Ponte Nova. Summer visitors to Obereggen are really spoiled: walk out the front door of the hotel and you're on lovely Trail 7. Just follow it to the 'Schwarzen Adler' — for a meal or a coffee, then take the next bus back.

Transport: **Parking** places in the village are limited; petrol is available further up the valley on the road to Lake Karer. There are up to 10 **buses** daily between Welschnofen and Bolzano, up to six a day to Lake Karer (three of which go further — to the Karer Pass and Vigo in the Fassatal as well as Moèna and Predazzo with connections to the San Pellegrino Pass and San Martino di Castrozza.) There are bus stops at the tourist office and the supermarket. There is also the free Eggental **walkers' bus** every Tuesday and Thursday in summer, linking the Karer Pass, Welschnofen, Birchabruck, Eggen and Obereggen, Deutschnofen and Petersberg (Weissenstein).

Sights: People come to Welschnofen for the exhilarating surroundings and activity holidays, not to see the village itself. Its 'sights' are quickly listed. There's the **parish church**, slightly above

Welschnofen/Nova Levante: the Frommerbachtal (top) and an old house in the centre

● **Walking tip: Elizabeth Promenade.** In 1897 Empress Elizabeth ('Sissi') of Austria spent a holiday at the Grand Hotel Carezza. One of the paths she used to walk has been upgraded and named the '**Elizabeth Promenade**'. There's a monument in memory of this glamourous but unlucky woman, who was murdered in Geneva a year later.

It's best to begin the walk at the Hotel Rosengarten in the Fromm Valley just northeast of Welschnofen (Tabacco 1:25,000 map N° 06): follow Trail 3 straight up to the monument (by Hof Zenai). From there you can pick up the Promenade itself (Trails 6/9) and stroll along to the Grand Hotel Carezza; the second part of the route is a track closed to motor traffic. Along the way you pass the Schönblick Inn (refreshments).

Reckon on 1h to reach the highest point of the walk, above the monument (ascent of 300m), and 1h30min from there (mostly contouring) to the hotel, where there is a bus stop for your return.

Rosengarten/Catinaccio

Rosengarten looks so steep that one would never dream of its **walking possibilities**. But there are several routes across the range which are suitable for the average hillwalker, and even inexperienced walkers can stroll from the top lift stations or places where they can be dropped off by the hut taxis — enjoying the high Alpine experience with little effort.

The most famous peaks of the Rosengarten group are not the highest (Kesselkogel/Catinaccio d'Antermoia, 3004m, with two

the centre and the road, with green meadows above it and views to Rosengarten. The **museum**, housed in the community centre next to the church, portrays farming life (changeable opening houses, ask at the tourist office).

King Laurin and the Rosengarten

The Germanic tribes who migrated from the Etschtal must have been astonished when they saw the red glow of sunset in the Dolomites — especially over the massif that is today known as Rosengarten/Catinaccio. They'd never seen anything like it. Clearly, they must have thought, this was not a natural phenomenon. It appeared to them that, in contrast to the tall blue-eyed Goths, the small dark alpine Romans (today's Ladins) must know some secret. It's all the stuff of legend — like the bit about the magical belt and hat. Dietrich von Bern, who would eventually become associated with the Rosengarten legend, was in fact the Goth King Theoderich, whose seat was in nearby Bern (Verona). And so (to make a long story short) here's the Rosengarten legend — or at least one version of it!

Where today there is only bare rock there was once the castle of the dwarf King Laurin. His pride and joy was his rose garden, in which red roses bloomed all year round. Laurin had a belt which gave him the strength of 12 men, and a magical hat which made him invisible. He was in love with the blond (naturally) Princess Simhilde; he kidnapped her and took her away to his castle, to live happily ever after. But her brother Dietleib turned to Dietrich von Bern, and the two of them rode off into the mountains with a large party to rescue Simhilde and punish Laurin. By trickery they managed to snatch the hat and destroy the belt.

Laurin could not fight any longer, but he could at least make his kingdom inaccessible, so that his conquerors went away with empty pockets (but with Simhilde, one supposes). He cast a magic spell: the castle disappeared and the rose garden faded away. But Laurin had made a mistake: he forgot about twilight. And that's why today we see the Rosengarten glow between day and night, full of glowing red roses, as it was back then, when it was the pride and joy of the unlucky dwarf king.

---

protected climbing paths), but the group called the Vajolet Towers in the north of the range. In the evening, when seen from the west, they are exceptionally beautiful in the red light — Ladins call this the 'Enrosadüra'. These three towers were first climbed under precarious conditions, as can be imagined, and still attract experienced climbers. The first to be climbed was the Winklerturm (1887; named for the Munich mountain climber Georg Winkler, who did it in three hours, climbing on his own). The Stabeler and Delago towers are also named for the first climbers to master them. Walks 27 and 30 come face-to-face with these towers.

Various lifts serve the huts on the mountain:

Paolina Hut: Paolina chair lift from Lake Karer (June to mid-Oct, 08.30-17.30, in high season 08.00-18.00, one way 12.50 €, up and back 18 €);

Kölner Hut: Laurin I cable car from Welschnofen to the Frommeralm (end May to mid-Oct, 08.15-17.45, in high season 08.00-18.15, one way 12.50 €, up and back 18 €), then **Laurin II cable car**: one way 12.50 €, up and back 18 €).

Rifugio Ciampedié: cable car

from Vigo di Fassa (Jun to end Sep, 08.30-18.00, midday break 13.00-14.00, one way 10.50 €, up and back 20 €);

Karersee/Lago di Carezza
Emerald-green Lake Karer, mirroring the wild rock towers of Latemar and surrounded by thick green forest, is one of the best-known images of the Alps. The downside is that the lake is so easily reached…

Sir Winston Churchill called for his paints when he spotted the lake en route to the Grand Hotel

The mesmerising colours of Lake Karer inspired Sir Winston Churchill to paint.

Carezza in the summer of 1949, and dashed off a very large canvas in 20 minutes!

Today the lake is surrounded by a fence, but there are many viewpoints and benches. Often in late summer and autumn there is so little water that its western part is cut off and the lake looks like a little pond. There's an ultramodern visitors' centre, café, souvenir shops, coachloads of tourists. But at least it is well blended into the landscape. A footpath leads under the road to a wooden viewing platform (open daily from 09.00-18.00). If you can escape the selfie-sticks, the reflection of Latemar in the lake's glassy surface is magical.

● **Walking tip: Lake Karer circuit.** There's a really pretty little **walk round the lake**, easily reached by descending to the water from either of the car parks. The circuit itself is only 25-30 minutes, but to climb to the viewpoints you should allow a good hour.

Latemar

The jagged limestone peaks of Latemar, so beautifully mirrored in Lake Karer, crumble so easily that the rock even breaks up in your hand. This means that the greatest level of care is needed for mountain- and rock-climbing here! And in fact there is only one **walking route over Latemar** — Trail 18, which runs to the Bivacco M Rigatti on the **Latemarspitze** (2791m). This isn't the highest peak on the mountain, but the most easterly tower.

On the other hand there are very beautiful **walks** at the foot of the mountain, between the Karer Pass, Latemar meadows, and in the 'Geplänk', the massive scree cirque at the northern foot of the walls. Another fine route runs from the Karer Pass over to Obereggen in 1h30min (Trail 21, then 21a).

Deutschnofen/Nova Ponente

Reached by road from the Eisack/Isarco Valley via Birchabruck/Ponte Nova, Deutschnofen has a brilliant view to Latemar, Rosengarten and Schlern; looking west one sees Mendel/Mendola and Adamello and in the northwest the Sarntaler/Sarentino and Texel/Tessa groups near Merano. The village, surrounded by fairly gentle terrain, is an ideal base for **easy walks**. And mountain bikers don't have to overcome any of the more difficult Dolomite routes; they can come here with their families and explore the Regglberg, the wooded hills south of Deutschnofen. On the other hand, mountain climbers and hillwalkers have challenging routes on their doorstep — easily reached by car or bus.

Transport: Deutschnofen has up to 10 **buses** a day to/from Bolzano and two a day with Obereggen in summer. There is also the free Eggental **walkers' bus** mentioned on page 59.

Sights and excursions: The late Gothic **parish church of St Ulrich** has a Gothic altar triptych (with neo-Gothic framing) by Hans von Judenburg (1421-24). It was once in the parish church at Bolzano — until they decided to have some fun with baroque and gave some of their 'old-fashioned' things to the people of Deutschnofen. Today this altar is the pride and joy of the village and surroundings; the five wooden reliefs work wonderfully in the high altar (and a side-altar), which are complemented by the beautiful net vault of the ceiling.

In the middle of the open fields in the east part of the village is the **chapel of St Helena** (key nearby in the Kreuzhof). Both the chapel and massive tower date from the 12th century. Inside is a wealth of frescoes from the Bolzano School (from 1410), showing scenes from the Old and New Testaments. It only takes about half an hour there and back on foot: follow the good lane closed to motor vehicles from the Gasthaus Pfösl on the road to Birchabruck or Obereggen.

The famous **pilgrimage church of Maria Weissenstein/Santuario di Pietralba** stands in an isolated position on a flat slope south of Deutschnofen, but it belongs to the village of Petersberg/Monte San Pietro. Its founding dates back to a vow. According to legend, one Leonhard, a farmer and probably an epileptic, was rescued by the St Mary after falling into a gorge and built the chapel in thanks. People seeking cures began to make pilgrimages to the place. Soon the little chapel was too small, so it was replaced by a church (1561), which was turned over to the Servite Order in 1718. They had the church enlarged, added the baroque touches in 1752 and built the two small towers and dome. The frescoes, by the 18th-century Viennese painter Adam Mölk, are the most interesting artistic features inside the church. The cloisters were built between 1787 and 1836, and both the cloisters and church have had some of their ornamentation stolen. On the left side of the church the old chapel still stands, with its collection of votive gifts. The church is the goal of tens of thousands of pilgrims on the saint's day, August 15.

The undulating hilly landscape south of Deutschnofen is called **Regglberg**. A wealth of forestry roads and **walking trails** crisscross this little-settled terrain. The only real 'mountain' rising up from the green woods in the area is **Weisshorn/Corno Bianco** (easily climbed from the Jochgrimm/Passo Oclini in the east). Regglberg is also ideal for mountain bikers, as long as they avoid the **Bletterbach Gorge** in the southwest. This steep valley is walkers' country — but keep away from the valley floor in wet weather. **Long Distance Trail E5**, a magnificent trail from Deutschnofen, crosses the gorge.

Although the little village of **Obereggen/San Floriano** belongs to Deutschnofen, it lies quite far out in the valley, below the rock needles of Latemar. It's best known for the Fiemme/Obereggen Skicircus. But while Obereggen is a very comfortable ski village, you can have a good summer holiday here too: **walks up Latemar** begin right in the centre — like the magnificent route to the Latemar Hut/Rifugio Torre di Pisa. Or you can take the **Oberholz chair lift** (operates from end Jun to end Sep, 08.30-18.00, one way 12.50 €, up and back 17 €) up to the Oberholz Hut and start there at 2150 m.

From **Rauth/Novale** a road runs up to a little lake at the **Lavazè Pass** (provincial border) and then down to **Cavalese**, the main village in the Fleimstal/Val di Fiemme. The lifts up here — and all those on the Reiterjoch and in Pampeago (reached from Obereggen via the road to Tèsero) — are included in the Fiemme/Obereggen Ski Pass. From the Lavazè Pass there is a road to the Jochgrimm under Weisshorn, from where Radein and Kaltenbrunn can be reached by mountain bike.

Walk 24: THE FARM TRAIL FROM PRÖSELS/PRESULE CASTLE TO ST KATHARINA/SANTA CATERINA

Distance/time: about 9.2km/ 5.7mi; 3h25min
Grade: ● easy-moderate, with an ascent of 520m/1705ft and descent of 465m/1525ft on tarred roads, tracks and some narrow paths. Can be muddy after rain; sun and shade

Waymarking: marked throughout with a square icon of two red houses in front of a red sky and mountain silhouette; after **11** also marked red/white Trail N° 6A
Equipment: sturdy shoes
Refreshments: numerous places en route, for instance in the Tommelehof (**6**), Fronthof (**10**; see the panel on page 171), etc. *In spring and winter, opening times are irregular, so take food and drink with you!* Many wine bars are closed on Mondays. Spring at **9**.
Walking map: Tabacco 029, Schlern-Sciliar/Rosengarten-Catinaccio-Latemar, 1:25,000
Transport: 🚗 large car park (signposted) at Prösels/Presule Castle (46° 30.237'N, 11° 29.760'E). 🚌 176 runs approximately every two hours between Seis/Siusi and St Zyprian/San Cipriano (alight at 'Prösels Dorf', from where it's just 200m to the start). So for instance 🚌 176 from Seis at 9.05, 11.05, 14.05 and 🚌 176 back from St Katharina 15.13, 17.13, 19.13.

This hike starts out from Prösels/Presule Castle and runs through woods and meadows, apple orchards and vineyards. You will pass many late-medieval farms and *enoteche* before coming to the little church of St Katharina. I particularly recommend this walk in autumn because of the glowing vines … and the 'Törggelen' (see panel on page 15)!

The walk begins at the lower end of the **Prösels/Presule car park** (**1**). There is a signpost ('Blumau/ Fronthof', Trail N° 3) and the symbol of this trail — known in German as the 'Oachner Höfeweg', in Italian as the 'Sentiero dei masi', and in English as the 'Aica Farm Trail'. Its **icon**, shown above, will be with you throughout and is particularly important because there are so many twists and turns in the route!

You hike through meadows below the castle and soon keep left uphill at a fork (**2**). At first you follow a fence, then the trail heads into a beech wood. Soon after, a brook babbles across the trail. You come back to meadows and now descend, with a beautiful view of the Eisack/Isarco Valley. If you're walking in summer, you'll see sheep grazing here.

At the next fork (**3**) take the right-hand, upper path signed to the 'Leitnerkeller'; this sets you hiking through dense conifers carpeted with moss and ferns. A few metres further on, on your left, is the medieval **Rieferkeller** — a stone structure known as a 'Wirtskeller' ('inn-keeper's cellar'). Due to its location at the lower end of a rockslide, it has a natural refrigeration system. Warmer air entering the rockfall from the top cools on its way down. In the storage area it is only 12-15°. There it blows out of specially created 'ice holes' (*Eislöcher*), so that cool air is always circulating. In the past, wine, bacon and cheese were stored here by the

landlord of the Rose Inn in Prösels.

Shortly after the Riefer cellar, you leave the forest and walk towards the beautiful old farmstead, the **Rieferhof**. The path swings left in front of the building, you pass a painted wayside shrine and dive back into the woods. After a few minutes the view opens up and you reach the Flungerhof, amidst apple orchards and grape vines. From here you're on a tarred road for a while, passing an orchard. At the end of the orchard, follow the by now familiar icon (4; **35min**) to the right.

Go through an underpass below the road in the Tiersertal/Val di Tires, then continue downhill through a beech grove to the **Zalterhöfl**. Once past an old barn, a vegetable patch and pear trees, you're again walking through woodland.

After a fork (where you keep straight ahead) the trail goes steeply downhill. At the end of the

Walk 24: Farm Trail from Prösels/Presule Castle 169

forest you reach a wide farm track (**5**) and climb uphill to the left through meadows. About five minutes later you come to another tarred road (**6**). Go left, to the **Tommelehof** (a *Buschenschank* or *agriturismo* see page 15), and turn right immediately past its impressive medieval stone facade (trail sign). You go through a garden gate (where a barking dog may frighten you!) and past the equally lovely **Psennerhof** with Gothic entrance door. The

Schloss Prösels/Castello Presule and Schlern/Sciliar

building dates from the 13th century, but what you see today was built in 1588.

A wooden fence leads you to southwest over a hill. The view extends back to the main Alpine ridge. At the end of a beech grove the trail takes you across a paved road, then you follow tar to the **Gemoaner Hof** (another *agriturismo*), whose origins go back to 1317.

After the farm the trail goes downhill past grape vines to a junction/viewpoint (**7**; **1h15min**). This is the westernmost point of the trail. Your view extends down into the Eisack Valley and south as far as the Bozen/Bolzano Valley. It's a good place for a leisurely break at the foot of the vineyard.

Then follow the path to the left (eastwards) through a beautiful beech and holm oak grove. A little later, the heart of the Tiers/Tires Valley opens up in front of you, with behind it the imposing rock massif of Rosengarten.

After this you continue downhill. Soon you reach a fork at a concrete terrace and take the left path (trail icon). It meanders above the Prackfoler Höfe. Shortly after the last building, your path turns sharp right (**8**; trail icon). About 10 minutes later it joins a wide trail with a wooden railing. A few metres further on, you come to a barn, next to which there's a **spring** (**9**) with cool drinking water. Above the Gschtatscher Hof you follow an artfully walled path through a meadow. Then you climb gently between grape vines. You pass the Ausser-perskoler Hof and immediately afterwards the

170 Dolomites, Book 1: North and West

Inner-perskoler Hof with a small chapel from 1736.

Once more the trail rises through vineyards, then runs through a mixed deciduous wood and over a small stream. Shortly afterwards you come to the **Zoarhof** and carry on uphill, again on a tarred road. There's a great view of the Bolzano Valley basin in the southwest and the your outgoing path. Soon after the farm, your tarred road joins another road, which you follow uphill to a crossroads (**10**; **2h15min**). Turn right here; after just a few metres you're in front of the impressive **Fronthof** (see panel opposite).

Not far past the Fronthof you cross a stream on a bridge and follow the trail past the medieval Fingerhof through undulating meadows and vineyards. Then you're in a dense deciduous wood, and a steep narrow path leads you into a small gorge. You cross its stream after five minutes on a bold **suspension bridge**.

On the far side, climb for about 10 minutes up to a tarred road. Then follow the road up to the left. Soon after the Unterharderhof, go right at a fork (**11**; 'St Kathrein'; Trail 6A, trail icon) and walk up to the main road to Tiers. On the far side of the road, continue to a crossroads (**12**; **3h**) with benches. Take the stony middle route (icon), which leads steeply into the

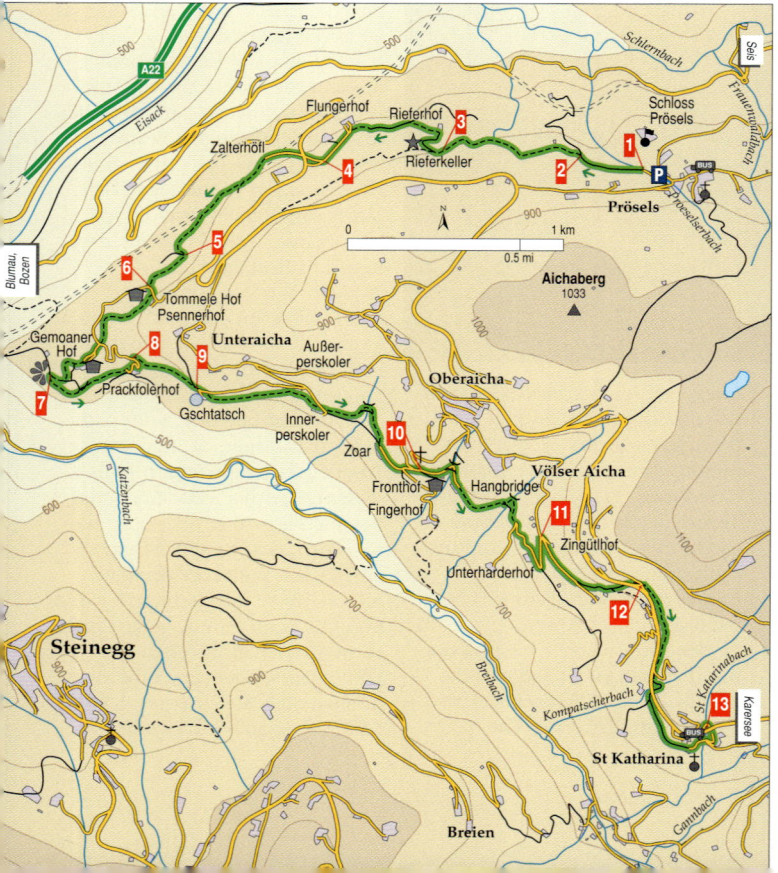

The Fronthof
The Fronthof is just one of several impressive medieval farms on this walk. What's special about it is the fact that it's the largest farm building in South Tyrol that has been preserved from the Gothic period and built from stone blocks.

The Fronthof is a 'Buschenschank' or 'agriturismo' (see page 15). It's run by the Compatscher family, who cook using their own locally produced ingredients. Their wines (silvaner and pinot noir grapes are cultivated, among others) mature in an impressive vaulted cellar. The wine can be bought from the farm (www.fronthof.com).

The Gothic arch at the entrance to the kitchen and the cozy wood-paneled room shown above round off the imposing picture.

---

forest and then through the meadows.

Eventually you descend a few wooden steps towards the main road. But just in front of it, your route (Trail 6A, signposted to 'St Kathrein', and with an icon) first heads left and then goes through an underpass. On the far side, turn left on a wide track.

A little later you're standing in front of the idyllic church of **St Katharina** with its colourful frescoes (1420).

Continue by walking left uphill behind the Michaeler Hof, to the main street. Going through a dark underpass, you reach the bus stop (**13**; **3h25min**) of **St Katharina** and the end of the Farm Trail at a bus stop.

Overleaf: the enchanting Farm Trail

Walk 25: TSCHAMINTAL/VAL DI CIAMIN

Distance/time: about 6.9km/ 4.3mi; 2h10min
Grade: ●❗ easy, with an ascent/ descent of 465m/1525ft; a mostly shady hike on good paths. Just a little exposed between **2** and **3**.
Waymarking: red/white; Trail N° 3 throughout
Equipment: sturdy shoes
Refreshments: at the start in the Tschaminschwaige: varied cuisine, including delicious Tyrolean 'Tris' (cheese dumplings, spinach dumplings and stuffed pasta dishes). Hot meals from 12.00-21.00, pizzas from 17.00-22.00. www.tschaminschwaige.com.

Walking map: Tabacco 029, Schlern-Sciliar/Rosengarten-Catinaccio-Latemar, 1:25,000
Transport: 🚗 follow signs to Weisslahnbad/Lavina Bianca. Go right at the roundabout, reaching the start of the walk after 200m (46° 28.784'N, 11° 33.749'E). Park at the side of the road between the roundabout and the start or west of the roundabout. Or 🚐 185 from Bolzano to St Zyprian/San Cipriano, hourly. From there it's 15 minutes on foot to Weisslahnbad. Last bus back at 20.01. (In summer the bus may also stop in Weisslahnbad, ask the driver.)

This varied out-and-back hike leads between vertical rock walls into the wild Tschamin/Ciamin Valley with spectacular views to the peaks of the western Rosengarten. Shady paths take you straight up to an idyllic alpine meadow — the Rechter Leger ... with tables and benches, a little wooden hut, and simply tremendous views.

Steger Saw Mill and Nature Park House

In addition to the rustic Tschaminschwaige/Malga Ciamin, there are two other interesting buildings to see at at the start of this hike: the medieval Steger Säge and the Schlern-Rosengarten Nature Park House.

The Steger Saw Mill is a restored medieval Venetian saw mill dating from 1598. It's open Wednesdays at 11.00, 15.00 and 16.30 with demonstrations of how the wood was processed in earlier times.

The Nature Park House has display boards and exhibits about the flora and fauna and the geological origin of this part of the Dolomites.

Both attractions are only open from June to October.

Steger Saw Mill

The hike starts on the paved terrace (**1**) between the dairy hut, **Tschaminschwaige/Malga Ciamin** and the **Steger Säge**. Take Trail N° 3 from the upper end of the terrace, signposted 'Tschamintal', and head into the forest under pine and spruce. You climb on log-supported steps, first on gravel, then on loose scree. The Tschamin Stream rushes below you in a narrow stream bed full of huge boulders.

About 10 minutes along, at a fork (**2**) keep left (northeast), and do the same at the next fork a few metres further on. From here, the path leads uphill in steep hairpins high above the Tschamin Gorge, offering repeated views into the depths. Log steps stabilise the path, and a handrail on the left protects the climb and helps allay feelings of vertigo among those who don't have a head for heights.

After about 15 minutes, the trail joins a wide motorable track (**3**). Follow this gently uphill to the left. At the next fork (**4**; **30min**), keep left in the direction of 'Rechter Leger'. Just under five minutes later — and despite its name — you can enjoy ice-cold mountain water from the splashing spring at the right of the path, called '**Schwarze Letten**' (or 'Black Mud').

Not far past the spring, you cross the **Tschamin** on a bridge and now continue walking gently uphill on the left bank of the stream below shady conifers. After 10 minutes you come to the small alpine pasture area of **Schaferter Leger** with a hut and benches inviting you to picnic. The northern walls of the valley rise vertically above you here. Weathered tree trunks cling to narrow rock gullies.

Walk 25: Tschamintal/Val di Ciamin 175

Back in the forest, there is a good opportunity to dip your toes in the icy water in the shallow stream bed! After about five minutes of gentle ascent, you cross another bridge and continue uphill, following the course of the valley. At this point the rock faces close in on each other — spectacular!

A good 100m after the bridge you come across another spring,

Relaxing on the Rechter Leger, with splendid views of the Grasleiten/ Cima del Principe peaks (in the northeast) and Tschamin/Ciamin peaks (in the east)

In the wild and romantic Tschamin/Ciamin Valley

called '**Am Hohen Steg**' (**5**). This one was buried beneath a landslide and has only been recovered and bubbling fairly recently.

Continue climbing alongside the narrow stream bed with its rocks and boulders. Having crossed the stream again on another bridge, you see the mighty Grasleiten/Cima del Principe peaks at the end of the valley for the first time.

The trail continues gently uphill through sparse trees, and about 10 minutes after the bridge you come to another small clearing with a bench. At the end of the clearing, climb stones over a flat stream, walk a few metres through the forest and you're there — at the **Rechter Leger** (**6**; **1h10min**). Immediately to the right of the path is a wooden hut, on your left there are several benches and tables. And rising in the middle of this wide alpine meadow is an old wayside cross. Signs point to ongoing trails to the Grasleiten Hut (1h40min) and Tierser Alpl Hut (2h30min). We leave them for another day (Walks 00 and 00 respectively), and call it a day at this point.

Whether you eat the snack you have brought with you, take a nap in the meadow, listen to the crickets and birds or enjoy the fascinating view of Grasleiten/Cima del Principe peaks (in the northeast) and Tschamin/Ciamin peaks (in the east) … is up to you.

Once you have take in the beauty of this atmospheric spot, you can wend your way back to the starting point in about an hour (**1**; **2h10min**).

Walk 26: FROM THE NIGER/NIGRA PASS TO ST ZYPRIAN/SAN CIPRIANO

Distance/time: about 9.9km/ 6.1mi; 3h35min
Grade: ● moderate, with an ascent of 390m/1280ft and descent of 945m/3100ft; a straightforward walk on forest tracks and alpine paths (some steep descents, especially after **5**). Shady at the start and end, sunny in the middle
Waymarking: red/white; Trail N° 1 to **3**, then Trail 7
Equipment: hiking boots, walking poles, sun protection
Refreshments: take provisions and enough water with you. Food is available at the dairy hut Haniger Schwaige/Malga Haniger (**5**) and at the Plafötsch Alm/Alpeggio Plafèc (**9**).

Walking map: Tabacco 029, Schlern-Sciliar/Rosengarten-Catinaccio-Latemar, 1:25,000
Transport: 🚌 It's a good idea to leave your car at the large car park for hikers at the Cyprianerhof (46° 28.237'N, 11° 33.664'E) and from the hotel take 🚌 185 to the Niger/Nigra Pass. Of course, it also works the other way around: park at the Niger Pass (46° 27.348'N, 11° 35.166'E) and when you finish the walk take the bus back to the start (last 🚌 in summer/autumn at 17.59, otherwise at 16.59). 🚌 185 runs about every hour between Bolzano and the Karer/Carezza Pass, last bus from St Zyprian back at 22.01.

This varied, mostly shady hike follows good paths at the foot of Rosengarten/Catinaccio through the dense Niger/Nigra Forest and flower-rich alpine meadows to the Haniger Schwaige/Malga Haniger, picturesquely sited at the foot of mighty rock faces. On the descent, the rustic Plafötsch Alm/Alpeggio Plafèc beckons with its fantastic panorama.

Start the walk at the **Nigerpass bus stop** (**1**), right next to the Niger Joch Haus/Rifugio Nigra and the hiking car park. Walk through the car park and, at its end, take the wide forest path (Trail N° 1, signed to the 'Hanicker Schwaige') up into a dense forest of mixed conifers. The rock walls of the Rosengarten emerge from the treetops again and again.

About 20 minutes along, keep left at a fork; then, almost immediately, at another fork (**2**) keep left again for 'Haniger Schwaige'. Now your view widens out to encompass the Schlern/Sciliar plateau in the north.

About 10 minutes after the last junction, you go through a cattle gate. Walking through firs and larch, shortly afterwards you reach the babbling Flötzer Stream and cross it on a boardwalk. After a few metres you then find a spring at the right of the path (according to the sign, the highest open spring in the Tiers/Tires Valley).

About 100m after the spring you cross the bed of the Weissbach/Rio Bianco on stones. Straight away the path forks (**3**). Climb up to the right on the now-steep mountain path beside the stream (Trail N° 7, 'Haniger Schwaige'). Boardwalks and steps make the ascent easier. Soon the path turns north, and you pass lichen-covered larches with huge trunks. About 10 minutes later you reach the edge of the forest. The Ploger Ridge and Plafötsch tower up ahead — a beautiful view!

For a few minutes the trail rises

via steep hairpin bends at the edge of the forest. Then it takes you through alpine meadows and below the mighty peaks of Rosengarten to a bench (**4**; **1h05min**) — at 2005m, this is the highest point of your hike and definitely worth a long rest! To the north the view extends to Plafötsch, to the west far out into the Eisack/Isarco Valley and as far as Bolzano! In the west the glaciated flanks of the Ortler/Ortles massif beckon from afar, in the south the striking peaks of Schwarzhorn/Corno Nero and Weisshorn/Corno Bianco.

About five minutes after the bench you go through a cattle gate. Then you climb steeply, but briefly, through mixed conifers. After crossing a stream on some small boulders, the trail descends steeply to the left — *take care on this stretch!* The forest clears, and about 10 minutes past the stream you're in a meadow.

At the end of the meadow, the path leads steeply downhill over rocks, then through a small stream bed. A little later you reach a wide alpine pasture called **Angelwiese**. In spring it is covered in flowers, in summer it's grazed by cows. On your right are the spectacular Vajolet Towers — a world-famous paradise for climbers!

After the meadow you descend steeply to a basin, in the middle of which the Haniger Schwaige (dairy) can already be seen between the larches. After about five minutes of descent you come to a spring at the right of the trail. Immediately afterwards your path joins a forestry track (Trail 7a), which brings you to **Haniger Schwaige/Malga Haniger** (**5**; **1h45min**) in a few minutes. Below the majestic walls of the Tschamin peaks, Vajolet Towers and Rosengarten, you can take a break on rustic wooden benches and enjoy generous portions of Austrian pancakes *(Kaiserschmarrn)* or cheese dumplings to get your strength back… Then perhaps try some of their home-made schnapps — 'on the house'.

Thus fortified, continue on Trail 7 towards 'Plafötsch/St Zyprian', passing the hut's stable building (with rabbits, pot-bellied pigs and donkeys) and a fountain. The trail goes steeply downhill on loose scree and after a few metres through the small bed of the Plafötsch Stream.

About 15 minutes after the hut you cross the Plafötsch on a wooden bridge, after which the trail forks (**6**). From here you're on a wide forestry track above the

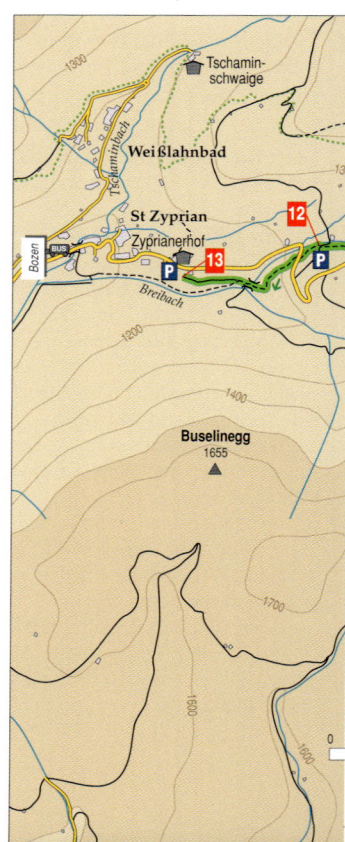

Walk 26: From the Niger Pass to St Zyprian 179

Angelbach, the bed of which gradually widens to a ravine. About 10 minutes later, take a path (**7**; **2h15min**) to the right (still Trail 7, signposted to 'Plafötsch'), first through forest, then through shrubs and bushes towards the stream bed.

After crossing the stream again, the trail continues as a beautifully laid-out path along the shore. You come to a bench with a wayside cross and follow an increasingly earthy path for about 10 minutes, to a fork (**8**). Head left here, on the wide forest track and *after just 10 metres* go right uphill on Trail 7 for 'Plafötsch'.

You go through two cattle gates, and shortly afterwards a motorable track takes you through meadows to the **Plafötsch Alm/Alpeggio Plafèc** (**9**; **2h45min**). This quiet hut, on a high, wide plateau, is far from the hustle and bustle. The few tables enjoy a breathtaking panorama — taking in the Tschamin peaks, Vajolet Towers and Rosengarten peaks.

Continuing on, you descend through woods alternating with meadows. The houses of Tiers and St Zyprian can be seen below. About 10 minutes from the Plafötsch Alm, at a fork (**10**), keep ahead (right) for 'St Zyprian'. Beyond a cattle gate, continue on a wide forest track under mighty larches and then descend a steep path through spruce and pine trees. About 15 minutes after the gate you cross a small stream and follow it a few metres to a fork. Go left on a motorable track for

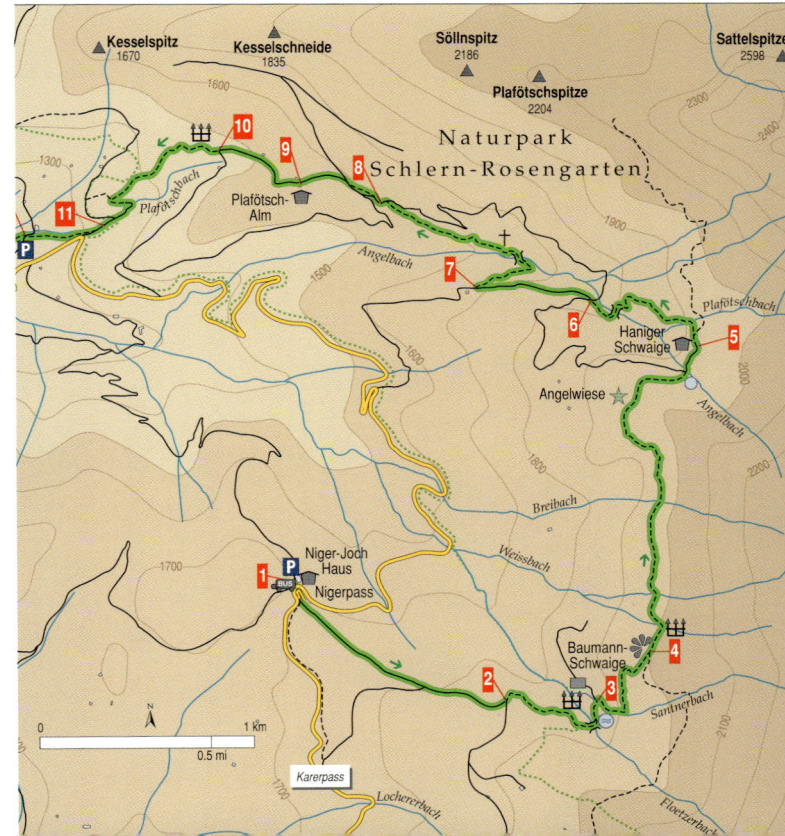

'St Zyprian'. Almost five minutes later turn right (**11**) just before the Niger Pass road.

The trail now runs above the stream, but below the road, heading down through the meadows. A little later you reach a hikers' car park (**12**). Trail 7 leads you past it to and across the Niger Pass road. At the end of a larch-covered meadow you go through a wooden gate and then downhill through conifers. Shortly after the gate you cross a wooden bridge over the Brei Stream. Just after crossing, keep right on a forest track (the signpost, 'Zyprianerhof', is low and easily missed). It takes about five minutes to the **car park** at the Zyprianerhof (**13**; **3h35min**).

Forest path over roots and rocks (with an onlooker at the left ...)

Walk 27: FROM THE KÖLNER HUT/RIFUGIO FRONZA THROUGH THE TSCHAMIN/CIAMIN VALLEY

Distance/time: about 15.3km/ 9.5mi; 6h50min
Grade: ●! strenuous; a high alpine hike with steep ascent of 840m/2755ft and descent of 2120m/6955ft, sometimes on scree-strewn paths. You must be sure-footed and have a head for heights (just at the start there is a tough passage with safety cables). I suggest splitting the hike over two days, with an overnight stay in a hut (see panel on page 185). If you don't want to do the whole walk, the last part of it, in the beautiful Tschamin/Ciamin Valley, is the same as Walk 25. The other possibility is to do Walk 30; the grade is even tougher, but it's much shorter.
Waymarking: red/white; Trail N° 550 to **4**, 541 to **6**, 584 to **7**, 11 to **8**, 3A to **10**, 3 to **13**, then Trail 2
Equipment: hiking boots, walking poles, sun protection *(hat, cream, glasses)*, plenty of drinking water!
Refreshments: available at the Kölner Hut/Rifugio Fronza (**1**), Preuss Hut (**5**), Vajolet Hut (**6**), Grasleitenpass Hut/Rifugio Passo Principe (**7**) and Grasleiten Hut/Rifugio Bergamo (**9**)
Walking map: Tabacco 029, Schlern-Sciliar/Rosengarten-Catinaccio-Latemar, 1:25,000
Transport: 🚗 via the Tiers/Tires or Eggen/Ega valleys to the free car park at the Frommer Alm (46° 26.652'N, 11° 35.294'E), then Laurin II cable car to the Kölner Hut (end May to mid-Oct, 08.15-17.45, in high season 08.00-18.15, 12.50 €). Or 🚌 185 from Bolzano via the Tiers Valley to the Frommer Alm (hourly; last bus from St Zyprian back to Bolzano at 22.01, back to the Frommer Alm in summer/ autumn at 17.59, otherwise 16.59)

This superlative mountain hike explores the heart of Rosengarten/Catinaccio. It goes over the steep Tschager Joch/Pas da le Coronele and past the towering east wall of the Rosengartenspitze/Cima Catinaccio. Then the route leads through the Vajolet Valley into the massive amphitheatre below 3004m-high Kesselkogel/Catinaccio d'Antermoia. The long descent through the wooded Tschamin/Ciamin Valley ends the walk on another high note. This grandiose hike can be spread over two days, with an overnight stay in the Vajolet Hut or Grasleitenpass Hut/Rifugio Passo Principe.

The hike starts at the **Kölner Hütte/Rifugio Fronza** (**1**), reached with the Laurin II cable car. Your trail (Nos. 550/542, signed 'Santnersteig/Tschagerjoch') begins at the back of the hut. Just after the start you're plunged into adventure with a first cable-assisted passage, climbing almost vertically over boulders and crags. You'll encounter cables again and again to help you over the rock.

About 15 minutes later, at a fork in a scree field, go right uphill below steep rock walls on Trail N° 550 ('Tschager Joch'). To the south there is a fine view of rugged Latemar. Soon after passing a bench, an extremely steep ascent through a narrowing corrie begins on a log-supported path; again, cables help with the strenuous ascent. After about 20 minutes, you reach a narrow gap between rock faces — the **Tschagerjoch/ Pas da le Coronele** (**2**; **45min**).

After climbing through this gap the view is spectacular — from the Pala de Mesdi to mighty Kesselkogel/Catinaccio d'Antermoia in the northeast — nothing but huge jagged rock faces! Further to the northeast, the Sella massif and the Marmolada glacier shine out.

The trail continues by descending steeply at the edge of a wide rubble corrie for about 15 minutes, down rocky steps. Then you come to a fork in the path (**3**; without any signposts at time of writing). A path branches off into the corrie, but keep left here.

The path soon swings north again and about 15 minutes past the unsignposted junction, you comes to another junction at the **Baumannpass/Forcella di Davoi** (**4**), where you leave Trail 550 running back down the valley, signposted to the easily recognised

The hike is steep and cable-assisted right from the start.

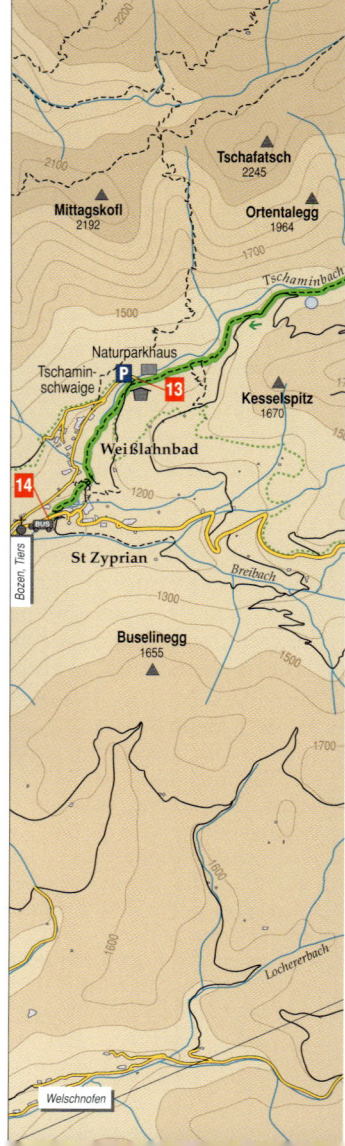

Walk 27: From the Kölner Hut through the Tschamin Valley 183

Kölner Hut ('Rifugio Catinaccio'). Keep to Trail 541 here, heading north to the Vajolet Hut.

The trail goes through rock-strewn meadows at the foot of the mighty **Rosengartenspitze/Cima Catinaccio** east wall — 600m high and 900m long, arguably the most impressive rock face in the group.

About 15 minutes after the pass, you cross a scree-filled depression, then you dedscend for another 15 minutes.

On the wide motor track in the valley, keep left on Trail 546 (**5**; **1h55min**) and climb uphill in steep bends for about 10 minutes. The little Preuss Hut clings to the

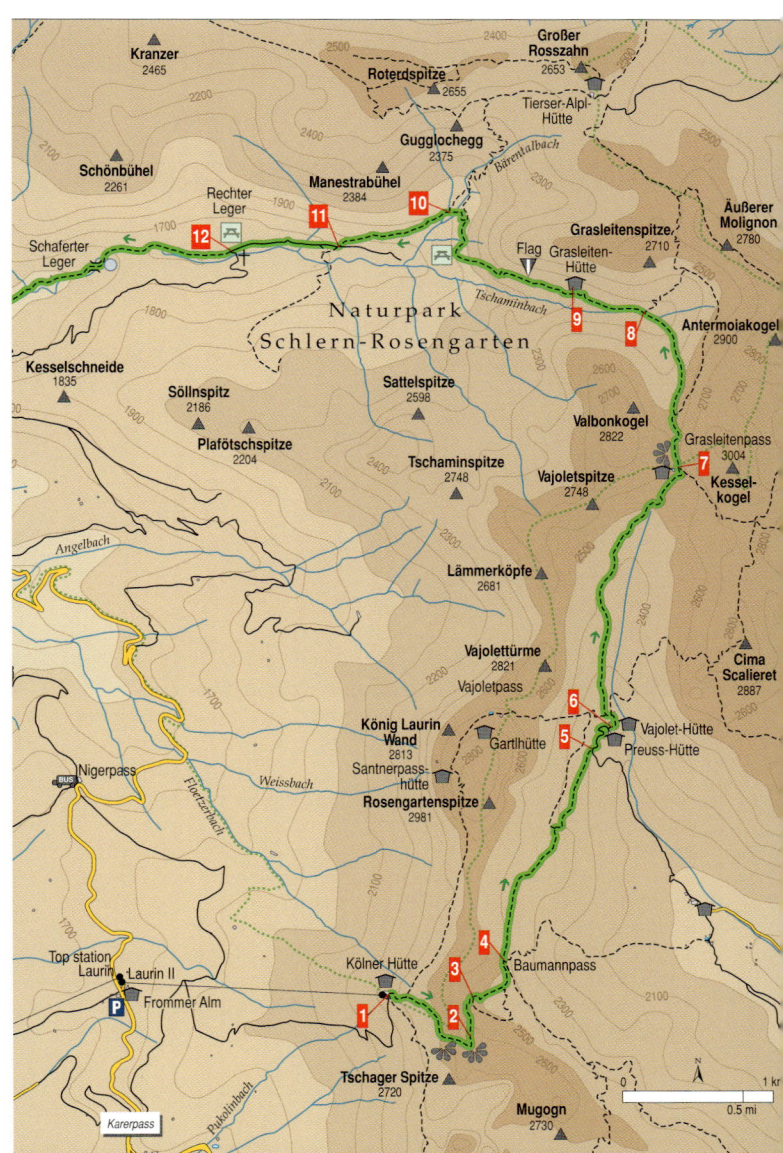

Climbing away from the Preuss and Vajolet huts on the way to the Grassleitenpass/Passo Principe, below the Vajolet Towers

rock above you like a bird's nest, and the massive Vajolet Hut comes into view.

From the **Vajolet Hut** (6; see panel opposite) keep on Trail 584, heading north towards 'Rifugio Principe' (the Grasleiten Pass Hut). A good 100m past the Vajolet Hut, Trail 542 branches off left, steeply uphill, to the Santner Pass Hut and further on to the eponymous and very popular *via ferrata* — see Walk 30 — where the Vajolet Towers, world-famous among climbers, dominate the landscape.

The well-surfaced trail now heads gently uphill past bizarre rock faces, boulders, rubble heaps and sparse grass (photo above).

Walk 27: From the Kölner Hut through the Tschamin Valley 185

About 20 minutes past the hut you reach a wide hollow. On the left a pathless scree field leads up to the Vajolet Pass and the entrance to the east face of the Vajolet north tower — a popular climbing route… You continue to hike through the Vajolet Valley towards the Grasleiten/Principe Pass and mighty Kesselkogel/Catinaccio d'Antermoia.

Shortly afterwards the pebbly and partly washed-out, tough ascent to the pass begins. After about 15 minutes you can already see the flag of the Grasleitenpass Hut flapping in the wind. The last few metres are steep hairpins up to the **Grasleitenpass Hut/Rifugio Passo Principe** (**7**; **3h10min**), sited right on the narrow notch of the Grasleiten Pass.

What a panorama! You look out south to the Vajolet Hut, Rosengartenspitze and Rotwand/ Roda di Vael with the Vajolon Pass. To the north, there's the gloomy rock labyrinth (from west to east) of Valbon Kogel/Cime Valbona, Grasleitenspitzen/Cime del Principe, the Molignon peaks and Antermoia Kogel/Croda dei Cirmei. No entrance to this labyrinth is visible from here…

After an airy rest in front of the hut, you nevertheless walk on to penetrate the labyrinth by following Trail 11 northwards in the direction of 'Grasleitenhütte/ Tierser Alpl Hütte'. The view opens onto a huge, steep field of scree that stretches down to the foot of the rock face. The best way to descend on slippery scree is *carefully*, using your hiking poles.

About 15 minutes past the hut, keep left downhill at a junction (a right would take you over to the Molignon Pass). The trail (not always easily visible) descends steeply for about 20 minutes, then crosses a field of rock debris. Shortly after it ends, you come to a fork (**8**).

Take trail 3A here, to hike at the edge of a gorge. In about 15 minutes you reach the boldly sited **Grasleiten Hut/Rifugio Bergamo** (**9**; **4h05min**). Its panoramic terrace offers a wide view to the west to Tschafatsch/ Monte Cavaccio and the distant Ortler/Ortles massif.

Hut hopping in Rosengarten/ Catinaccio

There are some great huts in the Rosengarten/Catinaccio massif that are not only worth a stop, but an overnight stay.

The Vajolet Hut, the first stop on our route, is very Italian in character and offers over 100 beds in two- to multi-bed rooms, as well as good, hearty cuisine — like polenta with venison goulash and strong red wine.

The small Grasleiten Pass Hut/ Rifugio Passo Pincipe is crouched against the rock at 2600m and impresses with its spectacular view.

The Grasleiten Hut/Rifugio Bergamo, on the edge of a narrow gorge, is more of a way-station (or a destination for those coming up the Tschamin/Ciamin Valley from the dairy Tschaminschwaige/ Malga Ciamin). In any case, according to the hut landlord, its beds are rarely fully occupied, even in the high season. What's more, this hut offers (in your author's opinion) the second-most delicious Kaiserschmarrn of any hut. I rate it at number two — just behind the incomparable Austrian pancakes on the menu at the Tierser Alpl Hut…

From the hut, take Trail 3A further west. Climbing, in about 10 minutes you reach a grassy hill with a large flag. To the west you can see far into the Tschamin/Ciamin Valley — your descent route. Follow the trail downhill via steep bends. After about 15 minutes you come to a beautifully carved bench on the left. From here descend on a scree-covered path between light pines and larches, then mountain pines. Keep left at a fork in the direction of 'Bärenloch/Weisslahnbad', staying on Trail 3A.

You walk for a few minutes through mountain pines, then the path forks again (**10**; **4h45min**). Here you're at the foot of the 'Bärenloch', the 'Bear Hole', a steep gorge leading up to the Tierser Alpl Joch. Follow Trail 3 west, towards 'Rechter Leger', descending steeply through shady mixed conifers forest for almost 25 minutes. To your right are the mighty rock faces of the Grasleitenspitzen/Cima del Principe — a notorious climbing area that has resulted in several deaths.

Eventually you follow a wide forestry track (**11**) out of the valley. Below, you can see the bed of the **Tschaminbach/Rio Ciamin** now and again between the trees. After about 15 minutes you reach the valley floor at the wide clearing shown on page 175, the **Rechter Leger** (**12**; **5h25min**). Chirping birds and crickets, and the rustling stream provide the appropriate acoustic background for a break.

Continue downhill on a wide forest trail through sparse mixed conifer forest in the company of Walk 25. Soon you cross the stream on a bridge and then walk along its banks. Shortly after the bridge you pass a spring, **Zum Hohen Steig**, on the left, with crystal-clear mountain water.

After you cross the stream bed again, continue steadily downhill to another meadow area, the **Schaferter Leger** with its hut (unmanned) and bench. A few minutes later you come to another spring, **Zum schwarzen Letten**, on the far bank of the stream.

Beyond a cattle gate, it's leisurely walking out of the valley on a wide motor track. The stream rushes deep below you and has cut a narrow gorge between the rocks. A good five minutes after the spring, fork off towards the valley floor on Trail 3. (The motor track continues as Trail 13 and reaches a bus stop on the Niger/Nigra Pass road in about 25 minutes.) Trail N° 3 leads you — more slowly but more beautifully — through tall conifers steeply downhill. Boardwalks and railings secure the path in several places. The view down to the stream is spectacular as you can see on page 176. Through dense forest, the last few metres take you down to the **Steger Säge** (see panel on page 173) and a dairy, the **Tschaminschwaige/Malga Ciamin** (**13**) — the perfect refreshment stop!

On the north side of this building, keep left on a forest path ('St Zyprian') and, a few metres further on, follow the **fitness trail** to the right. The woodland path runs above the stream, crossing small wooden footbridges and is secured with railings in several places. At a bridge, continue on Trail 2, pass an old weir, and soon after see the first houses of **St Zyprian/San Cipriano**. You meet the main Niger Pass road opposite the **Pension Rosengarten**; a few metres to the right is the bus stop (**14**; **6h50min**).

Walk 28: FROM THE PAOLINA HUT ROUND ROTWAND/RODA DI VAEL

Distance/time: about 6.8km/4.2mi; 3h
Grade: ●: moderate-strenuous, with a steep ascent of 655m/2150ft and corresponding very steep descent at the Vajolon Pass; some scree-strewn paths. You must be sure-footed and have a head for heights. No shade and very hot in summer
Waymarking: red/white; Trail N° 539 to **2**, 549 to **3**, 541 to **4**, 551 to **5**, 551/9 to **7**, then Trails 539/552 to the end
Equipment: hiking boots, walking poles, sun protection
Refreshments: available at the Paolina Hut at the start (**1**) or at **3** at the Rotwand Hut/Rifugio Roda di Vael or Pederiva Hut. But be sure to take drinks with you!
Walking map: Tabacco 029, Schlern-Sciliar/Rosengarten-Catinaccio-Latemar, 1:25,000
Transport: 🚗 via the Tiers/Tires or Eggen/Ega valleys to the free car park at the valley station of the Paolina chair lift at Lake Karer (46° 24.419'N, 11° 35.486'E), open June to mid-Oct, 08.30-17.30, in high season 08.00-18.00, one way 12.50 €, up and back 18 €).
Or 🚌 185 from Bolzano via the Tiers Valley to the Paolina lift (hourly; last bus back in summer/autumn at 18.35, otherwise 17.35)

This walk leads around the Rotwand/Roda di Vael massif, with spectacular panoramas. At the start it's just a high-altitude hike with modest ascents and descents, but after the Rotwand Hut/Rifugio Roda di Vael it turns into a mountain adventure. It goes through a huge rock basin up to the narrow Vajolon Pass. A steep and exposed descent is followed by a passage under black cliffs to end the circuit.

The walk starts at **Paolina Hut** (**1**). Take Trail N° 539 towards 'Christomannos/Rotwandhütte', initially heading uphill through flower-filled meadows in a south-easterly direction. On your right is the jagged labyrinth of Latemar, backed by Weisshorn/Corno Bianco and Schwarzhorn/Corno Nero.

About 10 minutes along you're in a stand of mountain pines. A short times after Trail 539 joins Trail 549 (**2**), you come to the setting shown on page 5, at the

In the heart of Rosengarten

Christomannos Eagle. Benches invite you to take a rest. The foot of the monument can be climbed and offers the chance for a splendid selfie, 'The Eagle and I' (see the panel on page 161 about the Great Dolomite Road).

The path leads you further east. Marmolada's mighty west face appears in front of you, and shortly afterwards, the Sella group with its highest point, the Boè peak. The path curves north and leads through grassy terrain dotted with huge boulders. About 15 minutes past the eagle, the small Pederiva Hut and a few metres above it, the massive Rotwand Hut/Rifugio Roda di Vael come into view. (On your right, Trail 548 leads through steep, grassy slopes full of **marmot burrows**. With a bit of luck you'll see these cute rodents dash from hole to hole and, if they see danger coming their way, stand up straight with a shrill whistle.) You reach both huts about five minutes later. Each has a panoramic terrace; the Pederiva Hut is more comfortable, the Rotwand Hut more lively.

From the **Rotwand Hut** (**3**; **40min**) well-built mountain Trail

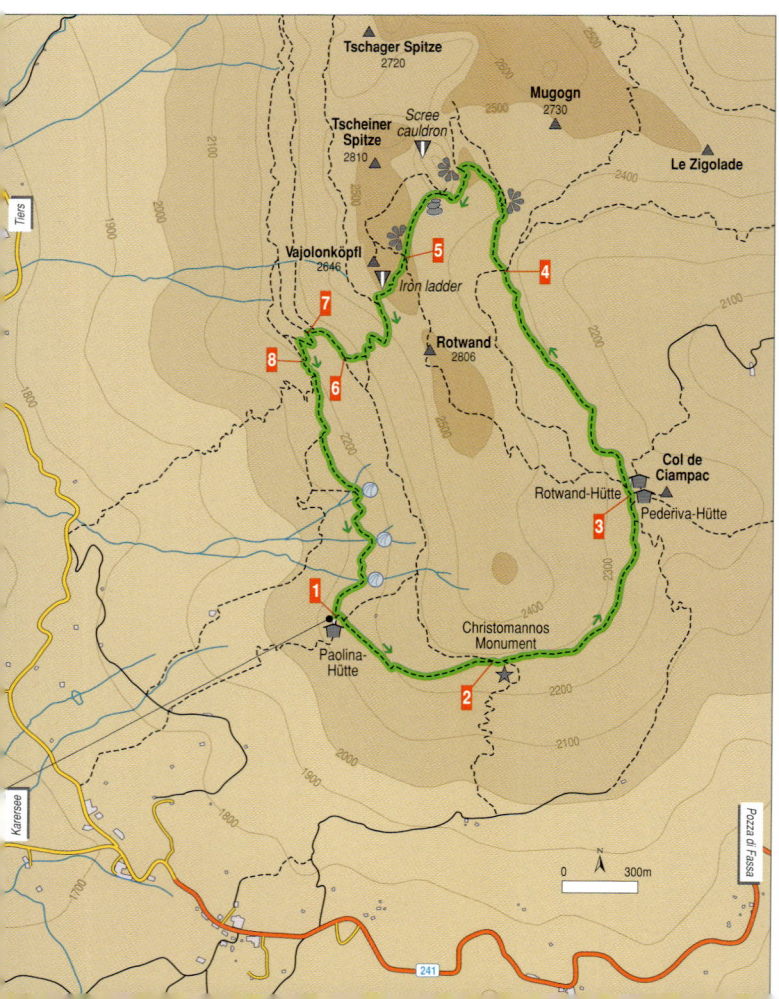

Walk 28: From the Paolina Hut round Rotwand

Rotwand Hut/Rifugio Roda di Vael in morning light

541 ('Vajolet/Vajolon Pass') leads you north — first across a scree field and then through a section with head-high boulders lying in the landscape as if thrown by a giant hand. On your left Rotwand's red and black eastern flank reaches for the sky. The calls of climbers mix with the whistling of marmots.

About 20 minutes after the huts, you reach a 3-way fork at the edge of a dip (**4**). Go straight ahead on Trail 551 ('Vajolon Pass'), which soon leads steeply and sweatily into a scree cirque. About 20 minutes later the cirque ends and a gigantic **cauldron full of scree** opens up in front of you with the Tschager peak/Le Coronele on the left and the Tschager and Mugoni passes on the right. What a sight!

You climb the edge of this basin for about 10 minutes. Then the path swings west and winds in sweeping bends up to a small pass. From here you have a great view of Rotwand's north ridge, which begins at the Vajolon Pass.

Continue by climbing to a hilltop with cairns. About 10 minutes later you reach the **Vajolon Pass** (**5**), a small gap in the rock with a fantastic view of Marmolada and towards Welschnofen/Nova Levante! From here the trail descends on loose scree into a narrow corrie *(take care!)*. Ten minutes later the **iron ladder** shown overleaf helps you climb over a boulder.

Continue through more loose scree on a slightly wider path until you reach a fork (**6**; **1h45min**) about 25 minutes past the boulder. Go right here on Trail 9 for 'Welschnofen/ Kölner Hütte'. Shortly afterwards, branch off left on Trail 552 for the Paolina Hut (**7**). Follow this for about 10 minutes through grassy, boulder-strewn slopes. At the next fork (**8**; **2h30min**) keep left again on Trail 552. After 10 minutes downhill, fork left one last time.

On a spectacular section of path below black rock walls streaming with waterfalls, you have to cross a steep rubble slope — you really need to be surefooted here! Shortly afterwards you're back at the **Paolina Hut** chair lift (**1**; **3h**).

Walk 29: FROM THE KÖLNER HUT/RIFUGIO FRONZA TO THE KARER/CAREZZA PASS

Distance/time: about 9km/5.6mi; 2h40min
Grade: ●! moderate; a high-altitude walk on mountain paths, with an ascent of 245m/800ft and descent of 885m/2900ft (with some steep sections); almost shadeless. You must be sure-footed and have a head for heights between ❸ and ❹.
Waymarking: red/white; Trail N° 549 and 'Hirzelsteig' to ❺, then Trail 548 and Trail 6 for the last metres to the bus stop
Equipment: hiking boots, walking poles, sun protection
Refreshments: available at the Kölner Hut/Rifugio Fronza (❶), the Rotwand Hut/Rifugio Roda di Vael or the Pederiva Hut at ❺ and at the Karer/Carezza Pass (❼)
Walking map: Tabacco 029, Schlern-Sciliar/Rosengarten-Catinaccio-Latemar, 1:25,000
Transport: 🚗 via the Tiers/Tires or Eggen/Ega valleys to the free car park at the Frommer Alm (46° 26.652'N, 11° 35.294'E), then Laurin II cable car to the Kölner Hut (end May to mid-Oct, 08.15-17.45, in high season 08.00-18.15, 12.50 €). Or 🚐 185 from Bolzano via the Tiers Valley to the Frommer Alm (hourly). Return by 🚐 185 from the Christomannos Alm: last return to Bolzano (via the Frommer Alm) in summer 18.36, otherwise 17.36.

This longish walk for all the family runs through extensive alpine meadows and mountain woodlands along Rosengarten's rock walls with spectacular views and a photo stop at the famous Christomannos monument. Be prepared for a narrow stretch of path demanding a head for heights and for a sometimes steep descent to the Karer/Carezza Pass.

Much-loved climbing boulder on the Hirzelsteig/Sentiero del Masarè

Walk 29: From the Kölner Hut to the Karer Pass 191

The hike starts at the **Kölner Hütte/Rifugio Fronza** (**1**). Walk to the southern end of the panorama terrace and head downhill on loose scree following Trail N° 549 to 'Hirzelsteig'. Your onward climb, below the mighty rust-brown walls of the Rosengarten massif is easy to see from here. In the south is jagged Latemar, in the southwest the peaks of Weisshorn/Corno Bianco and Schwarzhorn/Corno Nero.

After a first junction, you pass a rubble cirque and several large boulders; some 10 minutes later keep left at a fork (**2**). This is followed by a gentle ascent through scree and grassy sections. Soon you're scrambling over slabs of rock. Splashes of colour peep up through the rubble — the yellow of alpine anemones and the blue of bluebells.

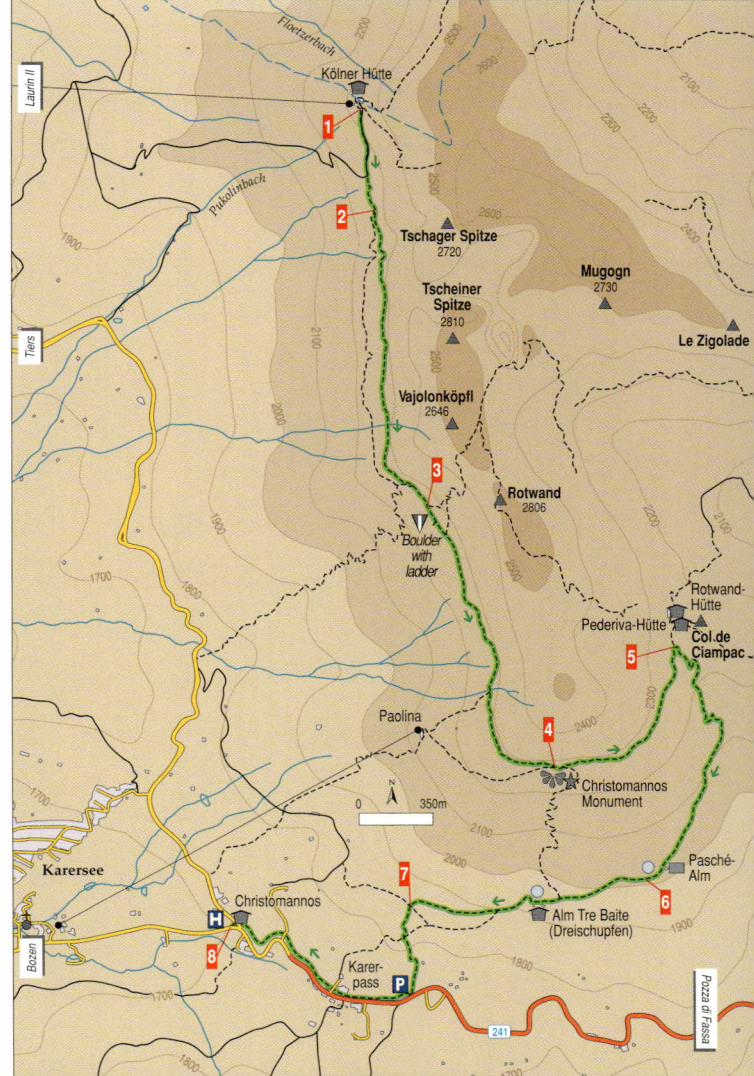

After crossing a small field of rock debris, you pass a crumbling wall at the end of which you come to a junction (**3**; **40min**). Straight ahead (right), the Hirzelsteig/Sentiero del Masarè leads you south. You pass a **gigantic boulder** on the right, with a rusty iron ladder attached. Ignore the faded sign 'No entry' sign (why else the ladder?); climb up and enjoy the view!

After that brief 'summitting', continue on the Hirzelsteig. Soon the path climbs gradually beside an exposed drop on the right. Take **care** here! After 10 minutes there is a short descent during which you cross a stream babbling from the rocky slope. Then the path rises again.

It gets increasingly windy. You have reached the eastern end of the magnificent mountain range and can see the Karer Pass and the Fassa Valley below. About 10 minutes after the stream crossing, at a junction (**4**), stay on Trail 549. The huge **Christomannos Eagle** is enthroned on a boulder in front of you — in the setting shown on page 5. The foot of the monument can be climbed and offers magnificent photo opportunities.

The path leads you further east. The mighty west face of Marmolada appears in front of you; then, shortly afterwards, the Sella group with its highest point, the Boè peak. The path describes a curve to the northeast and leads through grassy terrain where huge boulders lie scattered around as if

Walk 29: From the Kölner Hut to the Karer Pass 193

they had been tossed by a giant's hand.

About 15 minutes past the eagle, you pass a junction (**5**; **1h25min**) to the Karer Pass (your route later on) and shortly afterwards reach the **Pederiva Hut** and the massive **Rotwand Hut**, both with a panoramic terrace. The Pederiva Hut is cosier; the Rotwand Hut more lively.

After a long break, walk the few metres back to the junction and turn downhill on Trail 548 to the Karer Pass. It leads through steep, grassy slopes full of **marmot burrows**, and you may see some of these charming creatures whizzing from hole to hole. The trail descends via several steep bends, then crosses roots and scree below conifers and juniper. About 30 minutes after the junction, the forest clears. The meadows of the Pasché-Alm spread out in front of you. You pass the alm hut and a few metres further on come to a spring (**6**; **1h55min**) with deliciously clear, ice-cold water.

From here a wide alpine path leads steeply downhill after a short ascent. Beyond a cattle gate, follow a concrete lane for a good five minutes to the **Tre Baite Alm** hut with spring. You could get a hearty snack in the wood-paneled room here if you come in summer and find it open.

The trail continues downhill as a wide motor track through mixed conifers. About 10 minutes after the hut, at a fork (**7**), keep right on Trail 548 towards 'Karerpass'. In another 10 minutes you reach a

Far left: the large Rotwand Hut/ Rifugio Roda di Vael, with the small and cosy Pederiva Hut at the right. Left: Dr Theodor Christomannos (see panel about building the Great Dolomite Road on page 161) became known as the pioneer of South Tyrolean tourism. The year after he died in 1911, a monument in the form of a 2.70m/9ft-high bronze eagle was raised on the mountainside above the Karer Pass.

car park on the SS241. Follow the road to the right, and pass the **Karer/Carezza Pass** a few minutes later. From the pass follow Trail N° 6 for just under 10 minutes, to the **Christomannos Alm** (**8**; **2h40min**), with a bus stop.

Walk 30: BELOW THE VAJOLET TOWERS

Distance/time: about 7.5km/4.7mi; 4h30min
Grade: ●❗ strenuous; a high alpine hike with steep ascent/descent of 800m/2625ft, sometimes on scree-strewn paths. You must be sure-footed and have a head for heights (just at the start there is a tough passage with safety cables), as well as some *climbing experience: a few places are Grade 1*.
Waymarking: red/white; Trail 550 to ❷, 542 to to just before ❺, 541 to ❸, then 550 back to the start

Equipment: hiking boots, walking poles, sun protection; harness and helmet for inexperienced walkers on the *via ferrata*
Refreshments: available at the Kölner Hut/Rifugio Fronza (❶), Santner Pass Hut (❸), Gartl Hut/Rifugio Re Alberto (❹), Vajolet Hut (❺), and Preuss Hut (❻)
Walking map: Tabacco 029, Schlern-Sciliar/Rosengarten-Catinaccio-Latemar, 1:25,000
Transport: as Walk 27 on page 181

The Gartl Hut/Rifugio Re Alberto below the Vajolet Towers

Walk 30: Below the Vajolet Towers

Here's a hike even more exciting than Walk 27. You traverse the western side of the Baumann Ridge/Cresta di Davoi on a *via ferrata*, then climb to the Santner Pass Hut, before dropping to the eastern side of the ridge in the setting shown on page 184, where you follow Walk 27 in reverse back to the Kölner Hut.

The hike starts at the **Kölner Hütte/Rifugio Fronza** (**1**), reached with the Laurin II cable car. Your trail (Nos. 550/542, signed 'Santnersteig/Tschagerjoch') begins at the back of the hut. Just after the start you're plunged into adventure with a first cable-assisted passage (shown on page 182), climbing almost vertically over boulders and crags.

About 15 minutes later, at a fork in a scree field, go left on Trail N° 542 (**2**), the Santner Klettersteig/Via Ferrata Passo Santner, signed to the Santner Pass Hut), a wide rubble trail traversing below the western walls of Rosengarten.

The trail is fairly level walking initially, but after about 30 minutes starts to ascend. The going gets tricky now below the Santner Pass: there are iron ladders and handholds to help you climb the first rocky upthrust, and also cables at some of the most awkward places.

After a small saddle the route descends a bit in a steep ravine, usually at least partially filled with ice even in late summer. Then you have to get over another upthrust, helped by pegs and cables, before emerging at the Santner Pass and the **Santner Pass Hut/Rifugio Passo Santner** (**3**; 2h). Big sigh of relief and pause for refreshment!

From here go down through a corrie to the nearby **Gartl Hut** (**4**; and carry on — steeply again, but with less difficulty despite the occasional exposure — to the two huts below: **Vajolet** (**5**; left; 2h30min) and **Preuss** (**6**; right).

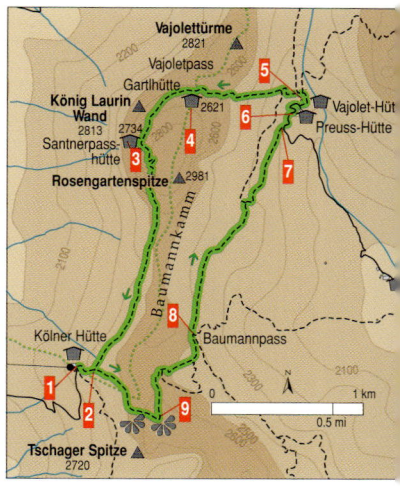

The route now descends just below the **Vajolet Towers**, which you can really appreciate when you get to the huts. From the huts take the wide motor track down the valley as far as the third curve, where you turn right (**7**) on Trail 541. This heads south, rising steadily below the rock walls of Rosengarten, culminating in the east wall of the Rosengartenspitze/Cima Catinaccio — rising 600m/2000ft above you.

When you approach the foot of the rock walls at the **Baumannpass/Forcella di Davoi** (**8**; 3h), fork right on Trail 550 to the Tschagerjoch — a steep climb, with scree and rocks on both sides. From the narrow **Tschagerjoch/Pas da le Coronele** (**9**) you dive back down to the start, again using the cables for this final, very steep descent to the **Kölner Hut** (**1**; 4h30min).

Index

Bold type indicates a photograph; *italic type* indicates a map or plan; both may be in addition to a text reference on the same page.

Adige *see* Etsch
Adolf Munkel Weg 84, 96, **97**, *98-9*, 101, *102*, 103-4
Aferer Geisler/Odles Deores 83-4, 89, 91-2, 94, 104, *106*, **108-9**, **109**, 110
Agriturismo 14
Ahr 42, 63, *70-1*, **71**
Ahrntal 20, 23, 27, 63-6, 67-71
Aica Farm Trail 21, **24**, 167, *170*, **171**, **172**
Airports 9
Almrosen Hut 153, 157
Alpe di Siusi *see* Seiser Alm
Alta Badia *see* Hochabteital
Alta Pusteria *see* Hochpustertal
Ampezzo 7, 12, 14, 18, 22, 26, 45, 161
Anterselva di Mezzo *see* Antholz Mittertal
Antholz Mittertal/Anterselva di Mezzo *72-4*
Antholzer Tal/Val di Anterselva 27, 72-3
Arnika Hut 131, *132-3*
Auronzo Hut 50, 54, *57*
Bad Moos 53-54, 59
Belluno 8-12, 14, 25, 50, 54, 59, 161
Bergbauernweg *87*, **88-9**
Birnlücke (pass, hut) *70-1*
Bolzano *see* Bozen
Bozen/Bolzano 9-10, 12, 18, 25-6, 121-2
Town plan 122
Brenner Pass 10-11, 24-6, 76
Brenta Dolomites 6, 8, 22
Bressanone *see* Brixen
Brixen/Bressanone 9-10, 12, 18, 20, 22-4, 76-7
Town plan 78-79
Brogles (alm, hut, stream) 96, *98-9*, **100**
Bruneck/Brunico 9, 12, 17, 20, 23, 36, **38**, 40-**42**, 43-4
Town plan 41
Brunico *see* Bruneck
Buchenstein 7, 14, 26, 161
Bullaccia *see* Puflatsch
Büllelejoch (pass, hut) 54, *57*-8
Buses 11-12
Cadipietra *see* Steinhaus
Cadore 7-8, 25, 50, 53-4

Campo Tures *see under* Sand
Carnic Alps 45, 51, 53-4, 61
Casere *see* Kasern
Castelrotto *see* Kastelruth
Catinaccio *see* Rosengarten
Catinaccio d'Antermoia *see* Kesselkogel
Chienes *see* Kiens
Chiusa *see* Klausen
Christomannos (alm, monument) **5**, *188*, 190, *191-2*, **193**
Ciamin *see* Tschamin
Climate and weather 16
Communications 16
Compatsch 115, 119, 131, *132*, 133-5, 137-9, *140*, 141, 143-4, 148-9, *152-3*, *154*, 155, 157
Cortina d'Ampezzo 6, 10, 12, 14-5, 17, 18, 22, 25-6, 45-6, 49-50, 161
Cristallo group 45, 49-50
Croda Rossa di Sesto *see* Sextener Rotwand
Cuisine 16
Cycling 6, 13
Deutschnofen/Nova Ponente 18, 23, 158, 161, 165-6
Dietenheim/San Theodone 18, 40, 42, 64
Dobbiaco *see* Toblach
Dolomites
 Great Dolomite Road 25, 59, 160-1, 171, 188, 193
 High Route 55-8, 93-**95**, 110
Dolomiti Superbike 49
Dolomiti Superski 8, 22-3
Drei Zinnen/Tre Cime di Lavaredo (peaks, hut) 6, 27, 45-7, 50, 53-4, *57*, **58**
Driving 9-11
Eggental/Valle d'Ega 158-161, 165
Eisacktal/Valle Isarco 22, 25, 27, 29, 36, 53, 76-7, 79-**82**, 83, 115, 161, 169
'Elizabeth Promenade' 158, 162
Emergencies 11, 16, 19, 33
Etsch (river, valley) 14, 24, 26, 28, 53, 76, 160, 163
Events 16-8
Falzàrego Pass 161

Fàlzes *see* Pfalzen
Fane Alm 36-38
Fanes group 32, 49-50, 109
Fassatal/Val di Fassa 12, 14, 17, 22, 160-1, 192
Festivals 16-8
Fiè *see* Völs
First World War 23, 25, 46-7, 50, 53-4, 58-61
Fischleintal/Val Fiscalina 45, 53-4, *57*, 59
Franziscusweg 66
Franzensfeste 9, 12, 36, 45, 53
Frommer Alm 163, 181, *182-3*, 190
Gampenalm 90, 91, 93-4, **95**, 96, 101, *106*, *108-9*
Gartl Hut **194-5**
Geisler (alm, hut) 101, *102*, 104
Geisler/Odle group **1**, **86**, 89, 94, *98-9*, *102*, 103-4, 107, **cover**
Gissbach 42
Gitschberg (mt/ski area) 36, 38
Glatschalm 96, 98, 101, *102*, 103-4
Gröden/Gardena (valley, holiday area) 6, 22, 69, 111
Gschnagenhardt Alm 96, *98-9*, 101, *102*, **102-3**, 104
Gsieser Tal/Valle di Casies (pass, valley) 72-4, **75**
Günther Messner Trail **108-9**, 110
Hahnspielhütte 61, *62*
Haniger Schwaige (hut) 28, 177, *178-9*
Hauenstein Castle 116, **128-9**, **130**
Haunold (peak, hut) 45, 51-2, 54
Hay baths 120
Helm/Monte Elmo 45, 51, 53-4, 61, *62*, **62**
Hirzelsteig **190-2**
History 24
Hochabteital/Alta Badia 22, 110

Index 197

Hochpustertal/Alta Pusteria 17, 22, 27, 45-54
Hofer Alpl 125, *126*, **127**
Höhlensteintal/Valle di Landro 45-6, 48-9
Horse-riding 23
Huts, mountain 14
Ibsen, Henrik 115-6
Illness 19
Innichen/San Candido 9, 12, 24, 45-6, 49-**51**, 52-4, 72, 74, 76, 81
Karer/Carezza (lake, pass) 12, 22, 158-161, 163-5, 177, 187, 190, *191*, 192-3
Kaserill/Caseril (alm, stream) 92, 96, **105**-*106*, *108-9*
Kasern/Casere 63-4, 67, 69, *70-1*, **71**
Kastelruth/Castelrotto **18**, 28, 115-6, **118**-9, *123*, 130, 132-3, 138
Kehrer Alm 69, 70
Kesselkogel/Catinaccio d'Antermoia 162, 181-2, 185
Kiens/Chienes 36, 43
Klausberg (peak, ski area) 68
Klausen/Chiusa 10, 12, 76, 80-**81**, 82-3, 90, 93, 96, 101, 105, 110
Kofler zwischen den Wänden 65
Kölner Hut/Rifugio Fronza 163, 181, **182**, *182-3*, 185, 189, 190-*191*, 193-*195*
'Krampus' 18, 47
Kreuzkofeljoch/Passo Poma 94, *95, 108-9*, **109**-110
Kreuztal/Valcroce 80, *85*-96
Krimmler Tauern (Austria) 63, 71
Kronplatz/Plan de Corones (mt/ski area) 22, 36, 40-2, **44**
La Villa/La Ila *see* Stern
Lace 20, 69
Ladin(s) 7, 15, 24, 26-7
Lajen/Laion 76, 82, **111**, *112-3*, 114, 119
Lake
  Antholz/Lago di Anterselva 72, 74
  Dürren/Lago di Landro 45-6, 50, 54
  Karer/Lago di Carezza 12, 22, 158-161, 163-**164**, 165, 187
  Klaus 63, 68
  Misurina 6, 50, 57
  Prags/Lago di Braies 45, 48-9, **55**, *56*
  Toblach 46, 50
  Vahrn 23

Völs 118, 125, *126*, **127**
Langental/Vallunga **32**
Langkofel/Sassolungo (peak) 85, 111-2, **113**, 119, 133-**134**, 148
Lappach/Lappago 66
Laranz Woods 115-6
Latemar group 8, 158, 160, 164-6, 181, 187, 191
Laurin Hut *136, 152, 154*
Laurin, King 28, 158, 163
Lienz (Austria) 23, 40, 45-6, 50, 52-3, 73-4
Lifts 8
Lindenweg 36-7
Lüsen/Luson (valley, alm) 76, 80, 110
Luttach/Lutago 63, 67
Mahler, Gustav 17, 46-8
Maps 19, 34-5
Mahlknecht Hut/Rifugio Molignon *146-7*, 153, *154*
Mahlknechtjoch/Passo Duron 146, 157
Maria Weissenstein 18, 158, 161, 166
Marinzenweg 123
Maranza *see* Meransen
Maria Weissenstein 158, 166
Marmolada group 8, 146, 182, 188-9, 192
Maximiliansteig *(via ferrata)* 136, 145, *146-7*
Meransen/Maranza 36-8
Messner, Reinhold 44, 83, 101, 104
Mills Nature Trail 36, 39-**40**
Mining 25, 68-9
Molini di Tures *see* Mühlen
Money/banks 20
Mongeulfo *see* Welsberg
Monte Elmo *see* Helm
Mühlbach/Rio di Pusteria 36-8, 43, 45, 52
Mühlen/Molini di Tures 63, 66
Mühlwalder Tal/Val dei Molini 63, 66
Nature Parks
  Fanes-Sennes-Prags 47
  Hohe Tauern (Austria) *70-1*
  Puez-Geisler/Odle 8, 76, 84, 90, **91**, **92**, **95**, *95*, **97**, *98-9*, **100**, **102**, **102-103**, **105**, *106*, **107**, *108-9*
  Rieserferner-Ahrn 63, 66, 68-9, *70-1*
  Schlern-Rosengarten 8, *126, 130, 136, **136-7**, *140, 146-7*, **150-1**, *152, 154*, **155**, 157, 159, 173, *174, 178-9*, **180**, **182**, *182-3*, **184**, **187**, **189**, **194**

Sexten Dolomites 25, 45, 47, 53, *57, 60*, 61
Neustift Monastery 24, 76-**78**
Niederdorf/Villabassa 45, 47-**48**, 49
Niger/Nigra Pass 177, *178-9*, 180, *182-3*, 186
Nova Levante *see* Welschnofen
Nova Ponente *see* Deutschnofen
Oachner Höfeweg *see* Aica Farm Trail
Obereggen/San Floriano 22, 161, 165-6
Odles Deores *see* Aferer Geisler
Olang/Valdaora 36, 44, 73-5
Ortisei *see* St Ulrich
Palmschoss/Plancios 80, *85*
Panorama Hotel *136, 152, 154*
Paolina Hut 163, 187, *188*, 189
Pederiva Hut 187-*188*, 190, 193
Peitlerkofel 80, 94, *108-9*, 110
Peitlerscharte *108-9*, **110**
Petz 139, *140*, **142-3**, 145
Pfalzen/Falzes 36, 39-40
Pfunderer Tal 36, 38
Pfunders/Fundres 39
Plafötsch/Plafec (alm, stream, hut) 177, *178-9*
Plan de Corones *see* Kronplatz
Plattkofel (peak, hut) 133-**134**, 139, 144, *146-7*, 148
Plätzwiese/Prato Piazza 45, 49-50
Plose (mt, ski area) 22-3, 44, 76, 79-80, *85*-**86**, 108, 110
Ponte Gardena *see* Waidbruck
Pontives *112-3*
Poststeig (trail) **111**-2, **113**, 114
Pragser Tal/Val di Braies (and lake) 45, 48-9, **55**-6
Prato Piazza *see* Plätzwiese
Predoi *see* Prettau
Presule (and castle) 118, 126-7, 167, 169
Prettau/Predoi 20, 63-4, 67-**69**
  Mining Museum **69**
Preuss Hut 181, *182-3*, **184**, 194, *195*
Primiero Valley 7, 18, 25
Prösels Castle 118, 127, **168-9**, *170*
Puez Group **120-1**, **123**
Puflatsch/Bullaccia (mt, hut) 34, 131, *132*, 133, **134**, 138, 141, 155
Pustertal/Val Pusteria 8-9, 12, 20, 23-5, 27, 36-**38**, 39, 44
Rail travel 9, 12-3

198 Dolomites, Book 1: North and West

Raschötz/Rasciesa (mt ridge) 82, 89
Rechter Leger 173, *174,* **175**, 176, *182-3,* 186
Regglberg 158, 165-6
Rein in Taufers/Riva di Tures 63, 65-6
Reischach/Riscone 23, 42, 44
Rienz (river, valley) 6, 36-7, 43, 45, **48**, 53
Rio di Pusteria *see* Mühlbach
Riscone *see* Reischach
Riva di Tures *see* Rein in Taufers
Rodella/Piz Rodela (peak) **133**, 147
Rodeneck/Rodengo **25**, 37
Rosengarten/Catinaccio group 24, 27-8, 142-3, 145, **147**, 151-3, 158-**160**, 161-3, 165, 169, 173, 177-9, 181, 185-7, 190-1, 195
Rosengarten-Latemar 125, 128, 158, 167, 173, 177, 181, 187, 190, 194
Rosengartenspitze/Cima Catinaccio 181, *182-3,* 185, 195
Rosszähne/Denti di Terrarossa 28, 119-21, 133, 136, 139, 144, 146, **151**, *152,* 154-5
Rosszahnscharte/Forcella Denti di Terrarossa *152-3, 154,* 155-6
Rotwand/Roda di Vael (peak, hut) 185, 187, *188,* **189**, 190, *191,* **192-3**
Rotwandwiesen Hut 53, 59-60
Runkelstein Castle 18, 122
Säben Monastery 80-**82**, 110
S Maddalena *see* St Magdalena
St Johann in Ranui (church) 83, **84**, *98-9, 108-9*
St Katharina/S Catarina 167, *170,* 171
St Magdalena/S Maddalena **1**, 48, 74-5, 83-4, *87,* **88-9**, 96, 100, *108-9,* 110, 119, **cover**
St Peter/San Pietro 47, 83, *87-***88**, 89-90, 93, 96, 101, 105, 107, 111-112
St Ulrich/Ortesei 22, 111, *112-3,* 114, 165
St Valentin (church) 116, *123,* **124**
St Zyprian 159, 167, 173, 177, *178-9,* 181, *182-3,* 186
Salegg (and castle) 116, 128-9, *130*
Saltner Hut 139, *140,* 141, *146-7,* 149-50, *152,* 154-5
San Candido *see* Innichen

San Floriano *see* Obereggen
San Pietro *see* St Peter
San Theodone *see* Dietenheim
Sand in Taufers/Campo Tures 63-**64**, 65-67
Santner peaks **27**, 115-6, **117**, 120-1, 123-**124**, 131, 136, 141, 154, 157, 184, 194-5
Santnersteig (trail) 181, 195
Sarntal Alps/Alpi Sarentine 80, 106
Sassolungo *see* Langkofel
Schlern/Sciliar 18, **27**, **117**, **124**, 125, 128, **140-1**, **142-3**, **144-5**, *152,* 167, 173, 177, 181, 187, 190, 194
Schlernhaus 139, *140,* 141-5, *146-7,* 149, **150-1**, *152*
Schlüter Hut 91, 93-4, *95,* 96-7, *108-9*
Sciliar *see* Schlern
Schwarzhorn/Corno Nero 178, 187, 191
Seasons 8, 13
Seceda (mt) 28, 99, 104
Seekofel (peak, hut) 49, 55-*6*
Seis/Siusi 17, *123,* **124**, *130,* 140
Seiser Alm **17**, **22**, **27**, **117**, *132, 136,* **136-7**, **138**, *140, 146-7,* **150-1**, *152,* **156**
Sella group 22-3, 111, 114, 133, 146-8, 182, 188, 192
Selva *see* Wolkenstein
Sentiero delle Odle *see* Adolf Munkel Weg
Sesto *see* Sexten
Sexten/Sesto (village, valley) 6, 8, 20, 25, 45, 47-9, 51, 53-4, 61
Sextener Rotwand/Croda Rossa di Sesto 45, 53-4, **59**, *60*
Shopping 20
Sillianer Hut 61, *62,* **62**
Siusi *see* Seis
Sonnenburg Nunnery 36, 43
Spitzbühl (peak, hut) 135, 137-8, *140*
Sports 21
Steger Sawmill **173**-4, 186
Steinegg 158-160, *170*
Steinhaus/Cadipietra 63, 68-9
Tagusens/Tagusa 115, 119
Taisten/Tésido 42, 47-8, 72, 75
Tauferer Tal/Val di Tures 23, 27, **38**, 63-7, 69
Telegraph (peak) *85*-86
Terenten/Terento 36, 39-**40**
Tésido *see* Taisten
Tiers/Tires 152, 158-9, 169-70, 177-9, 181, 187, 190

Tierser Alpl (alm, pass, hut) 121, 137, 139, 144-5, *146-7,* 149, **151**, *152, 154,* 157, 176, 185-6
Tierser Tal/Val di Tires 158, 181, 187, 190
Tires *see* Tiers, Tierser
Tisens/Tisana 115, **118-**9
Toblach/Dobbiaco 9, 12, 14, 17-8, 20, 23, 25, 45, **46-**8, 52-3, 55, 57, 59, 61, 74-5
'Törggelen' 15, 81, 167
Touristensteig (trail) 139, *140,* 141-3, 149-50, *152*
Transhumance 16-7
Tre Cime di Lavaredo *see* Drei Zinnen
Trentino 8-10, 11-2, 14-5, 17, 18, 20, 24-6, 161
Tschamin/Ciamin (valley, stream, hut) 28-9, 57, 146, 159, **173**, *174-***175**, **176**, 178-9, 181, *182-3,* 185-6
Tschantschenon (alm, stream) 91, 93-6, *99,* 101, *102*
Vajolet (valley, hut, pass, peaks) 163, 178-9, 181, *182-3,* **184**, 185, 189, 194-5
Valdaora *see* Olang
Vallunga *see* Langental
Valser Tal/Val di Valles 36-37
Via Ferrata Maximilian 136
Via Ferrata Passo Santner 195
Villabassa *see* Niederdorf
Villnöss/Funes (valley, stream) **1**, 18, 27, 29, **32**, 40, 76, 80-1, 83-4, *87,* 89, 90, 92-4, 96, 99-*102,* 104-8, **cover**
Völs/Fiè 14, 18, 23, 28, 115-6, 118, 120, 125, *126-7,* 130
Waidbruck/Ponte Gardena 74, 82-3, 120
Walking 6, 27
Weisshorn/Corno Bianco 166, 178, 187, 191
Weisslahnbad 158-9, 173, *174, 178-9, 182-3,* 186
Welsberg/Monguelfo (and castle) 72, 74-**75**
Welschnofen/Nova Levante 158, 160-**162**, 163, 189
Winter sports 23
Wolkenstein/Selva 17, 22, 82, 116, 128-**130**
Wolkenstein, Oswald von (poet, trail) 17, 82, 116, 129-**130**
Wood carving 23
Wörndleloch (alm, valley) 105, *106,* 107
Zans, Zanser Alm (and hut) 83, *90,* **91**, 92-*95, 96, 98-*9, 100-1, *102,* 104-*106,* 107-8